TRADING
WITH
INTERMARKET
ANALYSIS

Founded in 1807, John Wiley & Sons is the oldest independent publishing company in the United States. With offices in North America, Europe, Australia, and Asia, Wiley is globally committed to developing and marketing print and electronic products and services for our customers' professional and personal knowledge and understanding.

The Wiley Trading series features books by traders who have survived the market's ever-changing temperament and have prospered—some by reinventing systems, others by getting back to basics. Whether a novice trader, professional, or somewhere in-between, these books will provide the advice and strategies needed to prosper today and well into the future.

For a list of available titles, visit our web site at www.WileyFinance.com.

TRADING
WITH
INTERMARKET
ANALYSIS

A Visual Approach
to Beating the Financial Markets
Using Exchange-Traded Funds

John J. Murphy

John Wiley & Sons, Inc.

Cover image: © Istockphoto
Cover design: Paul McCarthy

Library of Congress Cataloging-in-Publication Data:

Murphy, John J.
   Trading with intermarket analysis: a visual approach to beating the financial markets using exchange-traded funds / John J. Murphy.
   p. cm.—(Wiley trading series)
   Includes index.
   ISBN 978-1-119-21001-6; ISBN 978–1–118–31437–1 (cloth); ISBN 978–1–118–41996–0 (ebk); ISBN 978–1–118–43399–7 (ebk); ISBN 978–1–118–42158–1 (ebk)
   1. Investment analysis. 2. Exchange traded funds. 3. Stocks. I. Title.
HG4529.M8625 2012332.63'27—dc23
                                                                    2012020566

Printed in the United States of America

10 9 8 7 6 5 4 3 2 1

To chartists everywhere.

I would like to begin by thanking Pamela Van Giessen, long-time Executive Editor at Wiley, for guiding me through several earlier books and for encouraging me to do one more. Her successor in that role, Burton Evan, convinced me that a new generation of e-books, with beautiful color graphics and digital enhancements, lent itself extremely well to visual market analysis, and would help bring inter-market analysis to a wider audience. I'm glad he did. I would also like to thank Judy Howarth at Wiley for working so closely with me in the complicated task of putting the book together, and for making my part in doing that much easier. All of the charts in this book were done on the StockCharts.com web site. I would like to thank the president of that organization, Chip Anderson, for creating new market indicators for my use in this book, and for providing historical market data that was extremely useful. I've learned from many other writers over the years. Special mention is owed to Sam Stovall, chief investment strategist for Standard & Poor's, for his work on sector rotation throughout the business cycle. Thanks also to John Creegan Jr. for his expertise in foreign exchange trading. Also to Ted Bonanno, my agent, who helped smooth the way. Finally, I'd like to thank readers of my earlier books on intermarket analysis who encouraged me to write something more current on that exciting field. This book is for them. And, of course, for newer readers interested in intermarket analysis.

My first book on this subject, entitled *Intermarket Technical Analysis: Trading Strategies for the Global Stock, Bond, Commodity, and Currency Markets* (Wiley & Sons), was published in 1991. The reason I wrote the book was to demonstrate that all global financial markets are closely linked and have an impact on each other. The book's main thesis was that technical analysts needed to broaden their chart horizon to take these intermarket relationships into consideration. Analysis of the stock market by itself, for example, was incomplete without taking into consideration existing trends in the dollar, bond, and commodity markets. That first book suggested that financial markets could often be used as leading indicators of trends in related markets or, at the very least, could provide confirmation (or nonconfirmation) of other existing trends.

Because the message of that earlier text challenged the *single market* focus of the technical community, some professional chartists questioned whether this newer and broader intermarket approach had any place in the technical field. Many questioned whether intermarket relationships existed at all or, if they did, whether they were consistent enough to provide any forecasting value. A paper on the subject that I once submitted to the Market Technicians Association (MTA) was rejected due to lack of proof. The seemingly revolutionary idea that all global markets are linked, and that American analysts could gain some edge by following trends in foreign markets, was also viewed with skepticism. How things have changed in the two decades since then.

Twenty years later, *intermarket analysis* is considered a branch of technical analysis and an increasingly popular one. A poll taken by the *Journal of Technical Analysis* asked the membership of the Market Technicians Association to rate the relative importance of various technical disciplines. Of the 14 technical disciplines included in the poll, intermarket analysis ranked fifth. In addition, my second book on the subject, entitled *Intermarket Analysis: Profiting from Global Market Relationships* (Wiley Trading, 2004), is now required reading for the MTA's Chartered Market Technician (CMT) program—the very program that rejected my earlier paper on the same subject. (The Chartered Market Technician program is a three-step certification process administered by the Market Technicians Association (mta.org) in which candidates are required to demonstrate proficiency in technical analysis. Successful candidates are awarded the professional designation of Chartered Market Technician.) It is certainly gratifying to see intermarket analysis come such a long way in the last two decades and to finally become such an accepted part of technical market analysis. After reading this book, I hope you'll agree with me that intermarket analysis has also become an increasingly indispensable part of it.

My first intermarket book (1991) reviewed the hyperinflationary decade of the 1970s ending with the bursting of the commodity bubble in 1980, which, in turn, led to major upturns in bonds and stocks in the early 1980s and ushered in two decades of *disinflation* and bull markets in bonds and stocks. It also analyzed the 1987 stock market crash, which, for me, turned intermarket theory into reality. It ended with a description of global events leading up to the start of the first Persian Gulf War as 1990 drew to a close. My second book on that subject (2004) took up where the first book left off and drew comparisons between the first Iraq war during 1990–1991 and the second war 13 years later, in 2002–2003. The actual start of both wars helped launch new bull markets in stocks during 1991 and 2003. The second book also described market trends in the 1990s, which included the *stealth* bear market during 1994, which offered another lesson in intermarket relationships. A huge spike in the price of oil was a big contributing factor to that year's losses in bonds and stocks.

Two watershed events took place during the 1990s that helped introduce a new word into the financial commentary: *deflation*. The collapse of the Japanese stock market in 1990 and the Asian currency crisis during 1997–1998 raised deflation concerns for the first time since the 1930s. My 2004 book described how the threat of deflation as the 1990s ended changed some important intermarket relationships, and contributed to the bursting of the Nasdaq bubble as the new century started. Many of those changes are still in effect more than a decade after that first market top of the new millennium. The 2004 book ended with the start of a new bull market in stocks during the spring of 2003 (caused partially by a collapse in oil prices at the start of the second Iraq war).

My next book, entitled *The Visual Investor, Second Edition* (Wiley Trading, 2009), covered market events surrounding the 2007–2008 financial meltdown, which was caused in no small part by the worst housing collapse since the Great Depression. That book showed how to combine traditional charting techniques with intermarket principles to get a complete picture of what was happening. As this book is being written nearly five years later, many of the effects of that global meltdown are still being felt.

This book will review events since 2000 with a view toward demonstrating that the threat of deflation throughout the past decade has dominated most intermarket relationships, as well as Federal Reserve policy. The start of the commodity boom during 2002 was the direct result of the Fed's devaluation of the U.S. dollar in an attempt to stem deflationary pressures (a technique that was also tried during the 1930s). One of the most important intermarket changes that will be described has to do with the changing relationship between bonds and stocks, which *decoupled* in the years after 1998. In the decades before 1998, rising bond prices supported rising stock prices. Starting in 1998, however, rising bond prices hurt stock values, which was a new phenomenon that became painfully evident from 2000 to 2002 during the worst stock plunge since the Great Depression, and again during the 2008 financial collapse.

A second intermarket change has been the increasingly close linkage between stock and commodity prices since the bursting of the housing bubble during 2007, which was also reminiscent of the deflationary 1930s. Since 2008, stocks and commodities have trended pretty much in lockstep. That's because both are tied to global economic trends. The events surrounding the 2008 market meltdown reinforced another economic lesson having to do with the link between markets and the economy. The stock market is a leading economic indicator. Stocks usually peak and trough ahead of the economy. The Great Recession following the housing collapse started in December 2007 (three months after stocks peaked) and ended in June 2009 (three months after stocks bottomed). It was also the longest and deepest economic downturn since the Great Depression of the 1930s. No wonder the Fed started to use the same playbook that was used back in that earlier era.

In my view, three major deflationary events have occurred over the last 20 years. The first was the peak in Japanese stocks starting in 1990, which turned into a deflationary spiral in the world's second biggest economy (at that time). The second was the Asian currency crisis during 1997–1998. The third event was the housing collapse during 2007. Those three deflationary events led to a *new normal* in intermarket relationships that exists as we enter the second decade of the new century. Explaining what those new normal relationships are, and how you can take advantage of them, is the purpose of this book.

Intermarket analysis is very visual. Although the relationships described herein are based on sound economic principles, and are backed up by correlation statistics, my approach relies heavily on being able to see those relationships on price charts. As a result, you're going to see a lot of charts. The use of color graphics in this edition will make those comparisons a lot easier to see and a lot more striking. Rest assured that you won't have to be a chart expert to understand the charts. All you'll need is the ability to tell up from down. And an open mind.

TRADING
WITH
INTERMARKET
ANALYSIS

PART I

THE OLD NORMAL

CHAPTER 1

Intermarket Analysis: The Study of Relationships

This chapter covers the main points of intermarket analysis, starting with the observation that all markets are related. It will also introduce asset allocation and sector rotation strategies at various stages of the business cycle, and explain how stocks peak and trough before the economy. Other points include the important role played by crude oil, how exchange traded funds have revolutionized intermarket trading, the advantage of using charts, why viewing the big picture is important, intermarket implications for technical analysis, how its adds a new dimension to technical work, why it's an evolutionary step, and why relationships change. It will end with a recap of intermarket principles.

3

■ All Markets Are Related

As the name implies, *intermarket analysis* is the study of how various financial markets are related to each other. This is a departure from prior forms of market analysis, which relied primarily on a *single-market* approach. Stock market analysts, for example, used to spend their time analyzing the stock market, which included market sectors as well as individual stocks. Stock traders didn't have much interest in what was happening in bonds, commodity markets, or the dollar (not to mention overseas markets). Fixed-income analysts and traders spent their time analyzing the bond market without worrying too much about other markets. Commodity traders had their hands full tracking the direction of those markets and didn't care much about other asset classes. Trading in currency markets was limited to futures specialists and interbank traders.

intermarket analysis is the study of how various financial markets are related to each other

That is no longer the case. Traditional chart analysis has taken a major evolutionary step over the last decade by adopting a more universal intermarket approach. I like to think that my two earlier books on intermarket analysis (published in 1991 and 2004) helped move things in that direction. It would be unthinkable today for a trader in any one of those four asset classes not to study trends in the other three.

Some understanding of how the different asset classes interact with each other is important for at least two reasons. First, such an understanding helps you appreciate how other financial markets influence whichever market you're primarily interested in. For example, it's crucial to know how bonds and stocks interact. If you're trading stocks, you should be watching bonds because bond prices usually trend in the opposite direction of stocks. In many cases, turns in the bond market actually precede turns in stocks. Bond yields are inversely correlated with bond prices. That being the case, falling bond yields (rising bond prices) can be a negative warning for stocks.

Figure 1.1 compares the yield on the 10-year Treasury note to the S&P 500 during 2000. After peaking that January (first arrow), the bond yield started falling a lot faster than the stock market. By that spring, the bond yield had fallen to the lowest level in a year while the S&P 500 was still trending sideways (although the Nasdaq peaked that spring). The S&P 500 didn't start falling until the fourth quarter of that year (second arrow) and entered a major bear market that lasted for more than two years. That's a pretty dramatic example of falling bond yields giving early warning that the stock market was in trouble. It demonstrates how the bond market usually changes direction before stocks at major turning points and is often a leading indicator of the stock market. Figure 1.1 also demonstrates why it's so important for stock analysts to take trends in the bond market into consideration.

If you're a bond trader, you should be watching trends in commodity markets. A jump in commodity prices, for example, is usually associated with a drop in bond values. In another illustration of how one market impacts on another, a falling U.S. dollar usually results in rising commodity prices. And, as you'll see later in the book, the direction of the U.S. currency helps determine the relative attractiveness of foreign stocks compared to those in the United States.

FIGURE 1.1   Drop in bond yield during 2000 warned of stock peak

■ Asset Allocation Strategies

A second reason why it's important to understand intermarket relationships is to help with the *asset allocation* process. There was a time not too long ago when investors' choices were limited to bonds, stocks, or cash. Asset allocation models were based on that limited philosophy. Over the last decade, however, investment choices have broadened considerably. Since 2002, for example, commodities have been the strongest asset class and are now recognized by Wall Street and the investing public as a viable alternative to bonds and stocks. The emergence of exchange-traded funds (ETFs) has had a lot to do with the increasingly popularity of commodity trading. The same is true for foreign currency markets, which have also had a strong run since 2002.

Consider the relative performance of those four asset classes since the start of 2002 when the U.S. dollar started a major decline that eventually took it to a record low. During the 10-year span starting in 2002, commodity prices gained 64 percent. By comparison, bond prices gained 23 percent, while U.S. stocks experienced a relatively modest gain of 9 percent. The main catalyst in the commodity upturn was a 32 percent drop in the U.S. dollar. That's because the dollar and commodities trend in opposite directions. A falling dollar results in higher commodity prices.

> ### JOHN'S TIPS
>
> Commodity prices and foreign currencies trend in the same direction and in the opposite direction of the U.S. dollar.

Figure 1.2 compares the trend of the U.S. Dollar Index to the CRB Index of commodity prices between 2000 and 2008. It's clear that the two markets trended in opposite directions. It can also be seen that the major upturn in commodity prices began during 2002 (up arrow) at the exact same time that the dollar started dropping (down arrow). The inverse relationship between the dollar and commodity markets is one of the most consistent and reliable relationships in intermarket work.

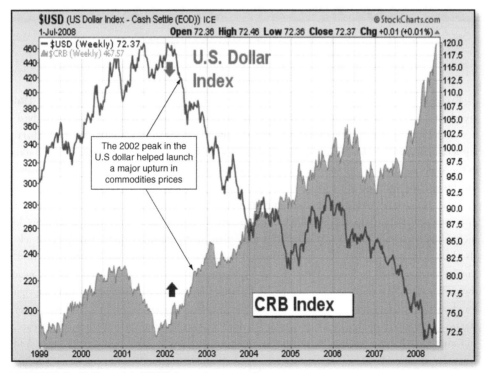

FIGURE 1.2   Dollar peak in 2002 led to major commodity upturn

Foreign currencies also benefit from a falling dollar. That's especially true for currencies tied to countries that export commodities like Australia and Canada. During the 10 years starting in 2002, the Aussie dollar (boosted by rising commodity prices) gained 101 percent versus 50 percent for the euro. It's clear that investors have benefited from the ability to expand their asset allocation choices beyond bonds and stocks. Exchange-traded funds are a big reason why.

ETFs Have Revolutionized Intermarket Trading

Exchange-traded funds have had a lot to do with expanding those choices into alternate assets like commodities and currencies. In fact, the explosive popularity of ETFs has revolutionized the world of intermarket trading and has made it increasingly easy to implement global intermarket strategies. During the 1990s, for example, the ability to incorporate commodities and currencies into one's portfolio was almost impossible outside of the futures markets. The growing availability of ETFs has made investing in commodity and currency markets as easy as buying a stock on a stock exchange. Exchange-traded funds can be used for virtually any asset class anywhere in the world. Mainly for that reason, we'll be relying very heavily on ETFs throughout this book to show how markets interact and how to take advantage of those interactions. Another place where ETFs have become extremely popular is in implementing sector rotation strategies.

Sector Rotation and the Business Cycle

Intermarket analysis plays an important role in *sector rotation* strategies. The U.S. stock market is divided into market sectors (which are further subdivided into industry groups).

JOHN'S TIPS

The stock market has 10 sectors and approximately 90 industry groups.

Exchange-traded funds are available that cover all market sectors (and most industry groups). That greatly facilitates the movement into and out of various market sectors at different stages of the business cycle. I'll show you later in the book how to use intermarket principles (and some simple charting techniques) to spot leading and lagging market sectors for the purpose of ensuring that you're in the leaders and out of the laggards. You'll also learn how tracking sector rotation offers valuable insights into the direction of the stock market and the economy.

Near the start of a new bull market in stocks, economically sensitive groups like consumer discretionary stocks (which include retailers) usually do better than most other stocks. So do technology and transportation stocks, which are tied to the business cycle. Small-cap stocks also lead at market bottoms. Near market tops, those very same groups usually turn down first. Energy stocks (which are tied to the price of oil) have a tendency to become market leaders near the end of a bull market in stocks. Energy leadership is almost always a dangerous warning sign for the stock market. One of the ways to tell that the stock market is peaking is when money starts to flow out of energy stocks and into defensive sectors like consumer staples, health care, and utilities. I'll show you how to spot those rotations and how to take advantage of them. And what they mean.

Stocks Peak and Trough before the Economy

Important tops in the stock market usually lead to periods of economic weakness (or recessions). The 2000 stock market top, for example, led to a recession the following spring. The October 2007 market top led to a recession that December. The same is true at market bottoms. The ending of the last two recessions during 2003 and 2009 followed market upturns a few months earlier. When the stock market weakens, money tends to rotate out of stocks and into bonds. At market bottoms, the opposite happens. Money rotates out of bonds and back into stocks. Fortunately, it's pretty easy to spot those shifts in investor sentiment, which we'll demonstrate later in the book. It's hard to separate trends in financial markets from trends in the economy. Intermarket analysis sheds light not only on market direction but the economy as well. You'll also see later in the book that bonds, stocks, and commodities have a history of peaking and troughing in a predictable order during turns in the business cycle.

JOHN'S TIPS

Bonds usually change direction first at tops and bottoms, stocks turn second, and commodities third.

That knowledge will help you determine where to be at different stages of the business cycle. It will also help you determine whether the business cycle is turning up or turning down.

The Role of Oil

Rising oil prices from the beginning of 2007 preceded a stock market downturn later that year. Oil's role in the 2007 market top wasn't an aberration. In fact, it was very normal. Rising oil prices have contributed to every U.S. recession in the last 40 years. Rising oil prices have also contributed to stock market peaks and resulting bear markets. That was certainly the case during the mid-1970s when a tripling in the price of crude during 1973 (during the Arab Oil Embargo) led to a 50 percent stock market loss the following year (1974). Spikes in the price of crude also preceded or accompanied stock market drops during 1987, 1990, 1994, and 2000. By contrast, sharp drops in the price of crude have usually had a bullish impact on stocks. That was the case at the start of the two Iraq wars in early 1991 and 2003, which helped launch new bull markets in stocks. That's why market leadership by stocks tied to oil is normally a danger to the stock market. That's also why our intermarket analysis has to always consider what the price of oil is doing. Upward spikes in oil prices have preceded most stock market peaks.

JOHN'S TIPS

Rising oil prices usually force the Fed to raise interest rates, which weakens the stock market and slows the economy.

Figure 1.3 compares the price of crude oil to the S&P 500 during 2007 and 2008. The chart shows two consistent intermarket tendencies. The first is that rising oil prices usually precede stock market peaks. Crude started climbing at the start of 2007 (first up arrow). After a modest pullback during August, crude turned up even more sharply that September (second up arrow). The stock market peaked a month later during October (first down arrow). Rising oil is usually a warning sign for stocks

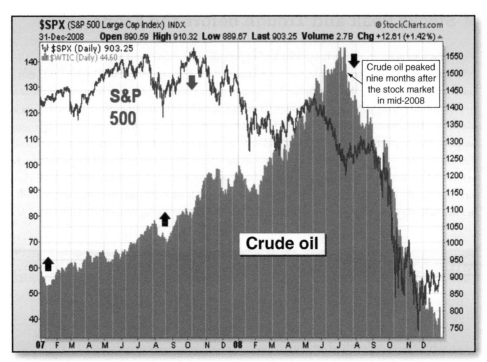

FIGURE 1.3 Rise in crude during 2007 contributed to stock peak

and has led to most market tops. The second intermarket lesson is that oil usually peaks after stocks do. Figure 1.3 shows crude peaking during July 2008 (second down arrow), nine months after the stock top.

■ Advantages of Using Charts

All of this talk about intermarket relationships may start sounding like a lot of economic theory. This is partially the case because intermarket analysis is based on economic principles. However, it is not theory. Intermarket work is market-driven. There is nothing theoretical about a profit-and-loss statement. Economists look at economic statistics to determine the direction of the economy and, by inference, the likely direction of financial markets. By contrast, chartists look at the markets themselves. That makes a big difference. Economic statistics by their very nature are *backward-looking*. What else could they be? They tell us what happened last month or last quarter. They tell us nothing about the future (or the present, for that matter). The markets, however, are *forward-looking* entities. That's why the markets are called *discounting* mechanisms. Stocks anticipate (or discount) economic trends six to nine months into the future. There's also a reason some markets are called *futures*. Which would you rather depend on: backward-looking statistics or forward-looking markets? Put another way, would you rather place your trust in a lagging or a leading indicator of future market trends? Economists rely on lagging economic indicators, while chartists place their trust in forward-looking financial markets.

> **JOHN'S TIPS**
>
> While stocks usually change direction before the economy, bonds usually change direction before stocks. That makes bonds an even earlier economic indicator than stocks.

This distinction goes to the heart of technical analysis, which is based on the premise that markets are leading indicators of their own fundamentals. In that sense, chart analysis is a shortcut form of economic and fundamental analysis. This is one reason why intermarket analysts use charts. Charts also offer a big advantage in intermarket work because they allow us to look at so many different markets. It's hard to imagine how anyone could study and compare markets all over the world in all asset classes without the use of charts. Besides making comparisons of so many markets much easier, it's not even necessary to be an expert in any of those markets. All one needs is knowledge of how to plot the charts and the ability to determine which markets are going up and which ones are dropping. Intermarket work goes a step further by determining if two related markets are moving in the same or in opposite directions.

Viewing the Big Picture Is Important

The biggest benefits of the visual tools described in this book are their universality and transferability. They can be applied to any market anywhere in the world—and to any time dimension. They can be applied to short-term trading as well as long-term investing. Any market that can be charted can be analyzed. That gives the chartist an enormous advantage over those who prefer to use some form of economic or fundamental analysis. Those two schools of analysis have a number of problems to deal with. The economist is forced to deal with old data. The fundamental analyst (who studies company and industry earnings) has a tremendous amount of data to deal with. That prevents the fundamental analyst from covering a wide variety of markets. As a result, fundamental analysts are forced to specialize. The intermarket chartist, by comparison, can follow any market he or she wishes to anywhere in the world without having to be an expert in any one of them. That's a pretty big advantage in an interrelated world of intermarket analysis and trading. More importantly, the ability to scan so many markets from different asset classes all over the world provides the intermarket chartist with a *big-picture* view of what's really happening. That's a huge advantage over the *tunnel vision* that's so often seen among market analysts who follow only a small portion of the financial spectrum.

Intermarket Implications for Technical Analysis

Because intermarket work involves looking at so many markets, it has to be done with price charts. Chart analysis is the easiest and most efficient way to study intermarket linkages. Intermarket work greatly expands the usefulness of technical analysis. It allows analysts like me to talk about things that used to be restricted to security analysts and economists, like inflation, deflation, the direction of interest rates, the impact of the dollar, and the state of the business cycle. Some understanding of how bonds, stocks, and commodities rotate during the business cycle, for example, allows us to talk about the state of the economy. Sector rotation also sheds light on whether the economy is contracting or expanding.

JOHN'S TIPS

Consumer discretionary stocks lead early in an economic expansion. Energy leadership occurs near the end of an expansion. Consumer staples are strongest during an economic downturn.

The financial markets are leading indicators of economic trends. It took the Federal Reserve until the spring of 2003 to acknowledge the threat of deflation. The markets had spotted the threat years earlier. It also took the Fed a lot longer than it took chart analysts to recognize the threat from the housing collapse during 2007. The events surrounding stock market peaks during 2000 and 2007 demonstrated the need to incorporate some chart and intermarket analysis into economic and fundamental forecasting. It took the Wall Street community too long to figure out what many chartists already knew during the first half of 2000 and 2007 when warning signs of a market top were clearly visible, and that the economy was headed for trouble (as you'll see in the following chapters). The idea that technical analysis is a shortcut form of fundamental analysis is based on the premise that price action in any market is a leading indicator of that market's fundamentals. A lot of Wall Street analysts (and their clients) paid a big price for ignoring the clear chart signals that the markets were giving off during 2000 and 2007. They also paid a price for ignoring intermarket signals.

■ A New Dimension to Technical Work

The greatest contribution made by intermarket analysis is that it improves the market analyst's peripheral trading vision. Trying to trade markets without intermarket awareness is like driving a car without looking at the side and rearview mirrors and windows. Intermarket analysis includes all markets everywhere on the globe. By turning the focus of the market analyst outward instead of inward, intermarket work provides a more rational understanding of forces at work in the marketplace. It provides a more unified view of global market behavior. Intermarket analysis uses activity in surrounding markets in much the same way that analysts use internal market indicators. Intermarket analysis doesn't replace traditional technical analysis; it adds another dimension to it.

■ Intermarket Work Is an Evolutionary Step

I like to think that intermarket analysis represents another step in the evolution of technical theory and practice. With the growing recognition that all global markets are linked, traders can take these linkages into consideration more and more in their analysis. Because of its flexibility and its universal application to all markets, technical analysis is uniquely suited to perform intermarket work.

Intermarket analysis provides a more useful framework for understanding how individual markets and sectors relate to one another. Throughout most of the 20th century, technical analysis had an inward focus. This new century has witnessed a much broader application of technical principles not just to financial markets themselves, but also to their wider implications for economic forecasting. Even the Federal Reserve looks to the financial markets to get clues about the future course of the economy. It has to use charts to do that. The intermarket principles presented in this book offer a much broader view of the future of technical analysis. I believe that intermarket analysis will play an increasingly important role in that future.

To ignore market interrelationships is to ignore enormously valuable price information. What is worse is that it leaves market analysts in the position of not understanding the external forces that move the market in which they are trading. The days of following only one market are gone. Market analysts need to know what is happening in all of the financial markets and must understand the impact of trends in those related markets all over the world. Technical analysis has enormous transferability in moving from one market to another, and is extremely useful in comparing the relative performance of those markets.

■ Why Relationships Change

Intermarket relationships are not static. While most remain constant over long periods of time, they sometimes change for short periods. Some changes are more long lasting. As you'll see shortly, that is what happened between bonds and stocks. Nothing changes, however, without a reason. The changing relationship between bonds and stocks that started as the old century came to a close signaled that business cycles after 2000 would be different from other downturns since World War II. That became especially true after the housing collapse during 2007, which precipitated the worst financial melt-down since the Great Depression. Government attempts to turn the business cycle back up relied on traditional fiscal and monetary measures, which had worked in the past. Unfortunately, they didn't work as well this time.

That was because the business cycle after 2000, and especially after 2007, wasn't like other traditional postwar business cycles. Deflationary pressures overrode those traditional government measures. Some of the intermarket changes that took place near the start of this century, and again after 2007, gave us plenty of warning that this time would be different.

The intermarket principles presented in this book are offered as guidelines, not rigid rules. The ability to adapt to changing market circumstances is one of the keys to profitability. This is as true in intermarket work as it is in any other form of market analysis. Although intermarket relationships are constant most of the time, there will be instances when some intermarket relationships (or correlations) may weaken for short periods of time. At such times, it's better to downplay those relationships until they start to strengthen again. Fortunately, we have tools to let us know when those correlations are strong and when they're weakening. Although the scope of intermarket analysis is broad, forcing us to stretch our imaginations and expand our vision, I remain excited about the prospects for its future. I hope you'll agree after finishing this book. Intermarket work is very fertile ground for market research and profitable trading opportunities.

■ Intermarket Principles

Before we begin our actual analysis of the various financial markets, let's review the main intermarket principles on which this approach is based. The principles are relatively few in number and easy to understand. All are based on sound economic principles and are supported by historical analysis. While most intermarket relationships listed below have remained very constant over the decades, some have changed from time to time. I'll explain why that happens and how you can tell when it is happening.

The basic intermarket principles are:

- All global markets are linked to each other.

- Analysis of any one market should include analysis of the others.

The four asset classes include:

- Stocks

- Bonds

- Commodities

- Currencies

Intermarket relationships:

- The dollar and commodities trend in opposite directions.

- Bond prices and commodities trend in opposite directions.

- Since 1998, bond and stock prices have trended inversely.

- Since 2008, stocks and commodities have been closely correlated.

How they interact:

- Bonds usually change direction before stocks.

- Stocks usually change direction before commodities.

- Bond yields peak first at tops, stocks second, and commodities last.

- Those rotations are less reliable at bottoms than at tops.

Foreign influence:

- All global stocks are closely correlated.

- A rising dollar benefits U.S. stocks.

- A weaker dollar favors foreign stocks.

- Emerging markets are closely tied to commodity trends.

Review of the Old Normal

Most of the intermarket principles just listed have remained pretty constant over the past few decades. Some, however, have undergone changes over the last decade. One change that has developed in recent years is that stock and commodity prices have become closely correlated. That's been especially true since the financial meltdown during 2008, which was caused mainly by a deflationary collapse in the housing industry. The more important intermarket change has to do with the relationship between bonds and stocks following the Asian currency crisis in the late 1990s. Since 1998, bond and stock prices have trended in opposite directions (which reversed their earlier relationship). That's also typical during a decade when deflation has remained a threat. Although the main focus of this book deals with the *new normal* in intermarket relationships that has existed since 2000 (and even more so since 2008), it's useful to briefly review intermarket relationships that existed in the final three decades of the prior century to lay a foundation for our intermarket work, and to examine market events that led to newer market relationships that exist in current time. We'll review those *old normal* relationships in the next chapter.

CHAPTER 2

Review of the Old Normal

This chapter reviews the *old normal* intermarket relationships that existed during the last three decades of the 20th century. A peak in commodity prices during 1980 ended the hyperinflationary 1970s and led to two decades of disinflation and bull markets in bonds and stocks. It will also show how the 1987 market crash reinforced intermarket trends, as did the first Iraq war at the start of 1991 and the second war 13 years later. Intermarket relationships held firm during the *stealth* bear market in stocks that took place during 1994. The Asian currency crisis during 1997–1998 introduced the threat of *deflation* for the first time since the 1930s and changed some key intermarket relationships. The collapse of the Japanese stock market in 1990, and resulting deflation in that country, also contributed to the growing deflation threat as the new century started.

▪ 1980 Was a Key Turning Point

The year 1980 is important in the history of intermarket relationships. The commodity bubble burst that year and ended the hyperinflation of the 1970s when hard assets like commodities soared and paper assets like bonds and stocks floundered. The 1980 peak in commodity prices (which coincided with a bottom in the U.S. dollar) began a two-decade disinflationary trend and launched major bull markets in bonds and stocks. The combination of a rising dollar and falling commodities during 1980 contributed to a major upturn in bond prices during 1981. The stock market began a major bull market a year later, during 1982, that lasted through the end of the 20th century. That important turning point in market history followed the traditional intermarket script very closely.

First, the major peak in commodities coincided with a major bottom in the U.S. dollar. That confirmed one of the most consistent intermarket principles that commodity prices and the dollar trend in opposite directions. Figure 2.1 shows that the 1980 peak in the CRB Index of commodity prices (down arrow) coincided exactly with a major upturn in the U.S. Dollar Index (up arrow). That major upturn in the dollar helped end the commodity inflationary spiral that characterized the 1970s.

JOHN'S TIPS

A rising dollar causes commodity prices to fall. Falling commodity prices usually produce higher bond prices.

FIGURE 2.1 Inverse correlation between commodities and the dollar

A second intermarket principle is that bond and commodity prices trend in opposite directions. The big drop in commodity prices during 1980 was a major reason why bond prices turned up so strongly during 1981. Figure 2.2 shows that major peak in commodity prices during 1980 (down arrow) contributing to a major upturn in Treasury bond prices a year later during 1981 (up arrow). A third intermarket principle that existed at that time was that bond and stock prices usually trended in the same direction. (That relationship changed in the late 1990s.) The 1981 bottom in bonds contributed to the 1982 upturn in stocks. Figure 2.3 shows that the 1981 upturn in Treasury bond prices (first up arrow) was followed by a major upturn the S&P 500 a year later during 1982 (second up arrow).

FIGURE 2.2 Inverse correlation between bond prices and commodities

FIGURE 2.3   Positive correlation between bond and stock prices

The fact that bonds turned up before stocks also followed the normal sequence in the sense that turns in the bond market usually precede turns in stocks. To summarize then, the decade of the 1980s started with a rising dollar, falling commodities, and rising bond and stocks prices (in that order). Those trends completely reversed intermarket trends from the 1970s.

■ The End of the Inflationary 1970s

To fully understand the dramatic turns in the financial markets that started in 1980, it's necessary to know something about the 1970s. That decade witnessed a virtual explosion in commodity markets, which led to spiraling inflation and rising interest rates. From 1971 to 1980, the CRB Index of commodity prices appreciated by 250 percent. Bond yields (which rise as bond prices fall) rose by 150 percent during the same period. The 1970s were not only bad for bonds. They were bad for stocks as well. The Dow Jones Industrial Average started and ended the decade near the same level of 1,000. In the middle of that 10-year period of stagflation, the U.S. stock market lost half of its value. That took place during 1974 as a result of a spike in oil that started the year before during 1973.

The 1970s was a decade for tangible assets like commodities; paper assets like bonds and stocks were out of favor. By the end of that decade, gold prices had soared above $700 an ounce. A weak dollar during that period also contributed to the upward spiral in gold and other commodities, as well as the relative weakness in bonds and stocks. Intermarket relationships during the 1970s also held intact. A

JOHN'S TIPS

Upward spikes in the price of oil usually produce lower stock market values.

falling dollar contributed to higher commodity prices, which contributed to lower bond and stock prices. The economic term used to describe the 1970s is *stagflation*, which occurs when high inflation combines with economic stagnation. Those trends completely reversed starting in 1980 with a peak in commodities. The CRB Index fell from a record high of 330 and began a 20-year decline, during which time it lost half of its value. During those same 20 years, gold prices fell from above $700 to $250, which was a loss of 60 percent from its 1980 peak. Within two years of the 1980 commodity top, the intermarket trends of the 1970s were completely reversed. The next two decades favored paper assets like bonds and stocks at the expense of tangible assets like commodities, which fell out of favor.

---

stagflation occurs when high inflation combines with economic stagnation

---

The 1987 Crash Reinforced Intermarket Trends

The biggest financial event of the 1980s—the 1987 stock market crash—provided another dramatic example of how markets are related to each other and the necessity for paying attention to all markets. Stock analysts who ignored the action in related markets like bonds and commodities during the first half of that year were blindsided by a market crash during the second half. In the four years after 1982, two of the main factors supporting rising stock prices were falling commodity prices (low inflation) and rising bond prices (falling interest rates).

During April 1987, however, commodity prices spiked higher while bond prices tumbled (rising commodities usually result in falling bond prices). The stock rally continued into that August before finally peaking. The fact that bond prices peaked four months before stocks once again demonstrated the tendency for bonds to change direction before stocks. The stock market finally crashed that October.

JOHN'S TIPS

The bond market usually changes direction before stocks.

I had given speeches that spring and summer on Wall Street, and written articles warning that intermarket trends in bonds and commodities had turned very dangerous for stocks. While the size of the stock downturn was a surprise, the fact that stocks did turn down shouldn't have been. Figure 2.4 shows an upward spike in commodity prices (up arrow) during the spring of 1987 coinciding with a plunge in bond prices (down arrow). The S&P 500 crashed that October (top portion).

The fact that the 1987 stock market crash was global in scope provided another lesson in intermarket work, which is that global stock markets become highly correlated during market downturns. That lesson was repeated again during 2000 and 2008. At such times, the benefits of global diversification are greatly diminished. As we'll see later in the book, a rising dollar during market downturns usually makes foreign stocks fall even faster than those in the United States.

The Two Iraq Wars

Three years after recovering from the 1987 collapse, global markets were forced to deal with Iraq's August 1990 invasion of Kuwait. Once again, financial markets reacted in predictable intermarket fashion. Gold and oil prices surged that summer and in the months following the invasion while bond and stock prices around the world tumbled. At the start of Desert Storm in January 1991, all those intermarket trends reversed. Global bonds and stocks resumed their uptrends, while gold and oil prices fell. Thirteen years later (during 2003), market analysts were facing the prospects for another Iraq war and were forced to study the 1990–1991 market reactions for guidance. It's a good thing

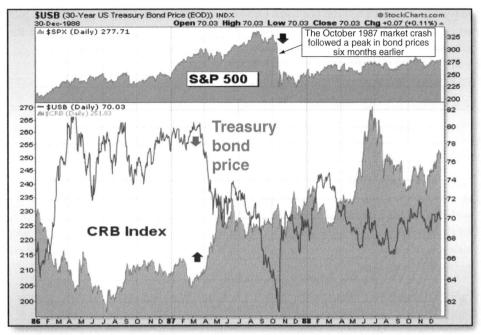

FIGURE 2.4 Intermarket trends leading to 1987 market crash

they did. Figure 2.5 shows the upward spike in crude oil (up arrow) during the second half of 1990 coinciding with a stock downturn. A plunge in crude oil (down arrow) the following January turned stock prices back up again.

Intermarket trends witnessed during the 1990–1991 Desert Storm era were remarkably similar to those witnessed during the second Iraq crisis over a decade later in 2002–2003. During the second conflict, gold and oil prices soared in the months leading up to the outbreak of the Iraq war while stocks and bonds fell (just as they had done during 1990). And, once again, the actual outbreak of hostilities saw a complete reversal of those intermarket trends. The week that hostilities started (March 17, 2003) the U.S. stock market surged 8 percent, which was the biggest weekly gain in

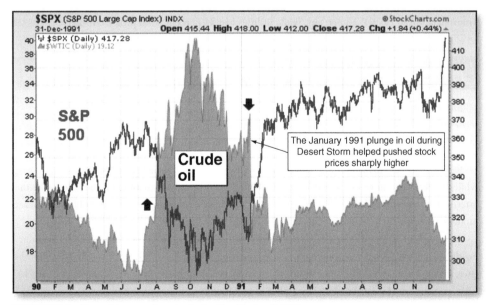

FIGURE 2.5 How oil impacted stocks during first Persian Gulf War

20 years (and started a bull run that lasted for four years). While global stocks were rallying, gold prices fell 15 percent. Crude oil prices tumbled 33 percent. A 4-percent jump in the U.S. dollar contributed to the drop in commodity prices.

Bond prices, which had attracted a safe haven bid in the months leading up the second Iraq crisis, turned down as a massive switch took place from the relative safety of Treasuries and back into stocks. In both Iraq conflicts, the four financial markets (bonds, stocks, commodities, and currencies) did exactly what they were expected to do from an intermarket perspective. Market analysts who studied market reactions during the first Iraq war for clues to what might happen during the second war weren't disappointed.

Did You Know. . .?

The fact that bonds and stocks trended inversely during the second Iraq crisis during 2002–2003 reflected the change in their relationship that started in 1998 when the two markets decoupled.

The 1994 Stealth Bear Market Follows Intermarket Script

The main event of the mid-1990s was the 1994 *stealth* bear market in stocks. Its name comes from the fact that major stock indexes lost little more than 10 percent (although bonds suffered their worst fall in decades). The relatively small declines in the major stock indexes, however, masked more serious damage suffered in some sectors of the market. Small-cap stocks, for example, lost 15 percent. Transportation stocks fell 26 percent, while utilities lost 34 percent from peak to trough.

Rising oil prices during that year contributed to the outsized losses in the fuel-sensitive transports, while the resulting jump in interest rates (and falling bond prices) contributed to huge losses in the interest rate–sensitive utilities. From the start of that bear market to the end, the old intermarket model held firm.

An upturn in commodity prices during the first half of 1993 led to a downturn in bond prices during the second half of that year. Bond prices peaked during September 1993. Stocks peaked five months later, during February 1994. Once again, the turn in the bond market preceded the turn in stocks. After peaking, stocks and bonds fell together as commodity prices rose, which was to be expected from an intermarket perspective. The dollar fell throughout that year, which contributed to the rise in

FIGURE 2.6   Utility stocks fell along with Treasury bond prices during 1994

commodity prices. Just as the upturn in commodity prices during 1993 started the topping process in bonds and stocks, a peak in the middle of 1994 started an intermarket rotation in the other direction.

A commodity peak in the middle of 1994 contributed to a bond bottom that November. Stocks turned up a month after bonds. Once again, the markets followed their normal rotation. A commodity drop led to higher bond prices, which, in turn, led to higher stock prices. From their fourth-quarter bottom of 1994, stocks began a phenomenal bull run that lasted until the end of that decade. After 1994, the stock market got help from a rising dollar and falling commodity prices. Treasury prices rose into the autumn of 1998, which also supported rising stock values. From an intermarket perspective, a rising dollar and falling commodities supported bull markets in bonds and stocks, which was the norm at the time. During 1998, however, one key intermarket relationship started to change. The reason for that change was the emergence of *deflation* for the first time since the 1930s. Figure 2.6 shows the close correlation between Treasury bond and utility stock prices during 1994 and 1995. Plunging bond prices during 1994 caused heavy losses in the rate-sensitive utilities. Both markets then rallied together during 1995.

■ Echoes from the 1930s

Starting in 1998, the word *deflation* was heard for the first time since the 1930s. That happened mainly because of the Asian currency crisis that gripped the world during 1997 and 1998. Another contributing (although less recognized factor) was the deflation that was starting to infect the Japanese economy as the old century ended. Within a couple of years after 1998, global deflation started to spread from Asia (*Asian contagion*) and started infecting global bond and stock markets everywhere else—including the United States. More than any other factor, the reappearance of deflation changed one key intermarket relationship that had existed through most of the postwar period. That intermarket change was that bond and stock prices became inversely correlated. In other words, they started trending in opposite directions, which was a departure from their prior tendency to trend in the same direction. What was good for bonds after 1998 became bad for stocks. That new bond-stock relationship became painfully clear during 2000 when bond yields not only fell with stocks, but actually turned down before stocks. While stocks fell, bond prices rose.

Bond yields turned down before stocks in 2000 and 2007 and gave early warning of a stock market decline.

A second intermarket change was that commodities started to become more closely correlated with stocks, just as they did in the deflationary 1930s. That closer link between stocks and commodities became even more pronounced after the collapse in the housing market during 2007, which led to the financial meltdown in 2008 (which brought back painful comparisons to the Great Depression of the 1930s). The deflationary implications of that historic event tightened the link between stocks and commodities after 2008. That was because both asset classes became closely tied to the global economic cycle. Rising commodities like copper and oil implied economic strength, which was good for stocks. Falling commodity markets suggested economic weakness, which hurt stock values.

The first decade of the new millennium witnessed the resurgence of hard assets (like gold and other commodities), which was largely the result of the Fed's weakening the dollar in order to combat the threat from deflation. That had also been tried during the 1930s when the dollar was devalued by taking the United States off the gold standard. The result in both instances was higher gold prices. Contrary to popular belief, gold assets do very well in a deflationary climate, as witnessed during the 1930s and the decade after 2000. In the four-year period from 1929 to 1932, stocks and commodities tumbled together. The only two assets that bucked that deflationary decline were Treasury bond prices and gold-mining stocks. I'll cover the upturn in commodities (and the collapse in the dollar) later in the book, at which time I'll draw more comparisons between the Fed's plan after 2002 and the 1930s.

■ The Deflation Scenario

In the 1999 revision of my book entitled *Technical Analysis of the Financial Markets*, I included a chapter on intermarket analysis, which reviewed the historic relationships that dominated the postwar era. I inserted a new section, however, entitled "The Deflation Scenario." That section described the collapse in Asian currency and stock markets that started in the middle of 1997 that had an especially depressing effect on global commodity markets. For the first time in a generation, that collapse in commodity prices to the lowest level in 20 years caused market analysts to start expressing concern that a beneficial era of *disinflation*, when prices of goods rise at a slower pace, might turn into a

---

disinflation when prices of goods rise at a slower pace

---

harmful period of *deflation*, when prices actually fall. How the financial markets reacted to that initial threat of deflation has defined the intermarket model since then.

---

deflation when prices actually fall

Commodity prices fell sharply while bond prices surged. That was nothing new, because falling commodity prices usually produce higher bond prices. What was new was how stocks reacted to the combination of falling commodities and rising bond prices. Instead of rising, stock prices fell. During 1998, stocks were sold all over the world while money poured into U.S. Treasury bonds in a global flight to safety. In other words, stocks fell while bonds rose. That was unusual and represented a huge departure from the old intermarket model (the *old normal*).

Disinflation that started with the commodity peak in 1980 and lasted for nearly two decades is bad for commodities but is good for bonds and stocks. Deflation (which started to emerge in the late 1990s) is also bad for commodities and good for bonds. Deflation, however, is also bad for stocks. Deflation changes the relationship between bonds and stocks. In a deflationary climate, bond prices rise while interest rates fall. Falling interest rates in that environment, however, don't help stocks. In fact, it's quite the opposite. Falling interest rates during a deflationary period are actually bad for stocks. That new relationship was evident during the two bear markets starting in 2000 and 2007, when bond yields fell right along with stocks.

The Japanese Bubble Bursts in 1990

Another important event that happened at the start of the 1990s is still having global repercussions two decades later. The bubble in the Japanese stock market burst that year, which started a 13-year descent that eventually turned into a deflationary spiral in the world's second-largest economy at the time. Over a decade later, central bankers in the West were busy studying the Japanese deflation model to find ways to combat increasing signs of deflation in their own economies. Japanese deflation is one of contributing factors to the *decoupling* of bonds and stocks that took place in the United States nearly a decade after the 1990 stock market top, and continues to influence intermarket trends to the present day.

While the plunge in the Japanese market at the start of the 1990s contributed to the growing deflation threat as the 20th century came to a close, the main event was the Asian currency crisis that lasted from 1997 to 1998. We'll examine that deflationary event in the next chapter, and I'll show how it changed at least one key intermarket relationship.

CHAPTER 3

The 1997–1998 Asian Currency Crisis

This chapter covers intermarket reactions to the Asian currency crisis that occurred between 1997 and 1998. The most important result of that crisis was the dramatic decoupling of bond and stock prices. Those market reactions were a dress rehearsal for the intermarket model that dominated the following decade. One intermarket lesson resulting from that crisis was a warning that falling bond yields (rising bond prices) after 2000 would not have the same positive effect on stocks that it had prior to 1998. The two deflationary events of the 1990s were the collapse in Japanese stocks in 1990 and the collapse of Asian currencies during 1997. Japanese deflation over the last two decades may help explain the persistent decline in bond yields in the United States. A positive correlation has existed between the trend of Japanese stocks and U.S. bond yields.

▣ The Asian Currency Crisis Starts in 1997

During the summer of 1997, the currency of Thailand started to tumble. It was a trend that soon spread to other currencies in that region. The collapse in Asian currency markets caused a corresponding collapse in Asian stock prices, which had a ripple effect around the globe. Fears of global deflation pushed commodity prices into a free fall and contributed to a worldwide rotation out of stocks and into Treasury bonds. Over the following year and a half, the CRB Index of commodity prices fell to the lowest level in 20 years.

25

> **JOHN'S TIPS**
>
> The CRB Index is a basket of 19 actively traded commodity markets and is the oldest measure of commodity price trends.

Figure 3.1 shows the CRB Index of 19 commodity markets during 1998 falling below its 1986 and 1992 lows to reach the lowest level in 20 years. That ended a plateau period in commodity prices that had

FIGURE 3.1   Commodity plunge to 20-year low during 1998 raised fear of deflation

lasted for more than a decade and had contributed to a benign period of disinflation. The 1998 plunge to a two-decade low threatened to turn that beneficial disinflation into a more dangerous deflation.

The reaction of Asian central bankers to the crisis provided a lesson in intermarket economics. In an attempt to stabilize their falling currencies, they raised interest rates. The hike in rates pushed Asian stocks into a steep decline that lasted for at least a year and had a pronounced effect on all global financial markets. Throughout those hectic two years, all traditional intermarket relationships held up quite well—except for one.

■ Bonds and Stocks Start to Decouple

The most important result of the events of 1997 and 1998 was the *decoupling* of bonds and stocks. *Decoupling* means that bond and stock prices trended in opposite directions, rather than adhering to their traditional tendency to trend in the same direction. During the second half of 1997, stock prices in the United States declined while Treasury bond prices rose. During the first half of the following year, stocks rose while bonds declined. During the third quarter of 1998, stocks fell even more sharply as Treasury bond prices soared. From July to October 1998, the Dow Industrials lost 20 percent. Stock markets sold off all over the world. While stocks were falling, U.S. Treasury bond prices surged to record highs. During those three months of panic in the second half of 1998, U.S. Treasuries became the strongest market in the world (a trend that we'll see again during subsequent stock market collapses in 2000 and 2008).

---

decoupling means that bond and stock prices trended in opposite directions, rather than adhering to their traditional tendency to trend in the same direction

---

JOHN'S TIPS

During financial panics, investors usually take money out of stocks and put it into U.S. Treasury bonds, which are considered to be one of the safest investments in the world.

By the end of 1998, perceptions that the crisis had passed caused bonds to tumble and stocks to soar in a complete role reversal of the prior three months. Bonds continued to fall throughout the entire year of 1999 while stocks soared to record highs. The events of 1997 and 1998 contributed to a major decoupling of bonds and stocks, which has lasted to this day. The changing relationship between bonds and stocks started in the midst of the Asian currency crisis when a new word started circulating in financial circles: *deflation.*

Figure 3.2 compares the trend of bond and stock prices during 1998 and part of 1999. During the height of the crisis from July to October 1998 (shaded area), stock prices plunged while bond prices soared. Global investors sold stocks all over the world and fled to the safety of U.S. Treasuries. When the crisis passed that October, those trends were reversed. Investors sold bonds and bought stocks. That decoupling of bonds and stocks during 1998 was a dress rehearsal for the coming decade.

During the Asian currency crisis that started in the middle of 1997, investors started selling stocks and buying bonds. The reason for that switch in trading patterns is that deflation changes some of the normal intermarket relationships, but not all. In a deflationary climate, bond prices rise while commodity prices fall (which also happens during disinflation). That's what happened from the middle of 1997 through the fourth quarter of 1998, and was not unusual. However, the stock market reacted negatively, which was unusual. My 1999 book, *Technical Analysis of the Financial Markets,* included the following quote on that period:

> The deflationary trend that started in Asia in mid-1997 spread to Russia and Latin America by mid-1998 and began to hurt all global equity markets. A plunge in commodity prices had an especially damaging impact on commodity exporters like Australia, Canada, Mexico, and Russia. The deflationary impact of falling commodity prices had a positive impact on Treasury bond prices, which hit record highs. Market events of 1998 were a dramatic example of the existence of global intermarket linkages and demonstrated how bonds and stocks can decouple in a deflationary world.

FIGURE 3.2   Bond and stock prices decouple during 1998 deflation scare

1997 and 1998 Were Only a Dress Rehearsal

The way the financial markets reacted to the initial deflationary threat during 1997 and 1998 was only a dress rehearsal for the devastating bear market in stocks that started in the spring of 2000. During the worst three stock market years since the Great Depression, bond prices rose continuously while stock prices fell. The Fed lowered interest rates 12 times over an 18-month period with no apparent effect on stocks. Those who heeded the warnings given during the Asian currency crisis a few years earlier were alerted to the fact that rising bond prices (and falling rates) don't necessarily help stocks in a deflationary climate.

JOHN'S TIPS

During an economic downturn, the Fed lowers interest rates, which helps to stabilize the stock market. During a deflationary downturn, however, Fed policy becomes much less effective.

Figure 3.3 compares the trend of stocks and bond yields before 1998 and after that watershed year. Prior to 1998, falling bond yields were positive for stocks (left arrow). Starting in 1998, however, bond yields started trending in the same direction of stocks (right arrow). After 1998, falling bond yields became bad for stocks. That can be seen very clearly in the three bear market years from 2000 through 2002. Figure 3.3 also shows bond yields turning down ahead of stocks during 2000. (They would do that again during 2007.) That maintained the historical tendency for bonds to change direction ahead of stocks—except that instead of bond *prices* turning down before stocks (which had been pattern prior to 1998), the new relationship between the two markets made bond *yields* the new leading indicator for stocks.

Did You Know. . .?

Since bond *yields* and bond *prices* trend inversely, that means that bond *prices* and stocks trended in opposite directions after 1998.

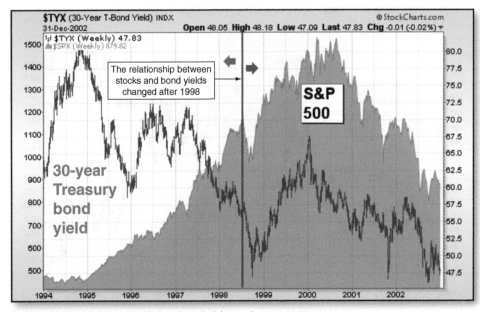

FIGURE 3.3 Falling bond yields have been bad for stocks since 1998

Intermarket Lessons of 1997 and 1998

Much was learned about intermarket relationships during the two watershed years that engulfed the Asian currency crisis. Those two years demonstrated the need to monitor global markets—not just in stocks, but in currencies as well. The collapse in a relatively obscure Asian currency started a ripple effect that eventually had a dramatic effect on the U.S. bond and stock markets. The most obvious impact was a flight out of stocks into bonds that lasted for 18 months. Sector rotations within the stock market were also influenced during the worst of the crisis. Investor funds rotated out of economically sensitive stocks and into more defensive stocks like consumer staples. Another effect of the *Asian contagion* was the collapse in commodity prices, which only served to intensify fears of global deflation.

JOHN'S TIPS

The existence of currency exchange-traded funds (ETFs) makes it much easier for investors to keep track of foreign currency trends and to participate in those trends.

Perhaps the most important lesson of all was that deflationary trends starting in Asia caused a major change in the relationship between bonds and stocks. Rising bond prices no longer helped stock prices. A rising bond market came at the expense of stocks. Put another way, falling bond yields now became bad for stocks. This would become even more pronounced during the bear market in stocks that started a couple of years later in 2000 (and again during 2008).

The Asian Effect Overrides the Fed

After the stock market bubble burst in the United States in 2000, the Federal Reserve lowered interest rates 12 times over 18 months in an attempt to stop the bear market in stocks and stabilize the American economy. The plan didn't work. Part of the reason it didn't work was the influence of deflationary trends coming from Asia. By 2002, even the Fed was using the "D" word (deflation), but only in denying that it was a real threat. That the Fed felt the need to issue the denial only strengthened the belief that the threat was real.

JOHN'S TIPS

A fine line exists between disinflation (when prices rise at a slower pace) and deflation (in which prices actually fall). While disinflation can help stock values, deflation usually hurts them.

Two Deflationary Events of the 1990s

Two deflationary events took place during the 1990s that gave warning that market and economic analysis would take on a different look in the years after 2000. The first deflationary event was the collapse in the Japanese stock market during 1990. The second was the Asian currency crisis during 1997 and 1998, which caused global commodity prices to collapse. While the Japanese stock collapse eventually led that country into a deflation that has lasted for more than two decades, the Asian currency crisis produced a more direct and immediate impact on financial markets.

FIGURE 3.4   Two deflationary events at the start and end of the 1990s

Figure 3.4 shows those two 1990 deflationary events that happened eight years apart. The first down arrow shows the collapse in Japanese stocks that started in 1990 and continued through the end of the decade. The Japanese stock market was the only major market in the world that didn't turn back up after the first Persian Gulf War during 1990–1991. The second down arrow shows commodity prices turning down during 1997 and falling below their 1992 low during 1998 in the midst of the Asian currency crisis (as did the Japanese market). That commodity plunge during 1998 had the more obvious and dramatic impact on bond yields.

■ Deflationary Effect on Bond Yields

Figure 3.5 shows the 10-year trend of the U.S. Treasury bond yield from 1990 to 1999. Bond yields had been dropping since 1981, which was the year after commodities peaked. The two arrows in Figure 3.5 show how the bond market reacted to the two deflationary events described previously. The first arrow shows bond yields falling after the Japanese stock market peak during 1990. After falling to 6 percent in 1993, bond yields rallied sharply during 1994 (which contributed to the stock market decline that year) and trended sideways for the next three years between its 1994 high and its 1993 low. The second arrow marks the point where commodity prices started dropping during the Asian crisis in 1997.

JOHN'S TIPS

Bond yields normally trend in the same direction as commodity prices.

Within a year, the long bond yield had fallen below its 1993 low to reach the lowest level in 20 years (just as the CRB Index did the same year). That plunge in the bond yield was a direct result of the two deflationary events that started in Asia.

FIGURE 3.5 Bond yields hit 20-year low during deflationary 1998

Japanese Deflation and U.S. Interest Rates

An argument can be made that Japanese deflation has had a much bigger impact on the direction of U.S. interest rates than it's given credit for. Figure 3.6 compares the trend in the Japanese stock market to the yield on the U.S. Treasury bond during the 20 years since 1990. There appears to be a remarkably close visual correlation between the two lines. In fact, a .75 correlation has existed between the two markets over that period. *Correlation* refers to the degree of linkage between two markets. The higher the reading is above .50, the stronger the linkage.

---

correlation refers to the degree of linkage between two markets. The higher the reading is above .50, the stronger the linkage

---

JOHN'S TIPS

Correlation between two markets can be positive or negative. Positive correlation means that two markets trend in the same direction. Negative correlation means that they trend in opposite directions.

While the Asian currency crisis of the late 1990s may have had a more dramatic impact on U.S. bond yields, the deflationary effects coming from Japan since 1990 may have had a more subtle but longer-lasting effect on the direction of falling U.S. interest rates.

$NIKK (Tokyo Nikkei Average (EOD)) INDX   © StockCharts.com
22-Mar-2012   Open 9771.34 High 10172.64 Low 9509.10 Close 10127.08 Chg +268.10 (+2.72%) ▲

U.S. Treasury bond yield

Nikkei 225 stock index

The deflationary impact of falling Japanese stocks may have had a depressing effect on U.S. rates.

FIGURE 3.6   Link between Japanese stocks and Treasury yields since 1990

◼ Summary

This concludes Part I of the book. Chapter 1 gives an introduction to intermarket analysis, and describes the impact it has on asset allocation and sector rotation strategies, as well as its role in economic forecasting. The emergence of exchange-traded funds (ETFs) has revolutionized intermarket trading. The first chapter also explained the advantages of using charts and how intermarket work adds a new dimension to technical analysis. The crucial role of oil was mentioned as well. The first chapter ended with a recap of intermarket principles. Chapter 2 reviews intermarket relationships that existed during the last three decades of the last century (the *old normal*). The year 1980 was a crucial turning point for the four asset classes (bonds, stocks, commodities, and currencies). A peak in commodity prices that year ended the hyperinflation of the 1970s, and ushered in two decades of disinflation and bull markets in bonds and stocks. Chapter 2 showed how intermarket relationships worked during the 1987 stock market crash, the 1990–1991 Iraq war, and the stealth bear market of 1994. Chapter 3 reviewed the Asian currency crisis during 1997 and 1998, and the emergence of deflation for the first time since the 1930s. The main result of that new deflationary threat was the decoupling of bond and stock prices, which remains to this day.

Part II moves into the 21st century, starting with events leading up to and following the 2000 stock market top in Chapter 4. Chapter 5 will show how a major decline in the U.S. dollar starting in 2002 led to a major upturn in commodity prices. Chapters 6 and 7 will review events leading up to the 2007–2008 stock market crash and will show how to combine intermarket analysis with traditional charting principles.

Answer the following multiple-choice questions.

1. The four asset classes included in intermarket analysis are _____.

   a. Bonds

   b. Stocks

   c. Commodities

   d. Currencies

   e. All of the above

2. A falling dollar normally causes commodity prices to _____.

   a. Fall

   b. Rise

   c. Trend sideways

   d. Has no effect

3. Falling commodity prices normally cause bond prices to _____.

   a. Fall

   b. Rise

   c. Trend sideways

   d. Has no effect

4. Deflation favors which asset class?

   a. Bonds

   b. Stocks

5. A falling stock market usually leads to _____.

   a. A weaker economy

   b. A stronger economy

   c. A flat economy

   c. Has no impact

ANSWERS:

1. e   2. b   3. b   4. a   5. a

PART II

THE 2000 AND 2007 TOPS

CHAPTER 4

Intermarket Events Surrounding the 2000 Top

This chapter covers events leading up to and surrounding the 2000 stock market top. A tripling in the price of oil during 1999 prompted the Fed to raise short-term rates enough to cause a dangerous inverted yield curve at the start of 2000. Money flowed into consumer staples and real estate investment trusts (REITs) that spring as the Nasdaq tumbled. Bond yields, stocks, and commodities peaked in that order. The Fed acknowledged the deflation threat in the spring of 2003. The falling dollar during 2002 caused commodities to bottom a year ahead of stocks.

■ Events Leading up to the 2000 Top

The previous chapter described how the global deflation fear that gripped the financial markets in 1998 caused a flight out of commodities and stocks and into the bond market. During 1999, those trends reversed. The stock market soared to a new record high while bond prices suffered one of their worst years in history. Part of the reason for the fall in bond prices was a sharp rise in the price of oil, which pushed interest rates higher around the globe. A collapse in Asian markets had pushed commodity prices sharply lower throughout 1997 and 1998. A rebound in those same markets in 1999 pushed commodity prices higher and resulted in heavy losses in global bond markets. While the rotation out of bonds helped stocks initially in 1999, the longer-lasting effects were more damaging. A recovery in Asian stock markets also contributed to global demand for industrial commodities like copper and aluminum. The rise in commodity prices prompted the Federal Reserve to start raising interest rates in the middle of 1999, a move that contributed to a major top in the stock market the following year (2000).

JOHN'S TIPS

Most stock market tops have been caused by the Fed raising short-term rates to stem the rise in the price of oil.

■ Crude Oil Triples in Price

As is usually the case in intermarket work, crude oil played a key role during 1999 in helping to set in motion a ripple effect that brought stocks down the following year. The price of crude oil tripled during 1999, which was a big reason why rates rose that year and bond prices fell. As is also normal, the rising price of oil had a positive effect on some market groups while hurting others. The biggest beneficiaries of rising oil prices were stocks tied to oil. During 1999, energy shares became the market's strongest sector. (You'll find out later in the book why energy leadership is almost always a warning sign that a stock bull market and an economic recovery are nearing completion.) Groups that suffered the most from rising oil were fuel-intensive transportation stocks and interest rate–sensitive financial stocks.

JOHN'S TIPS

When the price of oil is rising, stocks tied to energy usually become stock market leaders.

Those sector rotations were early warning signs of an approaching market top. In addition to causing those negative sector rotations, rising oil prices also prompted the Fed to start raising short-term rates in the middle of 1999, which was a major reason why the market topped the following year.

Did You Know…?

One way to tell when the economy has crossed the threshold from *late expansion* to *early contraction* is when leadership switches from energy stocks to more defensive groups like consumer staples, which is what happened during the spring of 2000.

■ A Rise in Short-Term Rates Leads to an Inverted Yield Curve

The Fed started raising short-term interest rates during the summer of 1999, as it usually does when commodity prices start rising too sharply. By the first quarter of 2000, that Fed tightening led to a condition known as an *inverted yield curve*. An inverted yield curve occurs when short-term interest rates rise above long-term rates. That situation usually arises after a round of Fed tightening (resulting from the rising price of oil and other commodities), and has usually been an early warning of a stock market top and economic weakness. The recessions of 1970, 1974, 1980, 1982, and 1990 had all been preceded by inverted yield curves. In a normal yield curve, long-term rates are higher than short-term rates. When the Fed tightens monetary policy to fight off an inflation threat, it raises short-term rates. The danger point for the economy (and the stock market) occurs when the Fed pushes short-term rates over long-term rates. That danger point was reached at the start of 2000.

Did You Know…?

An official inverted yield curve is present when the two-year rate rises above the 10-year rate.

When an inverted yield curve develops, stocks that become the most vulnerable are those with the highest price/earnings ratios (which are generally viewed as the market's most expensive stocks). At the start of the new millennium, those overvalued stocks happened to be in the dot-com world of Internet and technology that resided in the Nasdaq market. By that spring, the bubble finally burst in the Nasdaq market and ended the longest bull market in history.

Figure 4.1 shows the technology-dominated Nasdaq Composite Index peaking during the first quarter of 2000. It was the first major U.S. stock index to do so. By May, the Nasdaq had lost 40 percent of its value, which qualified as an official bear market. A *bear market* exists when a market falls 20 percent from a previous peak.

---

a **bear market** exists when a market falls 20 percent from a previous peak

---

It then rallied to the end of August before turning down again. Later that year, the Nasdaq fell below its late-spring low, which put it in a major downtrend. A *downtrend* is defined as a series of lower highs and lower lows.

---

a **downtrend** is a series of lower highs and lower lows

While this proved disastrous for the Nasdaq market, it benefited defensive market sectors that usually do better in the early stages of an economic slowdown, like consumer staples and utilities. (I'll cover sector rotation around market tops in a later chapter.) Real estate investment trusts also turned up as interest rates plunged along with the stock market. Stocks tied to housing did well during the ensuing bear market in stocks because of their sensitivity to falling rates.

JOHN'S TIPS

The rally in housing stocks helped the economy to escape more serious damage during the ensuing recession.

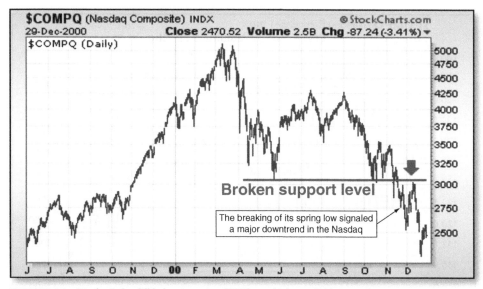

FIGURE 4.1 Nasdaq Index fell below its spring 2000 low, which signaled bear market

■ REITs Benefit from Falling Stocks

REITs were the top-performing stock group that April (as the Nasdaq was tumbling). Investors often turn to real estate stocks for bear market insurance. REITs have three things going for them. The first is that they pay high dividends, which have big appeal in a falling stock market (and a plunge in bond yields). REITs also have a low correlation with the stock market. As a result, they provide diversification value when the stock market is in decline. Third, REITs have historically had a negative correlation to technology stocks. That means that REITs have usually risen when technology stocks fall. And that's certainly what happened during the spring of 2000. REITs not only did better than the stock market in *relative* terms, but actually started to rise during April 2000 just as the Nasdaq was peaking. Homebuilding stocks, which also benefit from falling interest rates, turned up as well.

Figure 4.2 shows that REITs turned up in the spring of 2000 just as the Nasdaq was peaking (see arrows). REITs normally have a negative correlation to the Nasdaq market. Falling interest rates also increased the appeal of dividend-paying REITS. Rate-sensitive homebuilding stocks also benefited from falling interest rates during 2000. It could be argued that the bear market in stocks that started during 2000, and the aggressive Fed easing during that period to stabilize the stock market and the economy, helped create the housing boom that lasted for several years before bursting later that decade. Stocks tied to housing didn't benefit from the next major bear market in stocks during 2007 and 2008. In fact, the collapse in housing stocks helped create it.

JOHN'S TIPS

The collapse in the housing industry during 2007 made that market downturn much more serious than the one starting in 2000.

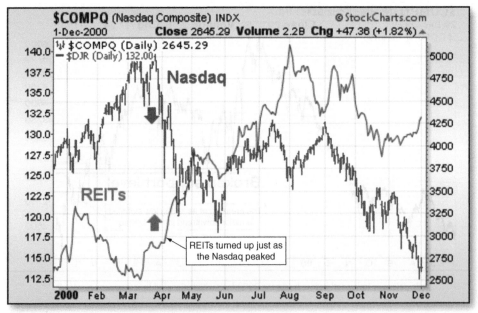

FIGURE 4.2 REITS turned up during 2000 as the Nasdaq peaked.

Consumer Staples Start to Outperform

Certain market sectors do better at different stages of the economic cycle. In the early stages of an economic downturn, one of the best performing sectors is *consumer staples*. Staples are considered to be defensive in nature and relatively resistant to turns in the business cycle. That's because the group contains stocks like beverages, food, tobacco, and household products. The reasoning is that people still have to use those products in good times and bad. Relative strength in this group often hints at economic slowing. (*Relative strength* refers to how a market group is doing compared to a market benchmark like the S&P 500.) A couple of other defensive groups that usually attract money in the early stages of an economic slowdown are health care and utilities. That's even truer if the stock market decline is accompanied by falling interest rates, which was the case during 2000. Falling bond yields make dividend-paying stocks more attractive. Most defensive stocks fall into that category.

---

relative strength refers to how a market group is doing compared to a market benchmark like the S&P 500

JOHN'S TIPS

When bond yields fall sharply, investors favor dividend-paying stocks in the search for a higher yield.

Figure 4.3 shows a basket of consumer staple stocks turning up during the spring of 2000 just as the Nasdaq was peaking. Defensive stocks usually do better in the early stages of a market top and an economic slowdown. Health care and utilities also benefit from a falling stock market. I'll explain how sector rotation strategies work at different stages of the business cycles in a later chapter. You'll also see that the same defensive rotation took place during the bear market starting in 2007.

FIGURE 4.3   Consumer staples turned up during 2000 as Nasdaq turned down

As I suggested earlier, one way we can tell when rising energy prices are starting to slow the economy is when market leadership starts to shift from *energy* stocks to *consumer staples*. Since that shift takes place gradually, the real danger becomes evident when energy and consumer staples are the two strongest sectors in the stock market. That was the case during the first half of 2000.

Market Lessons from 2000

If ever a year demonstrated how technical, intermarket, and economic analyses work together, 2000 was that year. Traditional technical signs of serious market deterioration were plainly evident. One of those signs was the breaking of 200-day moving averages by major U.S. stock indexes.

Figure 4.4 shows the S&P 500 falling deeply below its 200-day moving average during the second half of 2000. The 200-day moving average is the line that divides major uptrends from major downtrends. A significant drop below that long-term support line is a warning that a major decline has begun. The fact that the 200-day average for the S&P 500 itself turned down during the fourth quarter of 2000 was another clear sign that a major bear market had begun (see arrow). Most traditional stock market technical indicators were flashing *sell signals* during 2000.

Intermarket warning signs had been flashing during the second half of 1999 in the form of rising commodity prices and rising interest rates. The result was a round of Fed tightening that resulted in an inverted yield curve during the first quarter of 2000, which had led to every recession (and market top) since 1970. Sector rotations followed the sequence that normally takes place at the end of an

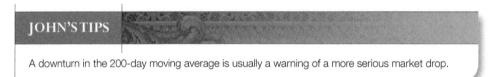

JOHN'S TIPS

A downturn in the 200-day moving average is usually a warning of a more serious market drop.

FIGURE 4.4   S&P 500 broke its 200-day moving average during 2000

economic expansion. What happened in 2000 was a textbook example of a stock market top and an economic recession in the making. Yet, incredibly, most of Wall Street and the economic community didn't see it coming—or pretended not to. They ignored all of the warning signs being given by deteriorating price charts and intermarket yellow flags. They even ignored the inverted yield curve. The most important lesson from 2000 is that it's very dangerous to rely exclusively on outdated economic and fundamental information, and to ignore the message being given by the financial markets themselves.

JOHN'S TIPS

Stocks are a better indicator of the economy than the economy is of stocks.

Bonds, Stocks, and Commodities Peaked in the Proper Order

The order in which the three markets peaked during 2000 is also instructive. Bonds, stocks, and commodities usually peak and trough in a predictable order. Bonds normally peak first, stocks second, and commodities third. They also tend to bottom in the same order. In that sense, bonds become a leader indicator for stocks, which, in turn, become a leading indicator for commodities. Stock prices usually peak six to nine months before the start of a recession. When commodities finally peak, that's usually a sign that a recession has started.

Figure 4.5 shows that the yield on the 10-year T-note yield peaked during January 2000 (first arrow). The previous chapter explained that falling bond yields after 1998 were actually bad for stocks, which became painfully clear during 2000 (and again during 2007). Although the Nasdaq market peaked that March, the rest of stock market held up for several more months. The S&P 500 didn't hit its final peak until the end of August before finally turning down during September (second arrow). Commodities didn't peak for another five months after the S&P 500.

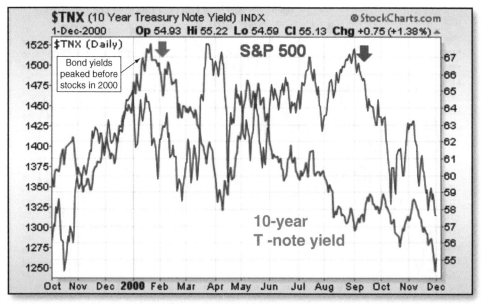

FIGURE 4.5   Bond yields peaked before stocks during 2000

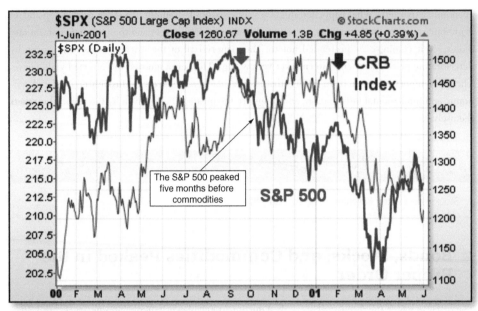

FIGURE 4.6 Stocks peaked before commodities during 2000

Figure 4.6 shows the CRB Index peaking during January of the following year (2001). That was five months after the S&P 500 peak around Labor Day of the previous year. The eventual drop in commodity prices is usually a sign that a recession has begun or is close to doing so. The official recession began two months later during March 2001.

Figure 4.7 puts all three markets on the same chart and shows them peaking in the normal order (bonds first, stocks second, and commodities last). We'll see later in the book that the three markets followed the same peaking order during the 2007–2008 period. Bond yields peaked during June 2007, which was four months before stocks peaked that October. Commodities didn't peak until the following July.

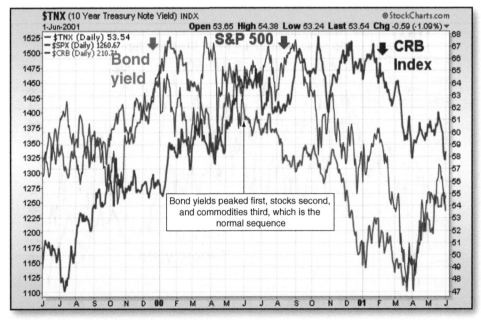

FIGURE 4.7 Bonds, stocks, and commodities peaked in that order during 2000

Before 1998, bond *prices* peaked before stocks. After 1998, bond *yields* have been peaking before stocks.

The 2002 and 2003 Bottoms Reverse Normal Order

Figure 4.8 shows commodities turning up at the start of 2002, while stocks didn't bottom until that October. Bond yields didn't turn up until the following June (2003). That sequence of bottoms was the exact opposite of the order in which those three markets usually bottom. When something unusual happens in intermarket work, there's usually a reason why. Part of the reason for the unusual activity in the bond market, and why yields bottomed so late in 2003, came from the Fed.

JOHN'S TIPS

The normal sequences at bottoms is for bond yields to turn up first, stocks second, and commodities third.

The Fed Discovers Deflation during 2003

Intermarket trends since the Asian currency crisis had been warning of a growing deflationary threat. The markets, which are discounting mechanisms, had been trading for several years on the assumption that the deflation threat was for real. Unfortunately, the economic community (including the Fed) kept referring to falling inflation and falling interest rates as *good things*. It took more than five

FIGURE 4.8 Three markets bottomed out of sequence during 2002 and 2003

years after the 1997 Asian crisis (and the worst bear market in stocks since the deflationary 1930s) for it to happen. In the spring of 2003, the Fed finally expressed concern about the threat from falling prices.

On Tuesday, May 6, 2003, the Federal Reserve announced its decision to leave short-term rates unchanged at the 1.25-percent level. That was expected. What wasn't expected was the statement released the same day that "the probability of an unwelcome substantial fall in inflation, though minor, exceeds that of a pickup in inflation from its already low level." That statement marked the first time since World War II that the Fed had expressed fear that *deflation* was a greater threat than *inflation*. The Fed had started lowering rates in January 2001 just as a new recession was about to start. By May 2003, it had lowered short-term rates 12 times to the lowest level in 40 years. It was running out of ammunition.

The reaction of the financial markets to the Fed's announcement of the deflation threat pushed the yield on the 10-year Treasury note to the lowest level in 45 years. Since the Fed couldn't lower short-term rates much more, there was talk that it might start buying bonds to lower long-term rates. That also contributed to the plunge in bond yields that spring. That plunge proved to be short-lived. By June, bond yields started to climb sharply. That rise in bond yields at midyear was helped along by a massive rotation out of bonds and back into the stock market, which had started a new bull market three months earlier.

JOHN'S TIPS

The Fed did resort to buying longer-maturity bonds during 2011 and 2012 as part of Operation Twist.

■ Commodities Turn Up during 2002

Although the Fed couldn't lower short-term rates much more to battle deflation, there was something else it could lower. That was the dollar. A falling dollar is one of the best cures for falling prices, since it helps boost inflation. Some market observers suspected that the Fed had been allowing the dollar to depreciate since the start of 2002 in an attempt to create some inflation. That suspicion was confirmed a couple weeks after the Fed issued its deflation warning when the Treasury Secretary hinted that the U.S. government had abandoned its policy of supporting a strong dollar. Traders took that as a sign that the government wanted the dollar to fall in order to *reflate* the economy. One place that strategy worked was in the commodity pits.

JOHN'S TIPS

Since commodities are priced in dollars, a falling dollar causes the prices of those commodities to increase.

Traders started selling the dollar and buying commodities more aggressively. Commodity prices had already been rising for over a year, thanks to the falling dollar. The U.S. dollar had in fact peaked near the start of 2002 and had started a major decline that lasted through the end of the decade. The dollar decline was the main reason that commodities turned up at the same time. That may explain why, in that instance, commodities turned up before stocks and bond yields. It seems ironic that the major bull market in commodities that started during 2002 was a direct result of the Fed's lowering the dollar to battle deflation.

CHAPTER 5

The 2002 Falling Dollar Boosts Commodities

This chapter deals with the major peak in the U.S. dollar during 2002, which led to a major up-trend in commodity markets. Gold experienced a major upside breakout as the dollar broke a seven-year support line. Gold ended a 20-year secular bear market just as stocks ended their secular bull market. Commodities outperformed stocks for the first time in two decades. A peak in crude oil during March 2003 contributed to the stock market upturn.

47

■ Commodities Inflate

The previous chapter mentioned the Fed's sudden concern about deflation in May 2003 and the U.S. government's abandonment of its strong dollar policy. The plan was to sacrifice the dollar in an attempt to boost prices. By the time the Fed became concerned that prices were falling, commodity markets had already been rallying for over a year. A lot of that had to do with the falling dollar.

The U.S. dollar hit its final peak during the first quarter of 2002. From that point, it dropped sharply for the balance of that year and for the rest of the decade. The CRB Index (a basket of commodity markets) turned up at the exact point that the dollar peaked. For the rest of 2002, commodity prices continued an uninterrupted advance (which was also to last for several years). That action was consistent with the intermarket principle that a falling dollar usually results in higher commodity prices. That's just what it did during 2002.

JOHN'S TIPS

The complete name for the CRB Index is the Thomson Reuters/Jefferies CRB Index.

Figure 5.1 shows the peaking process in the U.S. Dollar Index that lasted from October 2000 to spring 2002. Chartists refer to that type of topping pattern as a *head-and-shoulders top* that shows three peaks with the middle peak slightly higher than the two surrounding peaks (see arrows). That bearish pattern is completed when the trendline drawn under the two reaction lows is broken. During April 2002, the

FIGURE 5.1 Dollar completes topping pattern during 2002

U.S. Dollar Index fell below the trendline drawn under its January and September 2001 lows (see circle). That began the major decline in the U.S. dollar. At the same time, the CRB Index turned up.

---

a **head-and-shoulders top** shows three peaks with the middle peak slightly higher than the two surrounding peaks with that bearish pattern completed when the trendline drawn under the two reaction lows is broken

---

Figure 5.2 shows the CRB Index (of commodity prices) rising above its 200-day moving average during April 2002 just as the dollar was breaking down (see circle). The ability of the CRB Index to

FIGURE 5.2 CRB Index rises above 200-day average early in 2002

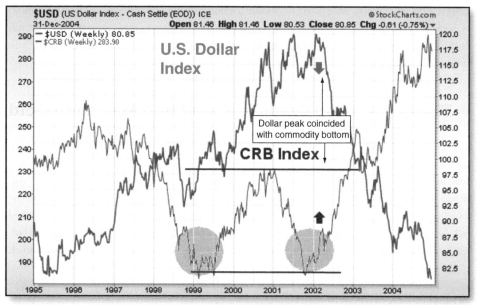

FIGURE 5.3 2002 dollar top coincides with major commodity bottom

climb above its 200-day line was a sign to chart followers that the trend in commodities was turning higher. The fact that it was happening while the dollar was breaking down gave the commodity upturn more credibility. Longer-range charts suggested that these weren't minor turns.

Figure 5.3 compares the trends of the U.S. Dollar Index to the CRB Index over the decade from 1995 through 2004. The peak in the dollar (down arrow) coincided exactly with the upturn in the CRB Index (up arrow) during spring 2002. From that point, the dollar fell to the lowest level in 10 years while the commodity index hit the highest level in more than a decade. The 2001 bottom in commodity prices represented a successful retest of its 1999 bottom. That formed a bullish *double bottom* reversal pattern that was completed when the CRB Index exceeded its 2000 peak near the end of 2002. Those trend changes were clearly visible on the price charts. That was a good example of how to blend traditional charting techniques with intermarket principles.

JOHN'S TIPS

The longer a chart pattern has been forming, the more significant it becomes.

Did You Know. . .?

A *double bottom* pattern exists when a market shows two prominent bottoms around the same price level (see circles) and is completed when prices exceed the middle peak.

Commodities Gain from Battle against Deflation

A falling dollar is normally considered to be inflationary. The collapsing dollar in the early part of 2002 had already started to push commodity prices sharply higher. By the end of 2002, the CRB Index had risen to the highest level in five years. That was clear evidence that the falling dollar was having the desired effect of creating some commodity inflation. That was good news for commodity traders. If the government was willing to devalue the dollar, that could only serve to boost commodity markets. A Fed preoccupied with deflation would also be reluctant to raise interest rates. That was also bullish for commodity prices. Ironically, that made commodity markets big winners in the Fed's battle against deflation.

■ The Dollar Drop Leads to a New Bull Market in Gold

Historically, the primary beneficiary of a falling dollar is the gold market and gold-mining shares. There usually exists a strong inverse relationship between the dollar and gold, meaning that they trend in opposite directions. The gold market had started rallying during spring 2001, just as the dollar was starting its peaking process. The final peak in the dollar in spring 2002 gave the new uptrend in bullion an even bigger boost. By that spring, the dollar was in major decline and gold had climbed back over $300 for the first time in two years. Gold-mining stocks were rallying right along with bullion. Gold was benefiting from more than a falling dollar. It also benefited from a falling stock market.

> **JOHN'S TIPS**
>
> Gold and mining shares generally trend in the same direction. The strongest moves take place when both are rising.

■ Falling Stocks Are Also Good for Gold

Gold peaked in 1980 over $700 and had been falling for 20 years. The stock market bottomed during 1982 and rose for the next two decades. That was consistent with another intermarket principle: that gold and the stock market usually trend in opposite directions. The S&P 500 had peaked near the end of August 2000. Gold stocks bottomed within three months (November 2000) while gold turned up the following April (2001). It seems clear that the bear market in stocks starting in 2000 helped usher in a new bull market in gold assets.

At the time, some skeptics questioned the staying power of the gold rally on the grounds that gold was an *inflation hedge* and there was more deflation than inflation. What they didn't realize was that gold assets have historically done well during both inflationary and deflationary periods. The inflationary period of the 1970s witnessed soaring gold prices and mining shares related to it. During the deflationary years from 1929 to 1932, gold bullion had been set at a fixed price. The price of Homestake Mining, however, gained 300 percent during those three years while the stock market lost 90 percent of its value. Gold is considered to be an alternative to paper assets. No one needed the insurance of gold during the big bull market in stocks during the last two decades of the 20th century. It was no accident that the end of the 20-year *bull market* in stocks coincided almost exactly with the ending of the 20-year *bear market* in gold. The combination of the start of the worst bear market in stocks since the Great Depression and another devaluation of the U.S. dollar a couple of years later made gold the world's strongest asset for the rest of that decade.

Did You Know. . .?

The dollar was essentially devalued during 1933 when the United States was taken off the gold standard and gold was allowed to rise in value.

Not a Lot of Alternatives

Some traders also took the view that gold wasn't much of an investment since it had done so poorly for 20 years. That, however, was one of the most compelling reasons why gold (and mining shares) were such a good investment. The two-decade bull market in stocks had just ended. What better time to consider an alternative market like gold? What other alternatives were there? Stocks were in major decline. Interest rates had fallen to the lowest level in 40 years, making fixed income investments less attractive. Twelve Fed easings since the start of 2001 had pushed U.S. short-term rates to the lowest level among major industrialized countries with the exception of Japan (whose rates were at zero). Money market funds were paying little more than 1 percent. With U.S. rates so much lower than rates in other countries, the dollar had nowhere to go but down. The falling dollar made U.S. bonds and stocks even less attractive to foreign investors. A climate of falling stock prices, a falling dollar, and historically low interest rates didn't leave people with a lot of investment alternatives. That is the exact type of intermarket climate that drives money to gold. That's exactly what it did.

Gold and the Dollar Experience Major Trend Changes

One of the main tasks of chart reading is to determine if a trend change is a relatively minor one or if it represents a major shift in the direction of any market. One of the ways to incorporate intermarket analysis into the picture is to compare the chart action of two related markets. First, one simply compares their direction to see if they're following the normal intermarket pattern. Recall that a falling dollar is bullish for gold. If gold is starting to rise, the first thing to do is to determine if the dollar is starting to drop. The next thing to do is to look at the separate charts of each market to determine the importance of their respective trend changes. A *minor* trend change in one may not justify a *major* change in the other. Their respective trend signals should be of similar magnitude. Figure 5.4 shows the rising trend in the U.S. dollar that lasted from 1995 to the end of

FIGURE 5.4 Dollar breaks major seven-year support line

2001. A trendline is drawn under the dollar's reaction lows. (Up trendlines are drawn upward and to the right under previous reaction lows. The longer it has been in effect, the more important it becomes.) The chart shows that the dollar had been dropping throughout 2002. During December 2002, the dollar broke the rising seven-year trendline (see circle). In chart work, that was a serious breakdown and was indicative of the start of a major decline in the U.S. currency. At the same time that the dollar was breaking down, the price of gold was achieving a bullish move of its own in the other direction.

JOHN'S TIPS

While *daily* charts are good for short-term trends, *weekly* and *monthly* charts are better for long-term trend analysis.

Figure 5.5 shows that the price of gold had been trending sideways in an apparent bottoming formation for several years. Near the end of 2002, the price of gold rose above its 1999 peak near $320, which put bullion at the highest level in five years. A five-year high qualifies as a major event in any market. That upside breakout signaled the start of a major bull market in gold. An *upside breakout* occurs when a price of a market rises above a previous peak. The further back in time the previous peak is, the more significant is the upside breakout. That's an excellent example of how to blend traditional chart work with intermarket principles. Both gold and the dollar were experiencing major trend changes at the same point in time. And they were trending in opposite directions.

---

an **upside breakout** occurs when a price of a market rises above a previous peak

---

FIGURE 5.5   Gold hits new five-year high near end of 2002

Shifting from Paper to Hard Assets

Gold is often viewed as a proxy for the entire commodity sector. This is probably due to its long history as a store of value and the fact that it is the most recognizable of all the commodity markets (with the possible exception of oil). Radio and television business shows quote the price of gold routinely, but not necessarily the price of cotton or soybeans. Major trends in the price of gold have either led to or coincided with major trends in the entire commodity group.

JOHN'S TIPS

Gold often has a tendency to change direction before other commodities. That's probably due to its stronger link to the dollar.

Gold surged over $700 during the 1970s when commodity markets as a group were in major uptrends. Gold peaked in 1980 just as the commodity bubble was bursting. It then declined for the next 20 years as commodity markets fell out of favor. Gold influences the direction of commodity prices and the public's perception of the attractiveness of commodities as an investment alternative to bonds and stocks. As the new millennium was just getting started, gold and other commodities were starting to attract new attention and money for the first time in 20 years—at the expense of bonds and stocks.

Did You Know. . .?

The emergence of commodity-related exchange-traded funds (ETFs) over the last decade has made investing in gold and other commodities much easier for the average investor and has also contributed to the growing popularity of commodities.

The Stock Peak Coincides with Gold Bottom

As mentioned earlier, there is a historical tendency for gold prices to trend in the opposite direction of stocks. Gold is considered to be a hedge against a falling stock market. It doesn't matter if the threat to stocks is coming from inflation (like the 1970s) or deflation (like the 1930s). The fact is that gold is tied to the stock market—but as an alternate investment. Gold prices peaked in 1980 and were in a bear market for nearly 20 years. Stocks bottomed during 1982 and were in a bull market for those same 20 years. In other words, the 20-year *bull market* in stocks coincided with a 20-year *bear market* in gold. Both of those long-term trends started changing direction right around the same time.

Figure 5.6 compares the 20-year trend of a rising stock market to a falling gold price. Notice that the 2000 peak in the S&P 500 (down arrow) coincided closely with a bottom in the price of gold (up arrow). It's no coincidence that gold bottomed just as stocks were peaking. Any historical comparison of the two markets will show that gold and stocks usually trend in opposite directions, and that the bull market in stocks ended just as the new bull market in gold was starting.

JOHN'S TIPS

One reason why Wall Street strategists are seldom bullish on gold is that they know that rising gold is usually bearish for stocks.

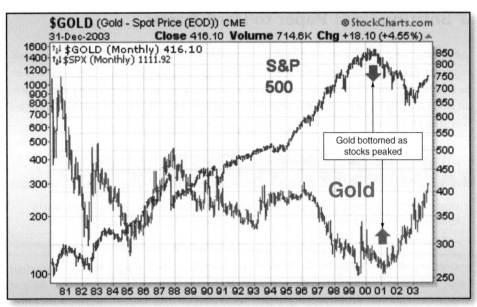

FIGURE 5.6   Gold bottom coincides with 2000 stock market top

■ Gold Breaks 15-Year Resistance Line

Long-term charts are most useful for spotting major trend changes. This is true for all markets. When prices break trendlines that have been in existence for several years, it is usually an indication that something important is happening. Earlier in this chapter, we talked about how the breaking of a seven-year rising trendline by the U.S. dollar during 2002 coincided with a bullish breakout in gold. However, that was only part of the intermarket story. As 2003 was starting, the price of gold had risen to the highest level in over five years. Even more impressive was the fact that bullion had risen above a 15-year trendline extending all the way back to 1987 (as you'll see shortly). That was another important chart sign that the rally in gold had staying power behind it and was more than just another rally in a long-term downtrend. Something else happened that gave even more credibility to the upturn in gold: Stocks were breaking a long-term support line.

■ Stocks End Secular Uptrend

Long-term chart analysis of the two markets also revealed that those trend changes that started in 2000 were very significant changes. In fact, they represented changes to each market's *secular* trend. *A secular trend* is a very long-term trend that can last for decades. In the case of gold and stocks, their secular trends had lasted for two decades. But each one of those secular trends was changing.

a **secular trend** is a very long-term trend that can last for decades

Figure 5.7 compares the 20-year trends of the S&P 500 and the gold market. The price scale to the right of the chart uses a *logarithmic scale*, which measures percentage price changes instead of absolute changes. Long-term trendline analysis is more valid on a log scale. A rising support line is drawn under the reaction lows that defined the 20-year secular bull market in stocks. To the upper right, you can see the S&P 500 falling below that long-term support line during 2002 (see circle). That signaled that the S&P 500 had ended its 20-year secular uptrend and was entering a secular bear market.

logarithmic scale measures percentage price changes instead of absolute changes

FIGURE 5.7   Gold breaks 15-year resistance line as stocks end 20-year bull market

> **JOHN'S TIPS**
>
> Logarithmic scaling works better on long-term charts extending back several years.

Figure 5.7 also shows the 20-year secular downtrend in the gold market. It also shows the price of gold rising above the falling 15-year trendline referred to earlier. The ability of the gold market to exceed that long-term trendline was a very convincing sign that gold had entered a new secular bull market.

Most impressive of all was the fact that gold was breaking a 15-year resistance line at the same time that stocks were breaking a 20-year support line. *Support and resistance* are used in chart analysis to represent a point above a market where resistance (selling) might occur, or below a market where support (buying) is likely to occur. Taken one at a time, each trend change looked important. Taken together, they reinforced each other's major trend reversals. Using traditional charting tools, it could be seen that each market had experienced a major change in trend. From an intermarket perspective, it could also be seen that both trend reversals were taking place at the same time, and they were traveling in opposite directions. What was bad for one market (stocks) was good for the other (gold). Because gold is also a harbinger of trends in other commodity markets, the bullish turnaround in bullion after 2000 also signaled a likely major upturn in commodity markets. That indicated a major change in the relationship between stocks and commodities.

support and resistance represent a point above a market where resistance (selling) might occur, or below a market where support (buying) is likely to occur.

> **JOHN'S TIPS**
>
> Ratio analysis is extremely helpful in spotting major shifts in leadership between asset classes.

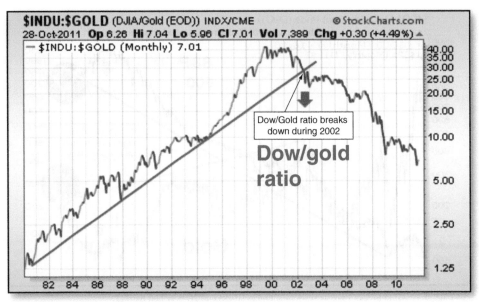

Dow/Gold ratio breaks down during 2002

Dow/gold ratio

FIGURE 5.8   Dow/Gold ratio peaked in 2000 after a 20-year rise

Gold Outperforms Stocks for the First Time in 20 Years

Figure 5.8 plots a popular intermarket indicator, which is the Dow/gold ratio. That ratio divides the Dow Jones Industrial Average by the price of gold. The Dow/gold ratio had peaked during 1966 and fell throughout the inflationary 1970s. Obviously, gold and other commodities were better investments than stocks during those years. The Dow/gold ratio bottomed during 1980 (when commodities peaked) and rose steadily until 2000, when it reached a record high near 40. During those 20 years, stocks were a much better investment than gold or commodities. Figure 5.8 shows the Dow/gold ratio peaking during 2000 (when stocks peaked). Within two years of that peak, the ratio broke a rising trendline that had lasted for the previous two decades (see arrow). A *logarithmic price scale* is used to produce a more reliable long-term trendline. The breaking of that long-term support line signaled a major change in the relationship between those two markets in favor of gold (and mining shares). That event signaled the need for an asset allocation shift out of stocks and into gold (and commodities in general). The chart also shows that gold continued to do better than stocks in the decade following the 2000 ratio peak.

a **logarithmic price scale** is used to produce a more reliable long-term trendline

From the start of 2000 to the end of 2011, the S&P 500 lost 15 percent. During that same time span, commodities as a group gained over 50 percent. Gold did much better than most commodities, with an 11-year rise of 490 percent. We'll explain in a later chapter that gold is more than just a commodity. Gold is also viewed by many traders as an alternate currency. That dual role also explains why gold has done much better than other commodities over the last decade.

Gold mining stocks are usually market leaders when the price of gold is rising. That has certainly been the case. Figure 5.9 compares the trend of the Market Vectors Gold Miners ETF (GDX) to the S&P 500 over the last decade. A visual comparison of the two lines shows that gold miners have done much better than other stocks since 2000. The performance numbers confirm the superior performance of gold miners. In the 11 years since the start of 2000, the Gold Miners ETF has gained more than 400 percent, versus a 15 percent loss in the S&P 500.

FIGURE 5.9 Gold miners have outperformed S&P 500 since 2000 by wide margin

The Oil Peak Coincides with the 2003 Stock Bottom

The previous chapter offered the falling dollar near the start of 2002 as an explanation as to why commodities turned up a year before stocks. That was unusual since stocks have a history of turning up first at bottoms. Interestingly, one key commodity played an important role in both bottoms (commodities and stocks). That key commodity is crude oil.

The price of crude oil turned up in spring 2002 (along with other commodities) as the dollar was peaking and continued to rally into the following spring. As usual, the rising price of oil was negative for stocks. Figure 5.10 compares the price of crude to the S&P 500 during that year.

FIGURE 5.10 Oil peak at start of Iraq war in March 2003 contributed to stock market bottom

You can see both lines trending in opposite directions from spring 2002 to spring 2003. The 50-percent spike in the price of crude from November 2002 to March 2003 (see box) was the result of a *war premium* built into its value in anticipation of a second Iraq war. That upward spike in the price of crude helped keep stock prices on the defensive during those five months. During the week that the war actually started (March 13, 2003), the price of oil tumbled 33 percent (down arrow). Interestingly, the plunge in the price of crude in spring 2003 coincided with (and probably contributed to) a major upturn in the stock market (up arrow). The ability of the S&P 500 to rise above a trendline drawn over the highs of the previous nine months during the second quarter of that year confirmed to chartists that a new bull market in stocks had begun—a bull market that lasted until 2007.

CHAPTER 6

Asset Allocation Rotations Leading to 2007 Top

This chapter shows how the use of the relative strength ratio can be used to spot changes in leadership between asset classes, which is necessary in making asset allocation choices. A major asset allocation shift took place from paper assets to hard assets during 2002. The bond/stock ratio tracked important changes in leadership between those two competing assets during 2000, 2003, 2007, and 2009. Rotations in 2007 followed the intermarket script very closely. Stocks and the dollar fell while gold and Treasuries rallied. Bonds, stocks, and commodities peaked in the proper order during 2007 and 2008. The 2007–2008 stock bear market was global. Global stocks become even more closely correlated during downtrends.

▮ Relative Strength between Asset Classes

The previous chapter used the Dow Industrial/gold ratio to compare the relative performance of gold and the stock market. This chapter will expand that analysis by using ratio charts to compare the relative strength between bonds, stocks, and commodities to show which of the three asset classes are doing better at any one time. The idea is to concentrate one's capital in the assets that are doing better and to avoid (or underweight) the ones that are doing the worst. Fortunately, ratio charts make it relatively easy to compare the strength or weakness of the three asset classes.

> **JOHN'S TIPS**
>
> Chart programs make it very easy to plot ratio charts.

Ratio charts can help warn of impending trend changes and can be an important supplement to traditional chart analysis. As you'll see in the following charts, one need not be a charting expert to learn how to spot such trend changes. Most of the trend changes can be easily spotted. Market developments since 2000 have provided several striking examples of why it is so important to know which markets are going up—and which ones are going down. As you'll also see, one of the most striking examples of why some markets go up when others go down took place during the months leading up to and following the 2007 stock market top.

Asset Allocation

Some understanding of how the different asset classes interact with each other is important for at least two reasons. First, such an understanding helps you appreciate how other financial markets influence whichever market you're interested in. For example, it's very useful to know how bonds and stocks interact. If you're trading stocks, you should be watching the direction of bond yields (and bond prices). That's because the direction of bond yields offers hints about the likely direction of stocks. If you're a bond trader, you should be monitoring the direction of stocks. A sudden jump in stock prices is usually associated with a drop in Treasury bond prices. The previous chapter showed that a falling dollar usually produces higher commodity prices. A later chapter will also demonstrate that the direction of the dollar helps determine the relative attractiveness of foreign stocks compared to those in the United States.

JOHN'S TIPS

A rising dollar favors U.S. stocks, while a weaker dollar favors foreign stocks.

A second reason why it's important to understand intermarket relationships is to help with the *asset allocation* process. There was a time not too long ago when investors' choices were limited to bonds, stocks, or cash. Asset allocation models were based on that limited philosophy. Over the last decade, however, investment choices have broadened considerably. Since 2002, commodities have been the strongest asset class, and are now recognized by Wall Street and the investing public as a viable alternative to bonds and stocks. The growing availability of exchange-traded funds (ETFs) has made investing in commodity markets as easy as buying a stock on a stock exchange.

The same is true for currency markets. Up until recently, currency trading was limited to professional interbank traders and futures specialists. That is no longer the case. Currency exchange-traded funds have put currency trading within easy reach of the average investor. Access to foreign currencies is especially valuable in a climate where the U.S. dollar is depreciating. Commodities aren't the only markets that rise when the dollar falls. Foreign currencies rise as well. Foreign currencies of countries that export commodities, like Australia and Canada, get a double boost from a falling dollar and rising commodity prices. I'll touch on foreign currency trading in more depth later in the book. I'll also talk about gold's role as an alternate currency, and why comparisons between gold and foreign currencies can be very useful. Both rise together, but not necessarily at the same pace.

The Relative Strength Ratio

This is perhaps the most important tool in asset allocation and sector rotation strategies. *Sector rotation* refers to movement of funds into and out of various stock market sectors depending on the state of the business cycle and the stock market. Most of my intermarket work is based on *relative* performance. Relative performance compares two asset classes (or markets) to determine which is the stronger of the two. That's done by plotting a *relative strength ratio* (which is also referred to as a *relative strength* [RS] *line*). The relative strength ratio (or line) is created by dividing the price of one market by the price of another, which is easily done with any charting program.

sector rotation is the movement of funds into and out of various stock market sectors depending on the state of the business cycle and the stock market

A *relative strength line* is most often plotted at the bottom of a stock chart to measure a stock's relative strength against the S&P 500. A rising RS line means that the stock is rising faster than the broader market. That's usually a positive sign for a stock. Ratio analysis can also be done on market sectors and industry groups, which is extremely useful in implementing sector rotation strategies. A rising ratio means that a market sector is outperforming the rest of the market. It's generally better to be in sectors with rising relative strength ratios (and out of ones with falling ratios). We'll deal with *sector rotation* in another chapter. In this chapter, we're using the relative strength ratio for *asset allocation* purposes.

JOHN'S TIPS

Any two markets can be compared with ratios.

2002 Shift from Paper to Hard Assets

The previous chapter employed a relative strength ratio in order to demonstrate that the price of gold started to outperform the stock market during 2002 for the first time in 20 years. In this chapter, we're going to apply the same analysis to the entire commodity asset class. In asset allocation work, the idea is to compare the relative performance between asset classes (which include bonds, stocks, and commodities) to determine which ones are doing better. Let's start with the relationship between stocks and commodities.

Figure 6.1 plots a ratio of the CRB Index of commodity prices divided by the S&P 500 (which is the benchmark for U.S. stocks). During the 20 years between 1980 and 2000, the falling commodity/stock ratio meant that stocks were the stronger asset class. That started to change in 2000 but didn't become obvious until 2002. During 2002, the CRB/S&P ratio broke a down trendline that had lasted for two decades. The upside break of that major trendline during 2002 signaled a generational shift out of stocks (paper assets) and into commodities (hard assets). By the middle of 2008, the commodity/stock ratio had risen to the highest level in six years. During the seven years between 2002 and 2008, gains in commodity markets outpaced stock gains by a factor of seven to one.

Did You Know. . .?

Figure 6.1 uses a *logarithmic* price scale, which is more suitable for long-term market comparisons.

JOHN'S TIPS

Simple trendline analysis is usually sufficient to spot important turns in relative strength ratios.

The Commodity/Bond Ratio Also Turned Up

The major upward shift in commodities starting in 2002 didn't come just at the expense of stocks. It came at the expense of bonds as well. Figure 6.2 plots a ratio of the CRB Index divided by the price of the 30-year Treasury bond. The commodity/bond ratio also bottomed during 2002 after declining for more than 20 years. From 1980 to 2000, paper assets (bonds and stocks) were in major bull markets, while commodities (hard assets) were in a major decline. Between 2000 and 2002, however,

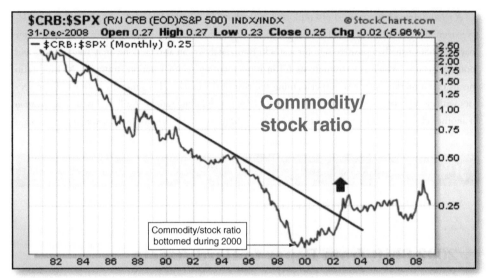

FIGURE 6.1   Upturn in commodity/stock ratio signaled major shift to commodities

the pendulum started to swing away from bonds and stocks, and back to commodities. During 2000, stocks started dropping sharply in anticipation of a possible recession. As a result, commodities started turning up against stocks in 2000. Bonds rallied from 2000 to the end of 2002 as stock prices fell. By the end of 2002, however, the bond rally stalled as stocks bottomed. That's when the commodity/bond ratio turned up in decisive fashion. Commodities continued to outperform bonds for six years after the ratio turned up in 2002.

■ Turns in the Bond/Stock Ratio

Let's now turn our attention to the relationship between bonds and stocks. Bonds and stocks are always competing for investor money. When investors are optimistic about the stock market and the economy, they usually put more into stocks and less into bonds. When they are more pessimistic, they usually commit more funds to bonds and less to stocks. Once again, the relative strength ratio is the best way to spot which of those two competing assets is doing better at any given time.

FIGURE 6.2   Upturn in commodity/bond ratio also signaled major shift to commodities

Figure 6.3 plots a ratio of the price of the 30-year T-bond divided by the S&P 500 from 1993 to 2006. The arrows show two important shifts in their relative performance. During most of the 1990s, the falling bond/stock ratio meant that stocks were the better performer. During 2000, however, the bond/stock ratio turned up (see up arrow) as stocks entered a major bear market. The upturn in the ratio became more obvious when it broke a down trendline drawn over the 1995/1998 tops. From 2000 to the end of 2002, bond prices rose as stocks fell. An investor using a bond/stock ratio could have benefited greatly by switching into bonds and out of stocks during those two years (or by increasing the bond/stock weighting in favor of bonds).

JOHN'S TIPS

Exchange-traded funds (ETFs) for bonds and stocks make it very easy to make switches between those two asset classes.

Did You Know. . .?

Trendline analysis is especially helpful in spotting turns in relative strength ratios.

During an economic slowdown or recession (like the period from 2000 to 2002), bond prices usually do better than stock prices as the Fed lowers short-term rates to stabilize the economy. Bond yields usually drop as well as bond prices rise. That makes Treasuries a safe haven in a slowing economy and a falling stock market. When the stock market turns back up (as in 2003), investors switch out of bonds and back into stocks. At that point, the bond/stock ratio turns down.

The circle in Figure 6.3 shows the bond/stock ratio peaking near the end of 2002 and the start of 2003. The downturn in the ratio was confirmed by the breaking of the rising trendline drawn under the 2000 and 2002 lows (down arrow). Although the breaking of that rising trendline during the

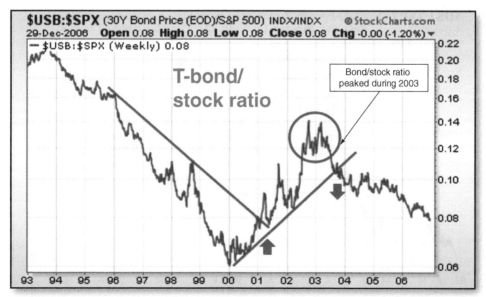

FIGURE 6.3   T-bond/stock ratio turned up during 2000

second half of 2003 came well after the peak that spring, chart evidence of that major peak in the bond/stock ratio was clearly evident much earlier.

Figure 6.4 shows the peak forming in the bond/stock ratio during 2003. The chart shows that the ratio peaked in two stages marked by two prominent peaks. The first was the peak formed during October 2002 (which was the start of the basing process in stocks). The second peak was formed the following March (when the stock market started a new bull market). Any astute chartist should have spotted the possibility of a double top in the ratio. A *double top* is present when a market or indicator starts to drop after forming two distinct peaks. The presence of the *double top* in the bond/stock ratio was pretty clear (see arrows).

---

a **double top** is when a market or indicator starts to drop after forming two distinct peaks

---

Did You Know. . .?

The bond/stock ratio uses the more widely followed 10-year T-note price in the numerator in place of the 30-year T-bond.

JOHN'S TIPS

Double tops appear very frequently on charts and are among the easiest patterns to spot

Confirmation of a completed top was more obvious during June when the ratio fell below the fourth quarter trough (see circle). Even if an investor waited that long to switch out of bonds and back into stocks, that strategy would have still worked for the next four years. Anyone with a basic knowledge of charting, however, should have spotted the turn in the bond/stock ratio a lot earlier.

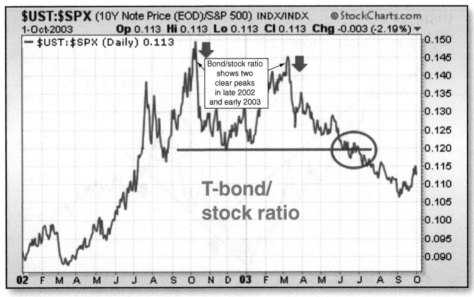

FIGURE 6.4 T-bond/stock ratio peaked in spring of 2003

The 2007 Bond/Stock Ratio Shifts Back to Bonds

The downturn in the bond/stock ratio during 2003 marked a major asset allocation switch out of bonds and back into stocks that continued for the next four years. During those four years, a heavier allocation to stocks (and a smaller allocation to bonds) was the correct asset allocation mix. It took a major bear market in stocks starting in 2007 to turn the asset allocation trend back in favor of bonds.

Figure 6.5 plots the ratio of the price of the 10-year T-note divided by the S&P 500 through the rest of that decade. After peaking during 2003, the bond/stock ratio didn't turn up again until 2007 (up arrow). In mid-2007, the ratio swung back in favor of bonds with a vengeance. Once again, however, the upturn in the ratio that year was pretty easy to spot. The most obvious sign was the breaking of the down trendline extending back to the 2004 peak. (Most of the turns in ratio lines are pretty easy to spot with trendlines or moving averages.)

> **JOHN'S TIPS**
>
> The 200-day moving average can be applied to ratio charts to help spot major trend changes.

During that summer, subprime mortgage problems first surfaced in the mortgage and banking sectors (together with a sharp slowdown in the housing industry), and threatened to undermine the U.S. economy and end the four-year bull market in stocks (which it eventually did). That prompted the Fed to start lowering interest rates during the second half of 2007 to stabilize the economy and the stock market, which was starting to weaken. As usually happens in times of financial stress, money started rotating out of stocks and into the relative safety of Treasuries. Fortunately, the upturn in the bond/stock ratio that started during the summer of 2007 was pretty easy to spot. Figure 6.5 also shows that the bond/stock ratio didn't turn back in favor of stocks until the spring of 2009 (down arrow).

> **JOHN'S TIPS**
>
> Turns in the bond/stock ratio also tell us something about the health of the U.S. economy.

FIGURE 6.5   T-bond/stock ratio turned back up during 2007

The use of relative strength ratios in the preceding charts is done for two reasons. The first is simply to demonstrate its usefulness in tracking the relative performance between competing asset classes. The relationships between bonds, stocks, and commodities aren't static. They change over time and often in a big way. It's important that the investor have tools, like the relative strength ratio, to help spot those changes. The second reason is to demonstrate that major turns in the ratios can usually be spotted with simple trendline analysis and some basic chart reading skills. Although you don't have to be an expert chartist to spot those turning points, some basic knowledge of charting techniques is a big help.

■ Bonds Rise as Stocks Fall During 2007

Let's now turn our attention to the intermarket reactions that took place in the months surrounding the 2007 stock market top. Before reviewing them, I'll let you know in advance that each and every market did exactly what it should have done from an intermarket perspective. That was especially true with bonds and stocks. One of the key intermarket relationships that has existed over the last decade is the inverse correlation between bond and stock prices. When one rises, the other falls. It's obviously very important to know which one is rising and which one is falling. That relationship also tells us something very important about the state of the stock market and the economy. And the message during 2007 wasn't good for either. Figure 6.6 compares the price of the 10-year T-note to the S&P 500 during 2007. During the first half of that year, stock prices rose as bond prices fell. During July, however, the stock market fell as subprime fears started to surface (down arrow). As one would expect, bond prices turned up immediately (up arrow). A second stock drop during October gave the bond uptrend another boost. The proper action at that time was to rotate out of the market turning down (stocks) and into the one turning up (bonds). But you had to spot the trend changes first.

> **JOHN'S TIPS**
>
> The most important trend changes are pretty easy to spot. You have to follow the charts, however, to see those changes.

FIGURE 6.6   T-note price rose during 2007 as stocks fell

It's important to combine intermarket work with traditional charting techniques.

You could have used ratio analysis to do that, as shown in Figure 6.5. Or, you could simply have compared the chart action in the two markets, as shown in Figure 6.6. I prefer to do both. A glance at those visual tools makes it clear that the turns in bonds and stocks should have been pretty obvious to the visual investor at the time. Some knowledge of intermarket principles also provided an understanding why that rotation happened—and what you could do about it.

A final glance at Figure 6.6 also reveals that the stock market was forming a top during that year. A number of technical market indicators were giving major warning signals. The actual chart breakdown took place during January 2008 when the S&P 500 fell below its November 2007 low and violated a trendline drawn under the August/November lows. A *trendline* is drawn under reaction lows. A downside violation of the trendline usually results in lower prices. There was little doubt at that point that a bear market in stocks was beginning. As had happened during 2000, however, the upturn in bond prices (and a corresponding plunge in bond yields) gave a much earlier warning that the bull market in stocks was coming to an end. The ominous bond/stock rotation that took place during summer and autumn 2007 was confirmed by a number of other intermarket warning signs.

a **trendline** is drawn under reaction lows and a downside violation of the trendline usually results in lower prices

Falling U.S. Rates Hurt the Dollar

Let's widen the intermarket net a bit wider during 2007 to explain the ripple effect that took place between short-term interest rates and the U.S. dollar. One of the reasons bond prices started rising (and bond yields dropping) that summer was the Fed's lowering of short-term rates to combat a weakening economy (and a falling stock market). When the Fed lowers short-term rates aggressively (and foreign central bankers don't), one usual side effect is a weaker dollar.

JOHN'S TIPS

The Federal Reserve influences the trend of the U.S. dollar by its control over the direction of interest rates.

Figure 6.7 shows a close correlation during 2007 between the two-year T-note yield and the price of the U.S Dollar Index. Both started to fall together during July and continued to drop into the first quarter of 2008 (pushing the U.S. currency to a record low). So here's another intermarket relationship to consider: When the Fed lowers short-term rates to combat a possible recession, the U.S. dollar usually suffers as a result. As you know by now, one asset class that benefits from a falling dollar is commodities, and gold in particular.

The Falling Dollar Pushes Gold to a Record High

While it's true that a falling dollar benefits most commodity markets, the one that's most closely linked to the greenback is gold. Part of the reason for that is that traders also view gold as an alternate currency. As a result, gold benefits from a falling dollar in its dual role as a commodity and a currency. Figure 6.8

FIGURE 6.7   Two-year T-note yield and dollar fell together during 2007

compares the price of gold to the dollar throughout 2007 and into the early part of 2008. The two markets are almost a perfect mirror image of one another. The two arrows in the middle of the chart show that bullion started to climb sharply during August 2007 (up arrow) just as the dollar started dropping (down arrow). Both moves were a direct result of the Fed's lowering of short-term rates (and the market's growing concern about possible damage from a housing collapse). By the first quarter of 2008, the dollar was trading at a record low and bullion at a record high. Gold wasn't just benefiting from a falling dollar. It also benefited from a falling stock market. Commodity prices kept rising until the middle of 2008 as the dollar kept dropping. A dollar bottom midway through 2008, however, caused

FIGURE 6.8   Gold turned up midway through 2007 as dollar fell

FIGURE 6.9 Bond yield, stocks, and commodities peaked in the proper order during 2007 and 2008

a plunge in commodity prices, which finally succumbed to fears of a possible depression engulfing the global economy. Gold held up better than other commodities but did suffer some profit-taking that summer.

The Three Markets Peaked in the Right Order

Just as they had done during 2000, the three main asset classes peaked in the proper order during 2007 and 2008. Figure 6.9 shows the 10-year bond yield peaking during June 2007 (first down arrow), while the second arrow shows stocks peaking four months later, during October. Once again, a downturn in bond yields acted as a leading indicator for the later downturn in stocks. The third down arrow shows that commodities didn't peak until the middle of 2008. That was a year after the peak in bond yields and more than a half-year after the stock peak. The falling dollar during the first half of 2008 kept the commodity rally going. The U.S. economy slipped into recession in December 2007, which was two months after stocks peaked. Once again, bond yields and stocks had proven to be reliable leading indicators for the economy.

No Such Thing as Global Decoupling

Global stock markets are pretty closely correlated. In other words, major bull and bear markets are usually global in scope. When the U.S. stock market started to weaken during the second half of 2007, a theory circulated throughout Wall Street and the financial media (as well as foreign traders) that foreign stocks were relatively immune from a drop in the U.S. stock market and a possible U.S.

FIGURE 6.10   All global stock markets fell together during 2008 bear market

recession. That misguided theory was predicated on the belief that U.S. housing problems resulting from the subprime mortgage crisis were domestic in nature, and carried little or no threat to foreign markets. That theory violated one of the principles of intermarket analysis, which is that global stock markets are closely linked to one another, especially during bear markets; 2008 was no exception.

JOHN'S TIPS

Since global economies are so closely linked, it's difficult for any of them to escape problems elsewhere in the world.

Figure 6.10 compares the S&P 500 to the MSCI World Stock Index ex USA (MSWORLD) from the end of 2007 to the spring of 2009. Although foreign stocks fell a bit more than U.S. stocks, it's hard to tell the two lines apart. The point of Figure 6.10 is to demonstrate that global stock markets fell together from late 2007 to early 2009. That's just another example of the intermarket principle that global stock markets are highly correlated, especially during a downtrend.

Proponents of *global decoupling* near the end of 2007 weren't market historians. If they were, they would (and should) have known that global stocks become even more closely correlated during bear markets.

Did You Know. . .?

I gave a speech in Switzerland in January 2008 to a group of European analysts. I had read local newspaper articles claiming that Europe was immune from a U.S. downturn. My speech, however, warned that any U.S. problems would soon become problems for Europe and everywhere else in the world. That warning was greeted with skepticism. So was the bearish chart analysis I presented that day. One of my hosts suggested discreetly that I tone down my negative views for a second speech in another European country. Unfortunately, those negative warnings turned out to be correct.

By the second quarter of 2008, many foreign stock markets had fallen even further than those in the United States. By the end of 2008, the S&P 500 had fallen 45 percent from its October 2007 peak. By contrast, EAFE iShares (which measure foreign developed markets) and Emerging Market iShares lost 50 percent and 55 percent, respectively. That earlier talk about *global decoupling* turned to fear of *global contagion*. As was the case during the 1987 stock market crash and the 2000–2002 bear market, the 2007–2008 stock collapse was global in scope. No foreign stock markets escaped those global downturns. The only safe havens at such times aren't stocks at all. They're usually Treasury bonds and gold.

CHAPTER 7

Visual Analysis of the 2007 Market Top

This chapter combines intermarket principles with traditional charting to demonstrate how they worked together to warn that the stock market was peaking during 2007. The S&P 500 was testing important resistance at its 2000 peak. Traditional breadth measures started to break down. Small caps, financials, retailers, and transports turned down first. Rising oil prices were part of the problem. Rising oil and falling homebuilding hurt the performance of retail stocks. The 2006 downturn in housing stocks was clearly evident on chart.

Combining Traditional Charting with Intermarket Warnings

The stock market top that started in 2007 led to a financial meltdown the following year that threatened to bring down the global financial system. For the first time in most people's lives, fears were being openly expressed that the global economy might be headed into another depression reminiscent of the 1930s. Because it was such an important financial and historical event, we're going to study the 2007 top in more detail in this chapter. To do that properly, however, it's necessary to blend intermarket warning signs that were clearly visible with some traditional charting. And, believe me, there were plenty of warning signs there as well.

> **JOHN'S TIPS**
>
> It's always a good idea to combine traditional charting techniques with intermarket analysis.

My 2009 book, *The Visual Investor, Second Edition* (Wiley Trading) covered the 2007 top very extensively along with the charting and intermarket warning signs that were evident as that book was being written. I've drawn from some of that material in this and the preceding chapter. While I'm going to include some traditional charting in this chapter, our main concern here is with intermarket influences. Anyone looking for a more extensive discussion of traditional charting techniques during the 2007 market top can consult that earlier book.

■ A Look at the S&P 500 Chart in 2007

Before discussing what happened to the stock market during and after 2007, let's begin by looking at where it was as it entered that historic year. To do that, it's necessary to look at a chart going back at least 10 years. Figure 7.1 is a monthly bar chart of the S&P 500 spanning the decade from 1998 to 2008. Anyone reasonably familiar with chart analysis knew going into 2007 that the S&P 500 had reached a dangerous area of resistance. *Resistance* is an area or level above a market where it usually meets with some selling. The most important resistance levels are at important previous peaks. The S&P 500 had reached the same level where it had peaked seven years earlier during 2000 (see circles).

---

resistance is an area or level above a market where it usually meets with some selling

---

In chart work, a *retest* of a prominent price peak is always dangerous. It's dangerous is because that's precisely where new market peaks are likely to form. In addition, the S&P 500 had doubled in price from its 2003 bottom, which was another warning sign of a dangerously overextended market. The trendlines drawn on the monthly bars define the bear market from 2000 to 2003, and the bull market from 2003 to 2007. The breaking of the downtrend line during 2003 (up arrow) signaled that the major trend had turned higher. The breaking of the uptrend line (down arrow) at the end of 2007 signaled that the major trend had turned down. The fact that the downturn took place at the same level as the 2000 peak made the downturn that much more credible and dangerous.

FIGURE 7.1   The S&P 500 was testing its 2000 peak during 2007

Market Breadth Warning Signs

As the year 2007 progressed, a number of dangerous warning signs were given that the market was in danger of peaking. One of the most important of those was the deterioration that developed in various measures of market breadth. *Market breadth* refers to the number of stocks that are rising on any given day versus the number that are falling. If there are more advances than declines, market breadth for that day is positive. More declines than advances translate into a negative breadth day. The most popular tool for measuring market breadth on the New York Stock Exchange (NYSE) is the *NYSE advance-decline (AD) line*. The AD line is simply a running cumulative total of advancing stocks minus declining stocks. When the AD line is rising, there are more advances than declines and the market is perceived to be in an uptrend. Market analysts usually compare the AD line to an index of stock prices like the S&P 500 Index. The reason for doing that is to ensure that the two lines are trending in the same direction.

market breadth refers to the number of stocks that are rising on any given day versus the number that are falling

At market tops, the advance-decline line usually turns down before the stock index does. (I'll explain later why that happens.) A warning of a possible market top is given when the AD line starts to fall while the market index is still rising. When that happens, chartists refer to that condition as a negative divergence. A *negative divergence* is present when two lines that should be rising in the same direction start to diverge from one another. That's exactly what happened during the second half of 2007.

a **negative divergence** is present when two lines that should be rising in the same direction start to diverge from one another

> **JOHN'S TIPS**
>
> The term *negative divergence* is very common in chart analysis and is used with several other technical indicators.

The NYSE Advance-Decline Line Shows Negative Divergence

The main reason for studying the NYSE advance-decline line is to ensure that it's trending in the same direction as the stock index it's being compared to. As long as both lines are rising (which had been the case since 2003), the market uptrend is considered to be healthy. When the AD line starts to drop before the price index, however, a dangerous negative divergence is created. That negative divergence is usually a warning sign that the stock market uptrend is on weak footing. Figure 7.2 compares the S&P 500 Index to the NYSE advance-decline line during 2007. Both lines peaked together during June and July, and dropped into August. The S&P 500 Index then started a rally that took it to a new high during October. Unfortunately, the AD line failed to do so. The AD line fell well short of its July high. That's when the trouble started. That lack of upside confirmation by the AD line created a negative divergence that warned that the new high recorded by the stock index was being supported by a smaller number of stocks than before.

The weaker performance by the AD line during October (relative to the S&P 500) can be seen by the declining trendline drawn over its July and October peaks. From that point on, the AD line led the stock index down from its October peak. That negative pattern of *lower highs* in the AD line gave an early warning that the market was peaking. The fact is that the deterioration in the advance-decline line was pretty obvious at the time. I remember showing it in several market reports during the

FIGURE 7.2   The falling NYSE advance-decline line during 2007 warned of market top

second half of that year. Yet, most of Wall Street either didn't see it or chose to ignore it. They ignored a lot of other warning signals that year.

What Caused the Divergence?

While it's important to know when the NYSE advance-decline line is diverging from market averages, it's also important to know what's causing that divergence. The reasons for knowing that are twofold. One is to know which groups to avoid (or rotate out of). The other reason is because certain market groups have a history of peaking first at market tops. (They're usually the same ones that turn up first at market bottoms.) Knowing that they're the ones leading the market lower is further evidence that the market is in fact peaking. It just so happens that four market groups that led the market lower in 2007 had a history of doing that in the past.

JOHN'S TIPS

At market tops, money tends to rotate out of economically sensitive stock groups first.

Those four lagging groups were small-cap stocks, financials, retailers, and transportation stocks. Homebuilders were in that group as well, but for a different reason. (I'll come back to homebuilders later.) None of those groups reached new highs during the fourth quarter of 2007, which helped create the negative divergence in the advance-decline line. Small caps have a history of turning up first at market bottoms (like 2003) and turning down first at market peaks (like 2007). In the final stages of a bull market, investors start rotating out of riskier small cap stocks into more stable large caps as a defensive maneuver. The move into large cap stocks is also a search for dividends to cushion a potential market decline. That's why large blue chip stocks are often the last to fall.

Financial stocks are also traditional leading indicators for the rest of the market. During 2007, financial stocks turned down with a vengeance. That was obviously a reaction to the fact that large financial stocks (like banks) were especially vulnerable to problems in the housing market. Retail stocks measure the strength of consumer spending and are often among the first to turn down at market tops. As you'll see shortly, the downturn in retail stocks was closely tied to rising oil prices and weakness in homebuilding stocks. Transportation stocks are another group that has a history of turning down first at market tops. That's also usually the result of rising energy costs, as was the case during 2007.

■ Rising Oil Hurts Transportation Stocks

During the bull market in stocks from 2003 to 2007, industrial and transportation stocks rose pretty much in tandem. That changed in a big way during 2007. Transportation stocks started to underperform badly that year. Rising oil prices were a big reason why. For reasons that should seem obvious, transports are especially vulnerable to rising oil. Airlines and truckers use huge amounts of fuel in their operations. Although railroads can pass most of their fuel costs on to their customers, even they couldn't withstand the type of soaring fuel costs that occurred during 2007 when crude oil doubled in price.

JOHN'S TIPS

Crude oil usually weakens during a market downturn, which is why transports usually turn up first at market bottoms.

Figure 7.3 compares the price of crude oil to a ratio of the Dow Transports divided by the Dow Industrials during 2007. An inverse relationship can be seen. Rising oil prices caused the transports to underperform industrial shares, especially during the second half of that year. Rising oil prices usually take place near the end of an economic expansion and usually lead to a stock market peak. The fact that transportation stocks are one of the most fuel-sensitive parts of the market explains their tendency to be one of the first parts of the stock market to start dropping in the early stages of a downtrend. That's what they did during 2007.

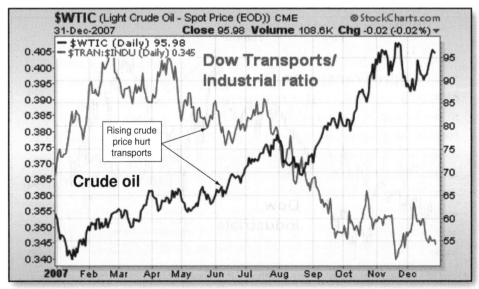

FIGURE 7.3   Dow Transports/Industrial ratio fell during 2007 because of rising crude oil

Another factor hurting transportation stocks during 2007 was a weakening economy (resulting from the start of a housing depression). That's because the transports are considered to be *economically sensitive* stocks. That means they're tied to the ups and downs of the business cycle. As such, they're especially vulnerable to early signs of an economic slowdown. The relative weakness in the Dow Transports during the second half of 2007 created a divergence between them and the Dow Industrials, which started to worry followers of the *Dow Theory*.

■ The Dow Theory

The venerable *Dow Theory* is one of the oldest and most influential pillars of technical analysis, and was originated by Charles Dow at the start of the 20th century. It was Charles Dow who created the first two stock indexes, which were the Dow Industrial and Transportation Averages. At first, the transports were limited to railroads. In time, however, airlines and truckers were added to the transportation index. Dow reasoned that, in a healthy economy, industrial and transportation stocks should be rising together. After all, the industrial companies made the products, while the transportation companies moved them to market. One couldn't function without the other. Although he intended his idea to be used mainly as an indicator of economic trends, it later became an indicator for the stock market itself.

JOHN'S TIPS

Railroad stocks benefit from demand for commodities like grains and coal, and suffer when that demand lessens.

Dow Theory holds that the Dow Industrial and Transportation Averages must rise together in an ongoing bull market. If one of them lags too far behind the other, or forms a serious negative divergence from the other, a stock market peak might be at hand. One of the first danger signs occurs when one of the two hits a new high and the other one doesn't. That's just what happened during 2007.

Figure 7.4 shows the two Dow averages rising together until the middle of 2007. During July and August, however, the transports fell further than the industrials. At first, that didn't seem too serious. During October, however, the Dow Industrials rose to a new high, while the transports didn't come

FIGURE 7.4   2007 Drop in Dow Transports caused negative divergence with industrials

close to matching that. While the industrials were at a new high during October 2007, the transports were trading nearly 10 percent below their summer high (see falling trendline). That divergence between the two Dow averages during the fourth quarter of 2007 was a Dow Theory warning that the market uptrend was in trouble.

Charles Dow had warned a century earlier that a downturn in either stock average was a bad sign for the economy and the stock market. Although Dow's ideas helped form the basis of modern technical analysis, he was also ahead of his time in suggesting that the stock market could be used as a leading indicator for the economy. The stock market has a history of peaking roughly six months ahead of the economy. The Dow Transports peaked in July of 2007. A U.S. recession started that December, which was five months after the transportation peak.

Consumers Are Also Squeezed by Rising Oil

During 2007, consumers were being hit from two different directions. Not only was the price of their homes falling for the first time in their lifetime, but energy prices were soaring to record heights. Figure 7.5 compares the price of crude oil to a ratio of the S&P 500 Retail Index divided by the S&P 500. From the start of 2006 to mid-2008, the two lines show a generally inverse correlation. In other words, they trended in opposite directions. A surge in oil prices near the start of 2007 was especially negative for retailers for the rest of that year.

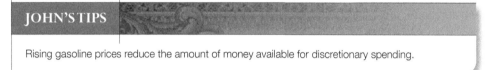

JOHN'S TIPS

Rising gasoline prices reduce the amount of money available for discretionary spending.

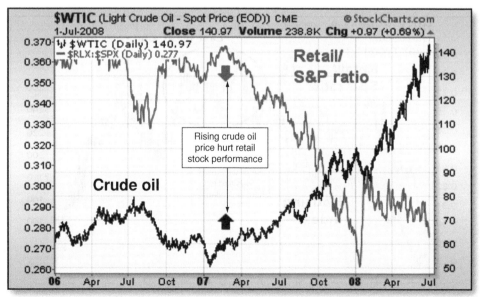

A doubling of crude oil from $50 at the start of 2007 to $100 at the end of the year accompanied a plunge in the relative performance of retail stocks (a falling relative strength ratio). The financial community at the time held to the mistaken belief that rising oil prices weren't having a negative impact on the consumer. Another mistaken belief at the time was that weakness in the housing industry wasn't having much of an impact either. They were wrong about both.

FIGURE 7.5   Rise in crude oil during 2007 contributed to drop in retail/S&P 500 ratio

■ Retailers and Homebuilders Were Linked

Throughout 2007, one of the mantras repeated over and over again in the financial media was that the U.S. economy was still healthy. Economists claimed that the fallout from a weakening housing sector wasn't having much of a negative impact on retail spending or the rest of the economy. As a result, there wasn't much concern about the downturn in housing infecting the economy or the stock market. Visual analysis of the financial markets, however, told a very different story.

Figure 7.6 compares weekly price bars for the PHLX Housing Index to a ratio of the S&P Retail Index divided by the S&P 500 (the same ratio shown in the previous chart). The chart shows that homebuilding stocks actually peaked in the middle of 2005, but really started dropping sharply during the first half of 2006 (see circle). They fell even more sharply during 2007. One of the reasons for looking at market charts is that financial markets have a way of *discounting* economic fundamentals before those fundamentals become generally known.

> **JOHN'S TIPS**
>
> Charts are a shortcut form of fundamental analysis.

The peak in housing stocks during 2005 and their downturn in early 2006 (which was so clear on the charts) gave two warnings. One warning was that it was time to exit homebuilding stocks that had been market leaders since 2000. A second warning was that a weaker housing sector was starting to have a negative impact on stocks tied to retail spending, which would eventually have a negative impact on the rest of the economy. That warning was given anywhere from one to two years before subprime problems surfaced in summer 2007 and was largely ignored by the financial community. Or maybe they just didn't look at the charts.

As already mentioned, the solid line in Figure 7.6 is a relative strength ratio of retail stocks divided by the S&P 500. That retail ratio line is overlaid on top of the index of housing stocks for a reason. By doing that, the close correlation between the two markets is both obvious and striking. Notice that the retail relative strength ratio peaked in the middle of 2005 right along with the Housing Index (see circle). They fell

FIGURE 7.6 Peak in housing stocks coincided with peak in retail/S&P 500 ratio

together during the first half of 2006 and throughout 2007. Figure 7.6 makes it clear that the peak in the relative performance of retail stocks, and the beginning of a period of relative weakness, was closely tied to the downturn in homebuilding stocks and the housing sector. The chart clearly shows that housing weakness was beginning to infect an important part of the stock market and the economy. And all of those early warning signs were clearly visible to the visual investor who looked at the charts and knew how to read them.

Retail Stocks Start to Underperform Long before 2007

Consumer spending accounts for 70 percent of the U.S. economy. That being the case, the trend of retail stocks tells us a lot about the health of the economy. And, as is the case with most common stocks, the trend of retail stocks is usually a leading indicator of trends in the retail industry itself—but not just the *absolute* trend of retail stocks; their *relative* trend is just as important. It was the downturn in their *relative* performance two years before 2007 that sent an early warning signal that the retail sector and, by inference, the economy was in trouble.

> **JOHN'S TIPS**
>
> *Absolute* performance measures the actual trend of a market. *Relative* performance measures its performance against other markets.

Figure 7.7 is an example of how to compare both the *absolute* and the *relative* performances of a market group, and how the two often give different messages. The price bars in that figure measure

---

Did You Know. . .?

Comparison between a relative strength ratio and a price index is much more revealing when the ratio is overlaid right over the price bars.

FIGURE 7.7   Falling retail/S&P 500 ratio during 2007 showed relative weakness

the *absolute* trend of the S&P Retail Index. The solid line is relative strength ratio of retail stocks divided by the S&P 500. That measures the group's *relative* performance versus the rest of the market.

Notice that retail stocks led the S&P 500 higher (rising ratio line) during the 2003 upturn and for two years after that. That's not unusual in the early stages of a bull market. Relative strength by retail stocks tells us that consumers have turned more optimistic on the economy and are spending more freely. That's why retail leadership is usually a good sign for the stock market and the economy. That's also why relative weakness by the retail group is bad for both.

The two performance measures started to diverge after 2005. The index of retail stocks turned higher during the second half of 2006 and reached a new high by the first half of 2007. That showed that their *absolute* performance was still rising. Unfortunately, their *relative* performance wasn't. The relative strength ratio peaked in the middle of 2005 (with homebuilding stocks) and started dropping into the middle of 2006. It then bounced into the early part of 2007. That's where a serious *negative divergence* became evident between the retail relative strength ratio and the actual price of retail stocks. While the Retail Index hit a record high, its relative strength ratio fell well short of its earlier peak (see falling trendline). That was convincing visual evidence that retail stocks were starting to underperform the rest of the market. Then things got even worse.

The relative strength ratio started dropping sharply during the second quarter of 2007 and by the third quarter had fallen to the lowest level in four years. That was a serious warning that retail stocks were starting to underperform, which would have negative implications for the economy and the stock market. This is a good example of why *relative* performance by a market group is often more telling than a chart showing a group's *absolute* trend. It also demonstrates why some knowledge of chart reading, together with an understanding of intermarket principles, offers insight not only into the health of the individual group, but into the health of the entire stock market.

■ The 2005 Homebuilding Top Gave Early Warning

Figure 7.8 is a weekly bar chart of the PHLX Housing Index. That index measures the trend of the homebuilding group (and some other stocks tied to the housing sector). It's a pretty simple chart, but it carried a lot of important messages. The first message is that the 2005 peak in housing stocks, and the 2006 downturn, was pretty obvious at the time. I've drawn a rising *trendline* under the 2003, 2004, and 2005 lows. The trendline in Figure 7.8 was touched three times (see up arrows). The last time was during October 2005 (third arrow). That important trendline was broken during the second quarter of 2006.

Did You Know. . .?

A rising *trendline* is drawn under previous reaction lows. The longer a trendline has been in effect, and the more times it has been touched, the more important it becomes—and the more important the breaking of the trendline becomes.

The main message from Figure 7.8 is that simple trendline analysis made it clear that a major trend reversal to the downside had taken place in the housing sector. A second signal that a new downtrend

FIGURE 7.8 Break of support line during 2006 marked peak in housing sector

had started was given when the 2006 price drop fell below its prior October's low (see circle). That formed a bearish pattern of *lower highs* and *lower lows*, which is the basic definition of a *downtrend*. One didn't need to be a charting expert to see that bearish trend reversal in housing. All one needed to do was look at the chart. It was pretty hard to miss at the time.

JOHN'S TIPS

An uptrend is a pattern of *higher highs* and *higher lows*.

Figure 7.9 shows a chart taken from a Market Message I wrote on StockCharts.com on June 5, 2006. The chart shows the Housing Index falling below its October 2005 low to complete a top. The caption on the chart reads: "Housing stocks are crumbling." As I said earlier, it was pretty hard to miss. But one did have to know where to look in order not to miss it. The HGX/S&P 500 ratio below Figure 7.9 shows that housing stocks started to underperform the S&P in the middle of 2005, and especially during 2006. It's been my experience in more than 40 years of charting markets that most important trend reversals are pretty obvious and hard to miss. You don't need a lot of fancy indicators to see them, but you do have to look at the charts. Some knowledge of basic charting and the ability to draw a trendline are usually more than enough.

A second message from Figures 7.8 and 7.9 is more subtle but equally important. I've already mentioned several times that financial markets are leading indicators of fundamental and economic information. Never was that more true than in 2005 and 2006 when the housing stocks rolled over to the downside. Anyone seeing the breakdown in housing stocks during 2006 had to suspect that something had gone wrong and that falling housing stocks were warning of future problems. It's amazing, however, that Wall Street analysts ignored those warnings and waited until 2007 to recognize the problem. Unfortunately, that was too late.

To cite another example that housing problems were becoming obvious during 2005, I'm going to quote the headline from a Market Message that I wrote on November 8 of that year: "Homebuilders Weigh on Market—Housing Index Peaked in July—Double Top in Bond Prices Signals End of

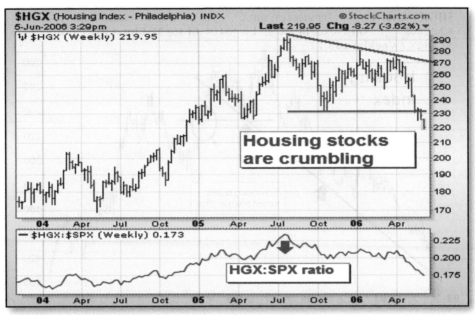

FIGURE 7.9   Housing stocks fall below chart support in spring 2006

Five-Year Housing Boom" (StockCharts.com). The reference to the bond price had to do with the fact that rising bond prices (falling bond yields) had been supporting interest rate-sensitive housing stocks since 2000. A drop in bond prices during 2005 (and an upturn in bond yields) threatened to damage a housing group that had already peaked.

JOHN'S TIPS

Homebuilding stocks are especially sensitive to trends in the bond market, which determine the cost of a home mortgage.

FIGURE 7.10   Housing stocks peaked two years before the S&P 500

Figure 7.10 shows the 2005 peak in the Housing Index taking place two years before the 2007 peak in the S&P 500. That was a pretty early warning that the housing boom was ending. It seemed obvious at the time and pretty hard to miss. Which makes it all the more incredible that so many professionals (including the Fed) did miss it. I'll deal with the implications of the resulting housing depression on the financial markets in the next chapter, and will put it into historical perspective. At that time, you'll also learn why the bursting of the housing bubble was another major deflationary event that helped define the way financial markets related to one another after 2008.

■ Another Bearish Warning During 2007

Let's end this visual study of the 2007 stock market top where we began it: with a look at another measure of *market breadth* that also gave a clear warning of a market peak. The indicator is the *percent of NYSE stocks that are trading above their 200-day moving average*. I explained earlier in the book that the 200-moving average (which is an average of the last 200 days' closing prices) is the dividing line between major uptrends and downtrends. A stock that falls below that long-term support line is judged to have entered a major downtrend. All of the U.S. stock indexes fell below their 200-day lines during the fourth quarter of 2007. By that time, however, a lot of money had already been lost. Most of the stocks on the New York Stock Exchange, however, fell below those lines a lot earlier.

Figure 7.11 compares the *percent of NYSE stocks trading above their 200-day average* to the NYSE Composite Index. In a healthy uptrend, both market measures should be rising together. Figure 7.11 shows that bullish percentage dropping sharply in the middle of the year (first arrow). The resulting *negative divergence* between the two lines was especially noticeable when the NYSE Index hit a new high during October and the breadth indicator didn't even come close to doing so (second arrow). While the stock index was hitting a new high, only two-thirds of its stocks were still in uptrends. That weakening in the breadth indicator was another warning that the stock market rally wasn't to be trusted. And it was right.

FIGURE 7.11 Percent of NYSE stocks above 200-day average fell below 40 percent during 2007

A bear market is signaled when the percentage of NYSE stocks above their 200-day averages drops below 40 percent.

The scale to the right of Figure 7.11 shows the actual percentage of stocks still in uptrends. Readings over 80 percent usually warn of a dangerously overextended market, which was the case during the first half of 2007. By that August, the indicator had fallen below 40 percent, which put most of the NYSE stocks in downtrends. In one of my market reports during that period, I questioned how a bull market could exist in the NYSE Composite Index when nearly two-thirds of the stocks in that index were in bear markets. As was the case with the NYSE advance-decline line shown earlier, the warning signs were clearly evident at the time. The breadth indicators worked. But they only worked for people who looked at them and knew what they meant.

◼ Why Breadth Measures Work

I explained earlier in this chapter that one of the reasons breadth measures turn down before the major stock indexes is because certain economically sensitive market groups usually peak before the rest of the market. That helps create the negative divergences that appear on breadth charts. There's another reason why measures of market breadth like the one shown in Figure 7.11, or the NYSE advance-decline line, start to fall before the major stock indexes.

Most major market indexes like the NYSE Composite and S&P 500 are *capitalization-weighted,* which means that bigger stocks are given greater weight in determining the daily value of those indexes. (The Dow Jones Industrial Average is *price-weighted.* That still means, however, that higher priced stocks are given greater weight.) I suggested earlier in the chapter that *small-cap* stocks usually fall faster than *large-cap* stocks in the early stages of a market downturn. It just so happens that there are more *small* and *midsize* stocks than there are *large* stocks. As a result, the *large-cap*-dominated stock indexes reported in the media tell us more about what the *large-cap* stocks are doing. They're usually the last ones to fall at a market top. The two breadth indicators described in this chapter tell us what most of the other stocks are doing. That's another reason why breadth indicators usually start dropping before the major stock indexes. That's what gives them their forecasting value. No analysts who looked at those indicators during 2007, and understood their meaning, can complain that they were surprised at what happened afterward.

◼ Summary

This chapter concludes Part II of the book. Chapter 4 examined events leading up to and surrounding the 2000 stock market top. Chapter 5 showed how a major drop in the U.S. dollar during 2002 contributed to a major upturn in commodities. Chapter 6 explained how to use relative strength analysis to determine asset allocation strategies among different asset classes. Chapter 7 combined intermarket principles with traditional charting techniques to perform a visual analysis of the 2007 stock market top. Part III will explain the important role the business cycle plays in intermarket analysis and sector rotation strategies. It will also devote a chapter to exploring the exciting world of exchange-traded funds (ETFs).

THE BUSINESS CYCLE AND ETFS

CHAPTER 8

Intermarket Analysis and the Business Cycle

This chapter examines various economic cycles that influence the financial markets and the economy. The presidential cycle helps explain the tendency for stocks to bottom every four years. The business cycle is also responsible for rotations that take place among the various asset classes. The Kondratieff Wave measures a long economic cycle, which turned down during 2000. A peak in the 18-year real estate cycle caused the housing collapse during 2007 and 2008. A bottom in homebuilding stocks suggests that the worst may be over for housing.

The Four-Year Business Cycle

The American economy goes through repeated up and down cycles. Sometimes those cycles have been dramatic, such as the Great Depression of the 1930s, the inflationary 1970s, and the housing-inspired collapse during 2008. At other times, their impact has been less extreme. These business cycles average four years in length. That means that every four years, on average, the economy normally goes through a period of expansion and contraction. Those contractions usually follow downturns in the stock market. The tendency for the stock market to bottom every four years (usually during the midterm election) is referred to as the *presidential cycle* because American presidents are elected every four years.

The Presidential Cycle

Figure 8.1 shows several examples of stock market bottoms tied to the four-year presidential cycle. The last six bottoms occurred during 1990, 1994, 1998, 2002, 2006, and 2010. Earlier four-year market bottoms occurred in 1970, 1974, 1982, and 1987 (the cycle skipped 1978, while the 1987 bottom was a year late). Most of those bottoms have taken place during the second half of those years and have coincided with midterm congressional elections. According to the *Stock Trader's Almanac*, the stock market performs better during the second half of presidential terms than the first half. Statistics also show that the third year of a president's term has seen the strongest stock market returns of the

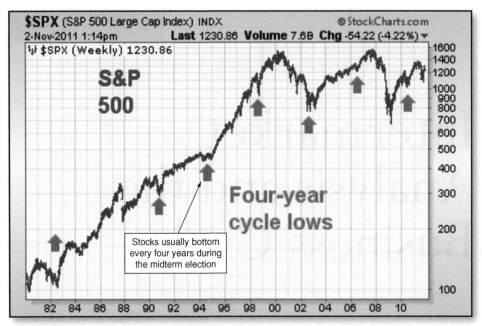

FIGURE 8.1   Examples of four-year stock market bottoms

four years. The fourth year is the second strongest. Since the stock market leads turns in the economy, it shouldn't come as a surprise to learn that the fourth year of a presidential term has historically shown the best economic growth. The rationale behind that four-year pattern is that presidents do everything in their power to stimulate the stock market and the economy in the two years before the next presidential election.

JOHN'S TIPS

The first two years of a president's term are usually the worst for the stock market.

The contraction phase of the business cycle often turns into a recession, which is a period of negative growth in the economy. The recession or slowdown inevitably leads to the next period of expansion. During an unusually long economic expansion when no recession takes place, the economy may undergo a slowdown before continuing into its next growth phase. When that happens, the time between actual recessions can stretch out to eight years. The recessions of 1970 and 1974 were exactly four years apart. The next scheduled recession during 1978 didn't arrive on schedule. And even though the 1980 recession arrived two years late, the 1982 recession occurred eight years after the 1974 recession.

Following the 1982 recession, it took eight years for the 1990 recession to arrive. After 1990, the U.S. economy entered the longest expansion on record (lasting just over 10 years), which exceeded the previous record of the 1960s. When no recessions actually occur, the timing of stock market downturns is helpful, since bear markets are usually associated with *expectations* for an economic slowdown. Based on the four-year business cycle, for example, the economy skipped scheduled downturns in 1986 and again in 1994. However, downturns in the stock market occurred during 1987 and 1994, which still adhered quite closely to the four-year business cycle model. The record expansion of the 1990s also skipped a scheduled economic downturn in 1998 (although stocks experienced a downturn during the second half of that year). That still left *scheduled* recessions for 2002 and 2006. As it turned out, the next two recessions began during 2001 and 2007. The first one was a year early, and the second one a year late.

Since World War II, the U.S. economy has experienced 11 recessions. Each recession lasted an average of 11 months. The Great Recession from December 2007 to June 2009 lasted 18 months, which made it the longest since the Great Depression. The last five recessions have resulted in stocks losing a little over a third of their value on average. Stocks lost half of their value during the Great Recession. While the four-year business cycle is the best known of the economic cycles, there are longer cycles that have come into play over the last decade that have intensified deflationary pressures, and have caused downturns in the business cycle to be more severe and upturns less robust. Before we get to those, however, let's study the impact the four-year cycle has on the financial markets.

JOHN'S TIPS

The stock market usually turns down before a recession starts and turns up before the recession ends.

■ The Business Cycle Explains Intermarket Rotation

The business cycle has an important bearing on the financial markets. Periods of expansion and contraction provide an economic framework that helps explain the linkages that exist between the bond, stock, and commodity markets. In addition, the business cycle explains the chronological sequence that develops among the three asset classes. Near the end of an economic expansion, bonds are usually the first to turn down. That happened during 2000 and again in 2007. Stocks usually peak second and commodities third. That also happened during 2000–2001 and again during the 2007–2008 period. The order of their troughs has been less reliable.

Did You Know. . .?

Prior to 1998, bond *prices* turned down before stocks and commodities. Since 1998, bond *yields* have been the first to peak.

A better understanding of the business cycle sheds light on the intermarket process, and confirms that what is seen on the price charts makes sense from an economic perspective. At the same time, intermarket analysis can be used to help determine the current state of the business cycle. That suggests that intermarket analysis can play a role in economic forecasting.

The stage of the business cycle is very important in determining *asset allocation* strategies. Different phases of the business cycle favor different asset classes. Periods of economic strength favor

Did You Know. . .?

As already noted in a previous chapter, the falling dollar during 2002 caused commodities to bottom a year ahead of stocks, while a deflation scare in spring 2003 caused bond yields to turn up three months after stocks.

stocks, while periods of weakness favor bonds. The beginning of an economic upswing usually favors stocks, while the latter part of an expansion favors commodities. Increased inflation pressures late in an expansion also favor inflation-sensitive stock groups like basic materials, gold, and oil stocks. Increased inflation pressures (usually from rising oil prices) prompt the Fed to start raising short-term rates, which eventually hurts stocks and the economy. That happened prior to the 2000 and 2007 market peaks and led to recessions both times.

Lessons from 2000 and 2007

Chapter 4 described how a tripling in the price of oil during 1999 prompted the Fed to start raising short-term rates during the second half of that year, which brought down the stock market the following year (2000) and the economy the year after that (2001). That's normal in the late stages of an economic expansion when commodities become the strongest asset class. Commodities didn't peak until the start of 2001, which was five months after stocks peaked. Bond yields also peaked before stocks during 2007, while commodities peaked last in the middle of 2008.

JOHN'S TIPS

Traders usually rotate into commodities and their related stocks in the late stages of a bull market in stocks.

Did You Know. . .?

When I discuss the impact of the business cycle on sector rotations within the stock market in the next chapter, you'll also learn why leadership by energy stocks is almost always a bad sign for the rest of the market.

Oil Leads to Higher Rates from 2004 to 2006

Oil is a key link in the intermarket chain and a focal point in the business cycle. It's amazing how many stock market peaks and business cycle downturns resulted from rising oil prices. During 2004, the price of oil rose above $40 for the first time in its history. Once again, the Fed embarked on a series of short-term rates hikes that lasted into 2006. The previous chapter showed housing stocks peaking in 2005 before tumbling during 2006. The combination of rising oil and higher short-term rates caused bond yields to spike higher during 2005 and 2006, which helped end the bull market in rate-sensitive housing stocks. We all know what happened after that. Figure 8.2 shows crude oil rising above $40 during 2004 (see circle). The Fed raised short-term rates (up arrow) between 2004 and 2006, which hurt homebuilders first and stocks a couple of years later.

Knowing the order in which the three markets normally peak offers all kinds of advantages. The topping process usually begins with an upturn in bond prices and a downturn in bond yields (which always move inversely). From an asset allocation standpoint, the peak in bond yields during 2000 and 2007 suggested that it was time to rotate out of stocks and into bonds. Knowing that commodities usually peak after stocks peak (which they did both times) also offers investors an alternate asset class to rotate into. In addition to helping investors make those asset allocation choices, the peaking process in the three asset classes also alerts everyone to the likelihood for a recession (which occurred in both instances).

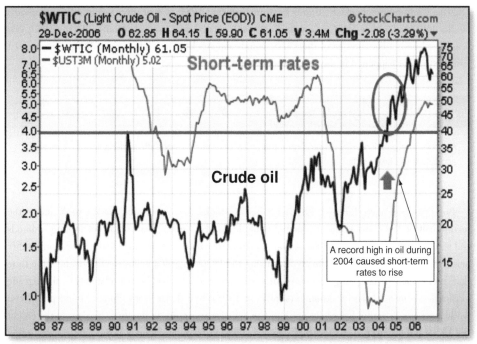

FIGURE 8.2 Short-term rates starting rising during 2004 after oil hit record high

JOHN'S TIPS

The position of the three asset classes helps determine the current state of the business cycle.

■ The 2001 Fed Easings Didn't Work

After the dot-com stock bubble burst in 2000, the Federal Reserve embarked on an aggressive series of rate cuts that should have stemmed the stock market's decline. By the time it was finished, the Fed had lowered rates 12 times. However, the usually beneficial impact of falling rates didn't help stocks as much as they had in the past. Bonds and stocks had completely decoupled. Something unusual was happening in that business cycle (and in the one after it). As already suggested, the unusual ingredient was the threat of global deflation, something that had not been experienced since the 1930s. The fact that none of that current generation of investors (or economists) had lived through that earlier deflationary cycle probably explains why so few of them recognized its dangerous symptoms.

■ Comparisons to the 1920s and 1930s

My 2004 book, *Intermarket Analysis,* revisited the era of the 1920s and 1930s to draw some comparisons between those and more recent decades. Here are some striking similarities drawn from that earlier text. After the inflationary World War I decade, commodities peaked in 1920 and, after an initial drop, trended sideways through the balance of that decade. (Commodities peaked 60 years later, during 1980, after the inflationary decade that included the Vietnam War). Bonds bottomed during

1920 as commodities peaked. (Bonds bottomed during 1981, a year after commodities peaked.) Stocks bottomed during 1921, one year after bonds turned up. (Stocks bottomed during 1982, one year after bonds.) For the rest of the 1920s, bonds and stocks rose while commodities remained flat (similar to what happened in the two decades after 1980).

Bond prices peaked during 1928, a year before stocks. After the stock market peak during the second half of 1929, stock prices plunged while bond prices rose. That major decoupling of bonds and stocks was caused largely by the action in commodity markets. Starting in late 1929, commodity prices (which had remained relatively flat during the 1920s) began a major decline at the same time that stocks peaked. That plunge in commodity prices turned what had been a relatively benign decade of *disinflation* into a harmful *deflation* (similar to 1998). In a deflationary climate, bond prices rise while stocks and commodities fall together. The deflationary trends in the three markets at the end of the 1920s and the start of the 1930s closely parallel their respective trends as the 1990s were ending and the new millennium was starting.

I wrote in an earlier chapter that the plunge in commodity prices during 1998 turned what had been a beneficial disinflation into a harmful deflation that changed several intermarket relationships. Quoting from my 2004 text: "When deflation is the main threat, stocks and commodities become closely correlated. . . . In a deflationary climate such as existed during the early 1930s, rising commodity prices are considered a plus for stocks and the economy." (That quote sheds light on the strategy of boosting commodities [by weakening the dollar] employed over the last decade by the head of the Federal Reserve, who is a student of that earlier deflationary era.) Stocks and commodities peaked together during 1929 and bottomed together during 1932, and stayed closely linked through the balance of the 1930s. I've already described the decoupling of bonds and stocks after the Asian currency crisis of 1997–1998. I'll have more to say a little later in the book on the close linkage that has developed between stocks and commodities, especially after the deflationary housing collapse that caused the 2008 financial meltdown.

■ Rotating Asset Classes over Decades

It's interesting to track the rotating leadership between bonds, stocks, and commodities over long periods of time. During the inflationary decade that included World War I, commodities were the strongest of the three markets. During the disinflationary 1920s, leadership passed to stocks. During the deflationary 1930s, bonds became the strongest asset. After World War II, stocks resumed a leadership role that lasted to the late 1960s. The inflationary spiral of the 1970s put commodities on center stage again. After commodities peaked in 1980, stocks and bonds came back into favor. The deflationary cycle that started in the late 1990s shifted leadership away from stocks and back to bonds for the following decade. What's even more impressive is that by the end of 2011, long-term government bonds had gained 11.5 percent a year on average over the prior three decades, beating the 10.8 percent increase in the S&P 500. That was the first time that bonds had outperformed stocks over a 30-year period since the Civil War (more on that shortly). Most of that generational bond strength took place after 2000, and was a reflection of global deflationary tendencies that existed during the first decade of the 21st century.

Lessons of Long Cycles

In looking back over these long cycles of rotation between bonds, stocks, and commodities, there are lessons to be learned. The most obvious is that each asset class has experienced long periods of outperformance. Those periods can last for decades. In the early stages of a long-term expansion (like the 1940s), rising commodity prices are positive for stocks. A little inflation is a good thing. It's when commodity prices start to spike higher (as they did during the 1970s) that a *little* inflation turns into *big* inflation, which is bad for stocks. While *rising* commodity prices can be good for stocks, *soaring* commodity prices are bad. Conversely, falling commodity prices can also be good stocks. Commodity prices peaked in 1920 and 1980 and, after initial declines, remained relatively flat for years afterward. Declining (or flat) commodity prices ushered in both eras of disinflation that carried stock prices higher during the 1920s and the two decades after 1980. *Collapsing* commodity prices are bad for stocks. In 1929 and 1998, a collapse in commodity prices to the lowest levels in decades turned a beneficial *disinflation* into a *deflation*, which is harmful to the economy and stock market.

The Kondratieff Wave

No treatment of long economic cycles can be complete without mentioning the *Kondratieff Wave*. This long cycle of economic activity lasts approximately 55 to 60 years and was discovered in the 1920s by Nikolai Kondratieff, a Russian economist. That *long wave* appears to exert a major influence on stock and commodity prices, as well as the direction of interest rates. Kondratieff tracked his long wave from 1789 and found three major peaks, with the third one occurring in 1920. The 1920 peak was marked by a major peak in commodity prices and eventually led to the deflationary era of the 1930s.

There have now been *four* Kondratieff Waves over the last two centuries. The four peaks occurred in 1816, 1864, 1920, and 1980. Each of those four economic expansions led to a burst of inflation (characterized by rising commodity prices and rising interest rates). Interestingly, all four inflations coincided with major American wars (the War of 1812, the Civil War, World War I, and the Vietnam War). Each burst of inflation ended with a peak in commodity prices. (The last two commodity peaks occurred in 1920 and 1980.) After peaking, commodities usually plateau for a decade or longer. During this plateau period, which we call *disinflation,* stock prices do especially well. That was the case during the 1920s and during the period from 1980 to 2000.

The danger point in the *long wave* comes when commodity prices end their *plateau* period and start falling again. That's when deflationary forces start to exert their negative influence on the stock market and the economy (which is what happened in 1929 and 1998). Interest rates also fall during the deflationary part of the cycle. The thirty year drop in bond yields after 1980 is matched by a similar decline that lasted from 1920 through the 1940s in that earlier deflationary era. Earlier reference was made to the strong performance of the long bond in the three decades since 1980 being reminiscent of the Civil War era. Bond yields also started a major decline after the Civil War, when that long wave peaked, and continued to decline through the remaining three decades of that century. It's truly amazing how history repeats itself. But we have to study that history in order to benefit from its lessons.

■ Dividing a Lifetime Cycle into Seasons

My 2004 book cited work done by Ian Gordon (then vice president of Canaccord Capital Corp., Vancouver, Canada) who published a newsletter entitled *The Long Wave Analyst*. Gordon divided the long wave into four parts, which he compared to the four seasons of the year. Each season lasts approximately a quarter of the length of the wave (about 15 years). The *spring* season (which Gordon put from 1949 to 1966) is characterized by a strengthening economy and benign inflation when stocks do well. *Summer* (which he measured from 1966 to 1980) is an inflationary period and is marked by rising commodity and real estate values. *Autumn* (which Gordon saw starting in 1980) sees the greatest speculation in bonds, stocks, and real estate. This speculative era also sees a massive buildup of debt. That is followed by Kondratieff *winter*, which Gordon identified as starting in 2000. The main characteristic of the economic winter (which is identified by a collapse in commodity prices) is deflation, which is made worse by the need to repay all of the debt built up during the autumn period. Stock prices plunge along with real estate during the Kondratieff winter. The best two defenses during the economic winter are bonds and gold. That's a pretty good description of the past decade.

Because the length of the Kondratieff Wave is approximately 60 years, it's often described as a *lifetime* cycle, because most people live through it only once. That explains why each generation is unprepared for its onset—and unfamiliar with its solution. People haven't experienced it before. Unfortunately, that *winter* can go on for a long time (15 years on average). After all the debt has been repaid, and confidence slowly restored, the *spring* season turns the long wave back up again.

Gordon's warnings about what might happen during a Kondratieff winter have proven to be extremely accurate. They also help explain why the last two business cycle upturns since 2000 have been so weak. That's normal on the downside of the *long wave*. The good news is that those predictions were made nearly a decade ago, which means that we're probably closer to the start of the *spring* season than the start of *winter*. If there's another silver lining, it's that the collapse in real estate values has taken place since then, which is one less deflationary event to worry about. That brings us to one final economic cycle that is needed to complete our comparison of events during the last decade and the deflationary era of the 1930s. That's the real estate cycle.

Housing Is Interest Rate Sensitive

Real estate and housing are closely tied to the direction of interest rates. That explains why housing has generally been considered to be *countercycle*; it moves in the opposite direction of the normal business cycle. Homebuilding activity tends to be strongest when interest rates are falling, which generally happens in a weaker economy. That explains why housing stocks turned up in 2000 and rose throughout that bear market and subsequent recession. They were reacting more to the falling rates than falling stocks. Tight monetary policy in a recovering economy has historically had a restraining effect on real estate. The raising of short-term rates during 2005 and 2006 helped end the housing boom of the prior decade. Figure 8.3 shows the jump on bond yields during 2005 coinciding with a peak in homebuilding stocks (see arrows). The homebuilding rally started during 2000 when bond yields plunged. The breaking of a three-year down trendline in bond yields during 2005 (second up arrow) raised fears of higher mortgage rates. Homebuilders tumbled during 2006 as bond yields reached a four-year high.

> ### JOHN'S TIPS
>
> Mortgage rates are determined by the yield on Treasury bonds.

Real Estate Doesn't Always Follow Rates

Real estate doesn't *always* follow interest rates. The collapse in real estate during the 1930s coincided with falling long-term rates. The housing boom of the 1970s took place while long-term rates were rising. In the latter case, the beneficial impact of an inflationary spiral during the 1970s appears to have overcome the harmful effects of rising interest rates. In the 1980s, housing and real estate values weakened as interest rates dropped. During the 1930s, the 1970s, and the 1980s, the real estate link to inflation appears to have been greater than the link to interest rates.

FIGURE 8.3 Jump in bond yields during 2005 contributed to homebuilder top

Real Estate Doesn't Always Follow Inflation

Real estate is also considered to be an *inflation hedge*. That's *often* been the case. Home prices and real estate values plunged during the deflationary years of the Great Depression. Home prices fell between 1925 and 1935, and didn't start rising until the late 1940s. Land values, especially in the Midwest, plunged during the 1930s as farm commodity prices collapsed; they started rising again with the rate of inflation during the 1940s and 1950s. That seems to support the view of housing and real estate as being both inflation and deflation sensitive.

JOHN'S TIPS

The direction of agricultural commodities has a big influence on the price of farmland.

Home values also soared during the inflationary 1970s and peaked with inflation in the early 1980s. The value of farmland plunged after 1981 when agricultural commodities peaked. This, too, supports the link with inflation. How, then, do we explain the surge in real estate and home values in the decade and a half after 1990 when inflation was low and deflation pressures emerged? The boom in housing in the years between 1998 and 2005 couldn't be tied to inflation.

It seems, then, that none of the historical reasons that are normally cited to explain real estate activity—inflation, interest rates, the direction of stock prices, or the business cycle—adequately explains the ebbs and flows of real estate and homebuilding. The answer to the real estate puzzle must lie elsewhere. The answer appears to lie in the fact that real estate and housing move according to a different cycle than all of the other financial markets and the economy.

The 18-Year Real Estate Cycle

Clarence Long discovered an 18-year real estate cycle in 1940. Long tracked the real estate cycle from 1870 to 1940. Since its length is 18 years (from peak to peak or trough to trough), approximately three real estate cycles take place in one Kondratieff Wave. In turn, each real estate cycle encompasses four normal business cycles. The Kondratieff Wave and Long's 18-year real estate cycle both turned down in the late 1920s. As a result of this downward convergence in two major economic cycles, stock values collapsed along the home and land values. The deflationary impact also caused commodities and interest rates to tumble.

JOHN'S TIPS

I've refrained from calling the real estate cycle the Long cycle to avoid confusion with the Kondratieff Wave.

That situation differed from what happened during the bear market lasting from 2000 to 2002. At that time, only one of the two cycles peaked. The Kondratieff Wave turned down during 2000 and ushered in the current deflationary cycle. The real estate cycle, however, kept rising. Because homebuilding is so important to economic activity, the ability of real estate and housing to keep rising after 2000 appears to have cushioned the downturn in the economy during the 2001 recession.

FIGURE 8.4 Falling housing stocks made 2008 stock plunge worse than 2000

Figure 8.4 compares the S&P 500 to a homebuilding stock from 1998 to 2011. Homebuilders rose during the first stock bear market that lasted from 2000 to the end of 2002 (because of falling interest rates) and helped cushion the economic downturn during 2001. After the collapse in housing stocks in 2006, the 2008 stock plunge was a lot more severe. So were the economic consequences.

■ The Real Estate Peak Was Overdue

Counting the 18-year cycles from a 1927 peak and 1945 trough suggested that major real estate upturns were *scheduled* for the 1970s and the 1990s. A major real estate peak was scheduled for 1981. All three arrived pretty close to schedule. The last major real estate trough occurred in the 1990–1992 time frame. That explains how the housing boom got started. It doesn't explain, however, why the housing boom lasted so long. The reason the last real estate cycle stretched out longer than usual was probably the unprecedented drop in long-term interest rates to the lowest levels in half a century. My 2004 book did note, however, that a peak in real estate was "overdue." Although the *peak* in the last 18-year cycle occurred late, its *trough* appears to be more on schedule.

A cycle's length can be measured between its peaks or between its troughs. Of the two, troughs are usually more reliable. An ideal 18-year cycle would have nine up years followed by nine down years. The last upswing in the real estate cycle lasted between 13 and 15 years, which was unusually long. The next cycle bottom (measured from the 1990–1992 trough) was scheduled to occur between 2008 and 2010. Chart patterns in homebuilding stocks suggest that bottom target may be more on time.

JOHN'S TIPS

The best way to measure the health of the housing industry is to study the trend of homebuilding stocks.

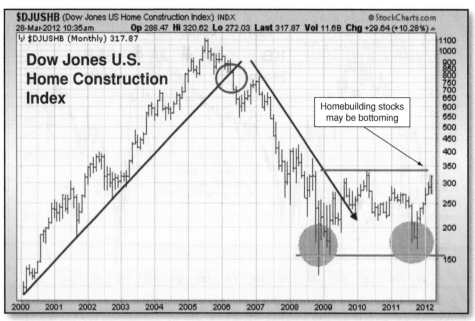

FIGURE 8.5 Index of homebuilding stocks forms bottoming pattern

Figure 8.5 plots the Dow Jones U.S. Home Construction Index between 2000 and 2012. That index measures the performance of homebuilding stocks. After rallying from 2000 to 2005, the index turned down during 2006 (upper circle), as discussed in an earlier chapter. The homebuilding index hit bottom in late 2008/early 2009 (first lower circle). It then rose above the falling trendline drawn over the 2007/2008 peaks, which ended the bear market. The index then trended sideways in a bottoming pattern (defined by the upper and lower horizontal trendlines). After forming a second bottom during the second half of 2011 (second lower circle), the index rallied back to its 2010 high during the first quarter of 2012. [Note: The index exceeded that 2010 peak three months later (June 2012), which established a new uptrend in homebuilding stocks.] That should carry good news for housing. The downturn in homebuilders during 2006 warned of trouble in the housing industry. A 2012 upturn in that same group sends the opposite message, namely that the housing industry is in for better days. That would also put the real estate cycle low in the 2008–2011 time frame, which isn't too far from the 2008–2010 target for the next real estate trough described in the previous paragraph.

The end of the last real estate boom started with a top in homebuilding stocks during 2005. Rising interest rates a year later finally pushed them over a cliff and into a major downtrend. The reason the peak in housing hit the economy so hard was because, for the first time since the Great Depression, both the 60-year Kondratieff Wave and the 18-year real estate cycle were falling together. The four-year business cycle also turned down at the end of 2007. But the nature of the business cycle since 2000 has changed. The downswings became more severe (especially after the housing collapse) and the upswings less robust. I believe that is largely due to downturns in the two longer economic cycles. The deflationary trend that emerged after 1998 had caused a major decoupling of bonds and stocks. The deflationary housing collapse during 2008 also had the effect of tightening the correlation between stocks and commodities. Both of those intermarket relationships were reminiscent of the deflationary 1930s.

JOHN'S TIPS

The good news is that the downturn in those longer economic cycles may be nearing completion.

Economic Cycles Set the Framework for Intermarket Work

This chapter's examination of the business cycle helps explain the rotation that takes place among various asset classes at different stages of that cycle. Our examination of the 55- to 60-year Kondratieff Wave and the 18-year real estate cycle helps explain changes that have taken place in that business cycle over the last decade and the intermarket relationships that go along with those changes. It's not enough to just look at the four-year cycle. It's also necessary to put that shorter cycle into a longer historical perspective. Those who don't do that remain baffled as to why the last two business cycles have been so different from previous ones, and why traditional fiscal and monetary steps to strengthen the business cycle have been mostly unsuccessful. As traders and investors, however, our main concern is with the financial markets. The main reason for this chapter's examination of the various economic cycles is to set the economic framework for our intermarket work, and to explain why some traditional intermarket relationships have changed over the last decade. As we examine those newer relationships in the following chapters, you'll have a better sense as to why they're happening.

CHAPTER 9

The Impact of the Business Cycle on Market Sectors

This chapter explains how various market sectors act at different stages of the business cycle. Shifts in sector leadership tell us a lot about the state of the business cycle and the stock market. A sector rotation model gives a visual representation of the business cycle's impact on rotating sector leadership. Other visual tools are shown that are helpful in spotting sector leaders and individual stocks within those sectors.

105

▮ Sector Rotation within the Business Cycle

The previous chapter showed how the business cycle has a major impact on the relationship between bonds, stocks, and commodities (and also how the position of those three markets tells us something about the position of the business cycle). This chapter shows how the business cycle impacts *sector rotations* within the stock market (and vice versa). There are two goals here. One is to show that different market sectors do better at different stages of the business cycle. By tracking the business cycle, one is able to anticipate which sectors should be upgraded in one's portfolio (and which ones to downgrade). The second goal is to show that sector rotations follow a repetitive pattern where money flows from one sector to another as the economy goes from expansion to contraction and back to expansion. By studying which sectors are leading the stock market at any given time, the trader can make a more reasonable estimate as to which way the business cycle is going.

More importantly, the trader has a better idea where the stock market is going.

▮ Sector Rotations during 2000 Favored Contraction

An earlier chapter covered the intermarket warnings surrounding the 2000 market top. Sector rotations during 2000 also signaled the end of the economic expansion of the 1990s and the start of an economic contraction. It was also pointed out how a jump in the price of oil during 1999 led to a series of rate hikes by the Fed that contributed to the 2000 market top. Reference was also made to energy stock leadership during 1999 (resulting from the rising price of oil) being a negative warning for the stock market. That's because energy sector leadership usually takes place near the end of an economic expansion.

One of the signs that the rising oil price is beginning to hurt the stock market is when sector leadership gradually starts to shift to a defensive group like *consumer staples*. That took place in spring 2000. Consumer staple leadership is a warning that the stock market is peaking. Since that defensive rotation from energy to staples takes place gradually, there comes a point when *energy* and *staples* are the two strongest market sectors. They were, in fact, the two top performing sectors during the first half of that year. You'll see later in the chapter why that was another bearish sign for the stock market. You'll also see that sequence following the exact rotation that normally takes place when the economy is moving from expansion to contraction.

JOHN'S TIPS

Market leadership by consumer staple stocks is almost always a negative warning sign for the stock market.

■ Sector Rotations during 2003 Favored Expansion

By contrast, sector rotations during 2003 favored economic expansion and a stock market upturn. Two sectors that normally show market leadership as the economy moves from contraction to expansion are *consumer discretionary* and *technology* stocks. That was the case during 2003 as the stock market was bottoming.

During the first six months of that year, two of the market's strongest sectors were the two just mentioned. Another positive sign that spring was that *consumer staples* became the market's weakest sector. That's normally a sign of increasing investor confidence when consumer staple stocks are the market's weakest sector and consumer discretionary stocks are among the strongest. That's good news for the stock market and the economy—and that was the case during the spring of 2003.

■ Technology Leadership Is Another Good Sign

From October 2002 (when the stock market hit bottom) until the following June (three months after it actually turned up), all of the major market indexes rallied. The two top performing indexes, however, were the Nasdaq Composite Index (+37 percent) and the Russell 2000 Small Cap Index (+24 percent). By contrast, the S&P 500 gained 19 percent. The fact that the technology-dominated Nasdaq led the market higher was another confirming sign that a new bull market had begun. That's because technology leadership is another symptom of a stronger stock market. The Nasdaq market is dominated by large technology stocks.

JOHN'S TIPS

The Nasdaq market is usually viewed as a proxy for the technology sector.

Smaller Stocks Lead at Bottoms

The fact that the Russell 2000 Small Cap Index was also in a leadership role during 2003 was another positive sign. That's because smaller stocks usually lead the stock market at important bottoms and when the economy is coming out of recession. The historical track record is impressive on that score. Six recessions occurred between 1960 and 1991. Small stocks outperformed large stocks in the first year following each of those previous recessions. They did the same following the two recessions that took place after 2000.

Transportation Leadership

Transportation stocks also play an important role at market tops and market bottoms. Earlier chapters, for example, mentioned how rising oil prices during 1999 and 2007 caused fuel-sensitive transportation stocks to turn down before the rest of the market. The good news is that the *economically sensitive* transports have a tendency to lead at market bottoms also. If the economy is going to produce goods, it has to also transport them, which is good for those stocks.

There's another element at work at that point in the economic cycle having to do with oil. During 1999, rising oil prices had put energy stocks in a leadership role and caused transportation stocks to weaken. Rising oil also contributed to the 2001 recession. After that economic slowdown, oil prices fell (which they usually do in a recession). As a result, energy stocks weakened along with the falling commodity. Weaker energy stocks, combined with stronger transportation stocks, are another sign that things are getting better. That was the case during 2003.

> **JOHN'S TIPS**
>
> Transportation stocks usually become market leaders in the early stages of a market upturn.

2007 Sector Rotation Showed Weakness

Chapter 7 examined the 2007 stock market top and explained that deterioration in *market breadth* indicators that year was caused by relative weakness in economically sensitive stock groups like small caps, retail stocks (consumer discretionary sector), and transportation stocks. Financials and homebuilders also fell hard that year, owing to the subprime housing crisis. Not surprisingly, defensive stocks like consumer staples took over a market leadership role (along with energy stocks and other stocks tied to commodities).

Figure 9.1 compares the S&P 500 to a ratio of the Consumer Staples SPDR (Standard & Poor's Depositary Receipts, an ETF that is based on that sector) divided by the S&P 500. That defensive ratio peaked at the end of 2002, just as the stock market was bottoming and continued to underperform during the subsequent bull market in stocks. That's perfectly normal. Defensive stocks lag behind when the market is strong. The ratio hit bottom, however, during 2006 and traded sideways for the next year. The staples/S&P ratio bottomed a second time during the summer of 2007, just the stock market was starting to peak. The ratio turned up sharply during the second half of that year as investors rotated into defensive stocks. By the end of 2007, the ratio had exceeded the peak formed in the middle of 2006. By

FIGURE 9.1 Consumer staple/S&P 500 ratio turned up during 2007

doing that, the ratio line completed a bullish double bottom reversal pattern. A *double bottom* is present when two prominent bottoms are visible after an extended price decline (see circles). The pattern is complete, and a new uptrend has begun, when the line rises above the peak in between the two bottoms.

a **double bottom** is present when two prominent bottoms are visible after an extended price decline

That chart sent two important messages at the time. One was that it was a good time to rotate into consumer staples and other defensive stock groups (like health care and utilities), and out of economically sensitive stock groups (more on that shortly). A second message was that leadership by consumer staples is usually associated with a market top. That would also have suggested rotating out of stocks and into bonds or gold. Consumer staples usually *underperform* the S&P 500 during bull markets and *outperform* it during bear markets. That makes the *consumer staples/S&P 500 ratio* an excellent contrary stock market indicator.

> **JOHN'S TIPS**
>
> Ratio analysis is the best way to compare a sector's performance to the rest of the market.

Did You Know. . .?

The staples/S&P ratio finally peaked in the spring of 2009 when the stock market bottomed and helped confirm that market bottom.

▪ Sector Rotation Has Two Sides

There are usually two sides to sector rotation. Money rotates out of one sector and into another. Figure 9.2 is an excellent example of that happening. The two lines on the chart compare the

Consumer Discretionary SPDR to the Consumer Staples SPDR during 2007. What's most obvious on the chart is that both lines moved in opposite directions in pretty dramatic fashion. That was especially clear at midyear when consumer discretionary stocks peaked (down arrow) and fell for the rest of that year. At the same time, consumer staples stocks turned up (up arrow) and rose through the balance of that year. The interplay between the two sectors is unmistakable. When subprime mortgage problems surfaced in July 2007, fear started to spread that contagion from a collapsing housing sector would bring down the stock market and the economy along with it (which it eventually did). That fear was reflected in a 10 percent drop in stock prices that summer.

Another manifestation of that fear, however, was the rotation out of *economically sensitive* consumer discretionary stocks (which include retailers and homebuilders) and into *economically resistant* stocks like consumer staples. As the name implies, consumer *staples* include food, beverages, and household products that consumers need to buy in good times and bad. By contrast, consumer *discretionary* stocks include products that consumers might *want*, but don't necessarily *need* (like a new car or house). They can defer those purchases until things start to get better. They can't defer food purchases.

The rotation shown in Figure 9.2 was a clear message that investors were turning defensive for the first time since the bull market in stocks began in the spring of 2003. The rotation that started in the middle of 2007 was clearly visible on the charts of the two competing sectors (as well as in the staples/S&P 500 ratio), and made it clear what needed to be done from a sector rotation standpoint. Figures 9.1 and 9.2 also demonstrate how the interplay between competing market sectors can offer clues about the state of the stock market and the business cycle. (You'll see shortly that those two sectors reversed roles during 2009.)

JOHN'S TIPS

Keeping track of which market sectors are the strongest is also a good way to keep track of how strong the stock market is.

FIGURE 9.2   Money rotated out of discretionary stocks during 2007 and into staples

It's Also a Market of Groups

It's often been said that the stock market is a market of *stocks*. It's equally true to say that the stock market is a market of *groups*. It's important to know what those groups are and how to measure their performance, because they don't always do the same thing at the same time. Some groups of stocks rise faster than others in market uptrends and fall faster during market corrections. Others rise slower during market uptrends and hold up better during downside corrections. Some groups fall while others rise. Most people would probably agree that the single most important question relating to stock investing is whether it's a good time to put new funds into the market (or take some out). An equally important question is *where* in the market to put your money.

One thing that stock investing has in common with real estate is that *location* is very important. In this case, however, we're referring to *where* in the stock market your money is *located*. Being in the right sectors and industry groups can enhance your overall performance. Being in the wrong ones can hurt it.

The Difference between Sectors and Industry Groups

The stock market is divided into *sectors* and *industry groups*. Select Sector SPDRs divide the S&P 500 into nine sector index funds. Those nine sectors are subdivided into approximately 90 industry groups. The basic materials sector, for example, is subdivided into industry groups like aluminum, chemicals, copper, precious metals, paper and forest products, and steel. The technology sector includes industry groups like Internet, software, networkers, semiconductors, and telecom.

Did You Know. . .?

Although telecommunications is considered to be a 10th sector with its own ETF, S&P also includes telecom stocks in its technology sector SPDR.

The nine S&P sector SPDRs cover basic materials, consumer staples, consumer discretionary, energy, industrials (which include transports), financials, health care, technology, and utilities. Each of those sectors has its own industries. It's important to know what industries are included in each sector as well as which stocks are included in those industries and sectors.

> **JOHN'S TIPS**
>
> When telecommunication stocks are treated separately, the stock market has 10 market sectors.

Sector Rotation Model

Figure 9.3 is a Sector Rotation Model that shows how the nine market sectors perform throughout the business cycle. The red line represents turns in the stock market while the green line represents the economy. Notice that turns in the stock market precede turns in the economy. The nine boxes along the top of the Sector Rotation Model show what each sector does as the stock market and the economy expand and contract.

At stock market bottoms (which signal that an economic recovery isn't far behind), economically sensitive cyclical groups and technology show market leadership. Cyclical stocks include consumer discretionary and transportation stocks. Later in an expansion when commodity prices are rising, leadership gradually switches to basic materials and energy. Energy leadership is usually a sign that the economic expansion is nearing completion (as well as the bull market in stocks). Energy group leadership is the result of the rising price of oil, which threatens the economic recovery. As has happened so often in recent years, rising energy prices cause the Fed to start raising short-term rates to stem inflationary pressures, which hurts the stock market and the economy. That scenario led to market tops in 2000 and 2007, and recessions shortly thereafter.

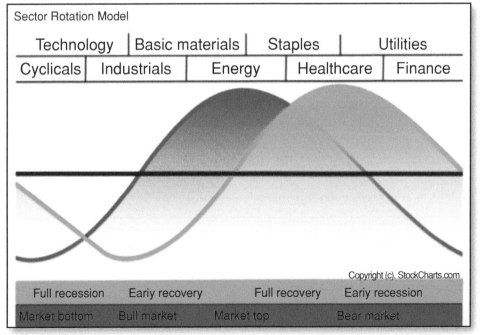

FIGURE 9.3   Sector Rotation Model

One way we can tell when rising energy prices are starting to hurt the economy (and when the stock market is starting to peak) is when sector leadership starts to gradually shift away from energy and into defensive sectors like consumer staples, healthcare, and utilities. As was explained earlier, that sector rotation usually takes place gradually. As a result, there usually comes a point where the top performing sectors are energy and staples. That was the case during 2000 and again during 2007.

◼ Sector Rotations during 2007

The two top sectors during 2007 were energy and consumer staples. That happened when the economic expansion and stock market rally were both in their fifth years and starting to weaken. Energy stock leadership came from rising crude oil prices during that year (which contributed to weakness in groups such as retailers and transportation). One of the weakest sectors was consumer discretionary. That's a recipe for a lower stock market and a slowing economy.

A closer scrutiny of sector performance during 2007 confirmed that negative warning. The top four sectors during that year were energy, materials, utilities, and consumer staples. If you check the Sector Rotation Model, you'll see that those four sectors are usually market leaders in the late stages of an economic expansion and the early stages of an economic contraction. As the economy starts to slow, money moves into defensive sectors like staples, healthcare, and utilities. That rotation is usually associated with a market top. The negative rotation is further characterized by relative weakness in consumer discretionary stocks. Those defensive rotations followed the Sector Rotation Model very closely during 2007.

The model can be used in several ways. If you know the position of the business cycle, you can adjust your sector rotation strategies accordingly. Most of the time, however, it's the other way around: Rotating sector leadership helps to determine the position of the business cycle. Since the stock market is also tied to the business cycle, the sector rotation model also tells us something about the current condition of the stock market. And the stock market leads turns in the economy.

◼ Industry Group Leadership

The term *sector rotation* is commonly used to describe flows of funds between various market sectors. That term is also often used in a broader sense, however, to describe rotations among industry groups as well. Just as it's good to know which *sectors* are leading the market, it's also instructive to know which *industry groups* are contributing to that leadership. During the second half of 2007, for example, two of the top industry groups were gold and oil service stocks, which are subsets of the basic materials and energy sectors. (That was due to rising commodity prices.) By contrast, the weakest industries were homebuilders, banks, retailers, semiconductors, brokers, and REITs (in that order).

Did you know. . .?

The term *group rotation* is also used to describe rotations among industries.

◼ Sector Rotations Turn Positive in 2009

Market rotations turned positive during spring 2009 as the market turned back up again. During that year, the technology-dominated Nasdaq market outperformed the S&P 500 by a 50 percent to 30 percent margin. The Russell 2000 Small Cap Index gained 40 percent by comparison. The Nasdaq and small caps did their usual thing of leading the market higher in the early stages of a new bull market. Sector rotations also turned positive that year. The two top sectors during that bullish year were technology (+58 percent) and consumer discretionary (+49 percent). That was normal at a market bottom. By contrast, the three weakest sectors during the market upturn were staples, utilities, and health care. That was also normal. When the stock market is rising, and investors turn more optimistic, they buy offensive-minded stocks (like consumer discretionary) and sell defensive stocks (like consumer staples). That's exactly what they did.

Figure 9.4 plots a relative strength ratio of the Consumer Discretionary SPDR divided by the Consumer Staples SPDR over a four-year period. As I've explained in earlier chapters, the *relative strength ratio* is one of the best tools for measuring one market sector against another. The message in Figure 9.4 is very clear: The ratio peaked in mid-2007 (down arrow) and bottomed during the fourth quarter of 2008. During those two bearish years, investors clearly favored defensive stocks. Staples were the better sector to own during that market downturn. The ratio formed a *higher low* during the following March and turned up decisively that April (up arrow). During April 2009, the ratio line broke a down trendline drawn along its 2007–2008 peaks. That left little doubt that a major change for the better had taken place in consumer discretionary stocks and the stock market.

FIGURE 9.4   Consumer discretionary/staples ratio turned up during 2009

Investors did just what they should have done at a market bottom. They stopped playing defense (holding consumer staples) and started playing offense (buying consumer discretionary stocks). That upturn in the *discretionary/staples ratio* in spring 2009 did at least three things. First, it told the visual investor it was time to rotate into discretionary stocks (and economically sensitive stocks in general). Second, it confirmed that a market bottom had been completed (which favored rotation out of bonds and into stocks). Third, it implied that the recession was nearing completion. The 2007–2009 recession ended three months later.

■ Sector Trends Need to Be Monitored

Keep in mind that sector trends need to be monitored on a regular basis. You can't just *buy and hold* a sector like you can the stock market. What worked for a given sector during one six-month period (or prior quarter) may not work during the next. In my experience, most sector trends last somewhere between three and six months. As a result, it's generally a good idea to review the performance rankings (and charts) at least once a week to see if some of the leaders are starting to slip in the rankings, or if some of the laggards are starting to move up.

Also keep in mind that the visual tools you'll be shown shortly are simply screening devices to ensure that you're always dealing with market leaders. The next step after that is to look at the actual charts of the leading sectors and industry groups to make sure that they're acting in a bullish fashion. Stock pickers can go a step further and isolate individual stocks within those leading groups. It's been estimated that as much as half of a stock's performance is tied to the group it belongs to. If you're looking for stock leaders, therefore, it's better to find the leading groups first. Then make sure the stock is a leader in one of those groups.

> **JOHN'S TIPS**
>
> The general rule to follow is to buy the strongest stocks in the strongest sectors or industry groups.

■ 2011 Rotations Follow Sector Rotation Model

The stock market rally continued into spring 2011, after which stock prices weakened. Sector rotations during that spring followed the Sector Rotation Model very closely and gave early warning of a stock market top. Since the previous August, energy stocks had led the market higher while healthcare, staples, and utilities lagged behind. That's normal during a market uptrend. As explained before, one of the signs that investors are turning more cautious is when those relative performance trends reverse. That's exactly what happened.

Figure 9.5 shows a *performance* chart that offers a visual way to compare sectors during 2011. (That line format allows us to plot market sectors on either an *absolute* or a *relative* basis, and makes their visual comparison a lot easier to track.) Figure 9.5 plots four sectors around the S&P 500, which is the flat zero line. That allows us to measure the *relative* performance of those sectors against the S&P 500. The lines above the zero line are doing better than the S&P, while the lines below the zero line are doing worse. It's also easier to spot turns in the relative strength lines. The chart shows energy stocks starting to underperform during that April (falling trendline). At the same time, the chart shows upturns in the relative performance of the three defensive sectors (up arrows).

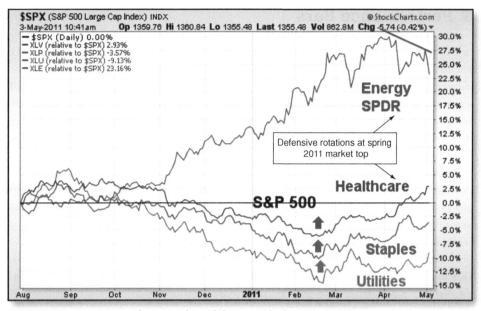

FIGURE 9.5   Rotation out of energy and into defensive stocks during spring 2011

During the six months that followed those turns, healthcare, staples, and utilities became the three strongest market sectors. At the same time that defensive stocks were strengthening, energy stocks went from the market's strongest sector to one of its weakest (as you'll see shortly).

JOHN'S TIPS

The S&P 500 lost 19 percent between April and October 2011, which just missed the bear market threshold of 20 percent.

Did You Know. . .?

Health care, staples, and utilities also pay dividends, which offers downside protection against a market correction. The fact that bond yields were also dropping at the time increased the value of dividend-paying stocks, which compete with bonds for yield.

Those very noticeable rotations sent out several warnings. From a sector rotation standpoint, it was a signal to rotate out of energy stocks (and economically sensitive stocks) and into defensive ones. It was also a warning that investors were starting to lose confidence in the market as a whole. From an asset allocation standpoint, that suggested some rotation out of stocks and into bonds (which rise when stocks fall). Within six months of those April rotations, the U.S. stock market had lost nearly 20 percent of its value. Treasury bond prices rose 7 percent during those same six months. Performance line charts like the one shown in Figure 9.5 are one of the best ways to spot sector rotations. There is, however, another way to view those relative performances. Figure 9.6 is an example of how to do that.

Performance Bars

Figure 9.6 shows the relative performance of five market sectors during the first nine months of 2011 in a bar format (instead of lines). Here again, performance bars can be viewed either in *absolute* or *relative* terms. The bars in Figure 9.6 show *relative* performance, which means that they're measured against the S&P 500, which is the zero line. Sector bars below the zero line show relative underperformance, while bars above the zero line show market leadership. During those first nine months of 2011, the market's three top performing sectors were utilities, health care, and consumer staples. By comparison, basic materials and energy were among the market's weakest groups.

The line chart in Figure 9.5 showed those defensive rotations beginning in April of that year. The performance bars in Figure 9.6 confirm that the market remained in a defensive mode for at least six months after its April 2011 peak (during which time it lost nearly 20 percent of its value). A glance back at the Sector Rotation Model in Figure 9.3 shows that market tops are usually associated with rotations out of basic materials and energy stocks and into staples, health care, and utilities. In other words, the defensive sector rotations that began in spring 2011 gave an early and accurate warning of stock market weakness. They also suggested not only how to protect oneself against a market downturn, but how to profit from it.

JOHN'S TIPS

Sector rotations generally last between three and six months and need to be monitored frequently.

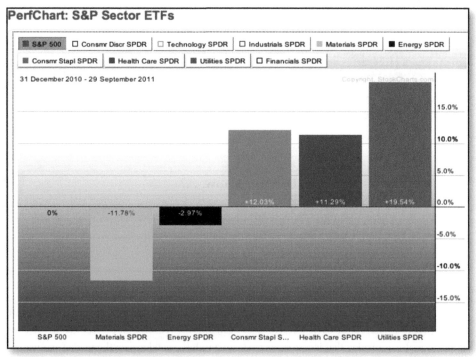

FIGURE 9.6   Relative sector performance.

Market Carpets

Figure 9.7 shows another tool that's very useful for tracking sector leadership. It's called a *market carpet*. Sector market carpets present a visually attractive way to determine which sectors are showing

THE IMPACT OF THE BUSINESS CYCLE ON MARKET SECTORS

better performance over a given period of time and which ones are lagging. This particular example is a snapshot taken over a period of a month. You can vary the time period by days, weeks, or months. Nine sector boxes are shown. The greener the box, the stronger is the sector performance. The redder the box, the weaker is the performance. *Heat maps* is another term used to refer to market carpets. In this example, the top four sectors during that month were consumer discretionary, industrials, technology, and utilities. Notice their greener colors. The three weakest were materials, energy, and healthcare. Notice their redder boxes. The box to the right of Figure 9.7 also ranks the four strongest and the four weakest sectors during the period under study.

---

heat maps is another term used to refer to market carpets

I generally view sector rankings at least once a week to determine if any significant changes are taking place. Sector rotations usually last only three to six months. That makes it a good idea to check them frequently enough to spot any changes. I usually measure their performance over the last one to two months. Once you've isolated the sector leaders, you can click on any box to see a chart of that sector. That allows you to quickly determine if the sector is doing anything significant from a charting standpoint.

JOHN'S TIPS

A market carpet is a screening device to help focus your attention on leading stocks within leading sectors.

■ Using Sector Carpets to Find Leading Stocks

There's another feature to the sector carpets that is especially useful for individual stock pickers. By clicking on any of the sector leaders, you'll be shown an additional carpet, which ranks the stocks within that sector. Figure 9.7 listed *consumer discretionary* as the top sector during the prior month.

FIGURE 9.7 Market carpets show which sectors are leading.

Figure 9.8 ranks the stocks within that sector. There again, the greener boxes show the strongest stocks in that leading sector. The box to the far right lists the five top percentage stock gainers during the month in question. By clicking on any of those five stocks, you can view a price chart to determine if you like the way it's acting. The value of doing things that way is that you're only looking at the five leading stocks in the market's strongest sector. The carpets allow you to filter your viewing choices. That saves an enormous amount of time. It also ensures that you're always looking at the market's strongest stocks in the strongest sectors.

You'll also notice that the stock boxes in Figure 9.8 are different sizes. You can view the stock carpet in *market cap* mode. The bigger boxes represent the most heavily weighted stocks in that particular sector. That allows you to pick the largest and most liquid stocks. That's especially useful in a defensive market, when large caps usually do better than small caps. The stocks in the largest boxes also exert the most influence on that particular sector. Even if you're not a stick picker, it's a good idea to keep an eye on what a sector's largest stocks are doing.

Comparing Absolute and Relative Performance

It's important to understand the different between a sector's *absolute* and *relative* performance. Both are important. They just measure different things. It's always better to be in a market that's rising in value (good *absolute* performance). Relative strength analysis, however, gives better insight into how a market or sector is doing *relative* to its peers. Figure 9.9, for example, compares the *absolute* trend of the healthcare SPDR to the S&P 500 from 2007 to 2011. It's clear from the chart that the health care line was stronger than the S&P 500. Both lines, however, generally trended in the same direction.

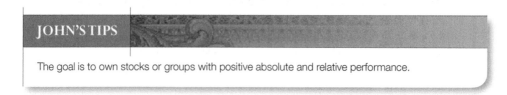

JOHN'S TIPS

The goal is to own stocks or groups with positive absolute and relative performance.

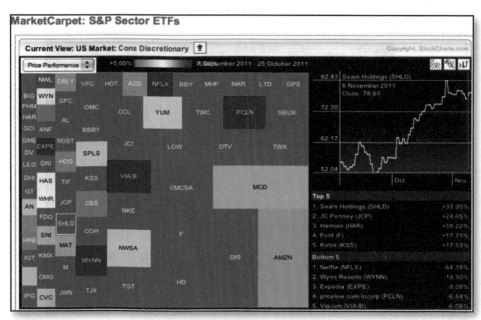

FIGURE 9.8 Market carpets show stock leadership within sectors.

Figure 9.10 shows the *relative* performance of the health care sector over the same five years. In that chart, the S&P 500 is plotted as the flat zero line. That allows us to see whether the health care SPDR (XLV) is doing better or worse than the S&P 500. In my view, Figure 9.10 is more revealing than the previous chart. The up arrow during 2008, for example, shows strong outperformance by that defensive group during that bearish year for stocks. The down arrow near the start of 2009 coincided with a strong upturn in the S&P 500. That was a signal to sell health care and buy the S&P 500. The up arrow in spring 2011 suggested the opposite. The right the thing to do in spring 2011 was to sell the S&P 500 and buy health care. Figure 9.10 demonstrates the real value of *relative strength* analysis. It not only tells us something about the strength of the sector in question, but of the market as a whole. While most of the emphasis in this chapter is on relative performance, that doesn't mean that absolute performance isn't important. The best asset to own is one that's showing good *absolute* and *relative* performance.

■ Sectors Are an Important Part of Intermarket Work

This chapter explains the importance of market sectors and industry groups. The stock market is divided into 10 sectors (which includes telecom) and approximately 90 industry groups. Investors familiar with those stock categories, and who know how to measure their performance, can greatly improve the overall performance of their portfolios. Fortunately, there are visual tools that make the task of finding group leaders relatively easy, like relative strength ratios, performance line and bar charts, and sector carpets (or heat maps). Being in the right sectors (and out of the wrong ones) is very important. You need tools to help to determine how to do that. This chapter presents examples of some of the best ones.

| | Did You Know. . .? | |

Investor's Business Daily, a financial newspaper and web site, actually tracks 197 market subgroups.

Sector rotations also play an important role in *intermarket* analysis. Knowing which market sectors are in a leadership role tells us a lot about the condition of the stock market and the business cycle.

FIGURE 9.9 Comparing absolute performance between health care SPDR and S&P 500

$SPX (S&P 500 Large Cap Index) INDX
9-Nov-2011 12:12pm   **Open** 1275.18 **High** 1275.18 **Low** 1239.58 **Last** 1247.96 **Chg** -27.96 (-2.19%) ▾

— $SPX (Daily) 0.00%
— XLV (relative to $SPX) 19.57%

Relative performance of health care stocks reveals more about shifts in market leadership

Healthcare SPDR (XLV)

Relative performance

S&P 500

FIGURE 9.10   XLV/SPX ratio shows relative performance of health care sector

Knowledge of whether the economy is expanding or contracting (which is associated with the direction of the stock market) helps in deciding whether to allocate money into bonds or stocks. Economic expansion favors stocks, while contraction favors bonds.

JOHN'S TIPS

By helping measure the strength of the stock market, sector rotation strategies also influence asset allocation decisions.

■ The Emergence of Exchange-Traded Funds

In addition to the visual tools shown in this and earlier chapters, which make sector rotation and asset allocation decisions a lot easier, the emergence over the last decade of a new trading vehicle has also made the implementation of those strategies a lot simpler. I'm referring to *exchange-traded funds (ETFs)*. Every market shown in this book can be traded with an ETF. That includes every asset class, every market sector, and most industry groups. The ETF universe has also placed alternate asset classes like commodities and currencies within easy reach of the average investor. ETFs have also made investing in foreign markets much simpler. Exchange-traded funds also lend themselves very well to traditional chart analysis. We'll take a closer look at them in the next chapter, and I'll explain why ETFs can be used to implement just about any type of trade you can imagine.

Answer the following questions.

1. Which groups usually turn up first at market bottoms?

   a. Small-cap stocks

   b. Technology stocks

   c. Transportation stocks

   d. Consumer discretionary stocks

   e. All of the above

2. True or False: Market sectors are subdivided into industry groups.

   a. True

   b. False

3. Which normally changes direction first?

   a. The stock market

   b. The economy

4. Sector rotations usually last for how long?

   a. One to two months

   b. Three to six months

   c. Nine to 12 months

5. Which is more revealing of shifts in leadership?

   a. Absolute performance

   b. Relative performance

ANSWERS:

1. e   2. a   3. a   4. b   5. b

121

CHAPTER 10

Exchange-Traded Funds

Although *exchange-traded funds (ETFs)* first appeared in 1993, they didn't start attracting serious attention until after 2000. Funds invested in ETFs grew at an impressive pace of 30 percent per year between 2000 and 2010. By 2012, ETF assets had grown to $1.5 trillion. Some industry estimates called for that number to double by 2015. The growth of ETFs has represented a huge step in the evolution of the financial markets and has made the task of investors a good deal easier. That's especially true in the area of intermarket work. When I first wrote about intermarket relationships 20 years ago, it wasn't that easy to implement all of the strategies involved. That's because intermarket analysis encompassed bonds, commodities, currencies, foreign markets, and the U.S. stock market. It also included market sectors and industry groups.

123

Outside of the futures markets, it wasn't easy to trade commodities or currencies. Sector trading wasn't that easy either. Although mutual funds offered a large menu of sector funds to their clients, they made it difficult to move in and out of those sectors. Frequent trading is discouraged in the mutual fund industry. That's not true with exchange-traded funds. You can trade them as often as you want. Buying or selling an ETF is as simple as buying or selling a stock. That has been a giant leap forward for the more active trader and investor.

What Is an ETF?

An *exchange-traded fund (ETF)* is an investment vehicle that combines key features of traditional mutual funds and individual stocks. Like mutual funds, ETFs represent diversified portfolios of securities that track specific indexes. Just like stocks, they can be bought and sold throughout the trading day on a stock exchange. It's also possible to sell an ETF short. *Selling short* means selling an ETF at a higher price in hopes of buying it back at a lower price. In addition, ETFs offer lower expenses, tax efficiency, and more

---

selling short means selling an ETF at a higher price in hopes of buying it back at a lower price

---

transparency of holdings than mutual funds. ETF providers publish their stock holdings on a daily basis and make that information available on their web sites. Mutual funds only provide that information on a quarterly basis. While those features make ETFs an attractive alternative to traditional mutual funds, the main benefit to more active traders and investors is the fact that ETFs cover the entire universe of investment choices in all markets, and make it much easier to move into and out of those markets.

■ Mutual Funds versus ETFs

Mutual funds still offer a simple way for most long-term investors to participate in the financial markets. Exchange-traded funds, however, offer advantages that mutual funds don't. That's especially true for investors who take a more active role in managing their assets. The main advantage of ETFs is what they can do better than traditional mutual funds from a trading standpoint. Most importantly, ETFs trade like any stock on a stock exchange. That offers more active traders and investors the ability to take quicker positions in the financial markets, and then to exit those positions when they wish to do so. They can execute those trades during the trading day and can trade from either side of the market (long or short). Mutual fund investors have to settle for the fund's closing price no matter what time of the day the order is submitted. The ability to move in and out of trades more quickly is especially important in fast-moving markets like commodities and currencies. Speed is also important in sector rotation strategies.

Mutual funds discourage frequent trading and penalize investors who attempt to do so. *Market timing* is frowned on in the mutual fund industry. Trading restrictions applied by mutual funds greatly diminish the value of sector mutual funds for sector rotation purposes. While an investor might choose to buy and hold a diversified stock mutual fund, that investor might not wish to do so with a sector fund. That's because sector trends usually last for only a few months. The active investor needs to be able to get into a rising sector as early as possible, and rotate somewhere else when the time is right. That involves moving out of a sector that's starting to fall and into one that's starting to rise. ETFs make doing that a good deal easier than a sector mutual fund.

ETFs offer exposure to individual commodity and currency markets that isn't available through a mutual fund. The ability to buy an *inverse* (or bear) ETF for the general market (and market sectors) also makes for a complete set of trading alternatives. You can also sell an ETF short, which you can't do with a mutual fund. For all of those reasons, ETFs are ideal for implementing intermarket trading plans, asset allocation choices, and sector rotation strategies. That's why this book relies so heavily on ETFs to demonstrate intermarket linkages and strategies.

■ Top ETF Providers

There are at present at least a dozen providers of exchange-traded funds. The three that dominate the industry are iShares, State Street Global Advisors, and Vanguard. According to Morningstar, those three providers account for 80 percent of the ETF market. iShares is the biggest provider, with a market share of 43 percent of all ETF assets (versus 24 percent for State Street and 15 percent for Vanguard). Other ETF providers include PowerShares, ProShares, Van Eck, WisdomTree, Rydex, iPath, Direxion Funds, and Guggenheim Investments.

Those providers offer ETFs that cover the entire financial landscape. That includes domestic stock indexes, market sectors, and industry groups, as well as international markets. Every choice of investing is covered, including size (large, midcap, and small) and style (growth versus value). ETFs are offered for all bond categories (such as Treasuries, investment grade corporates, high yield, municipal, and TIPS [Treasury Inflation Protected Securities]. Bond ETFs also exist all along the yield curve. ETFs cover commodity baskets as well as individual commodities. Currency ETFs offer trading in the U.S. dollar and most of the world's larger currencies. *Inverse* funds are offered for those who wish to profit from falling markets (or to hedge their current holdings). Inverse funds trend in the opposite direction of their benchmark index. *Ultra* funds offer more leverage by moving two or three times faster than their benchmark index. That's why they're also called *leveraged* funds. Direxion, Rydex, and ProShares are the biggest managers of leveraged ETFs.

International ETFs cover all of the major stock markets around the globe by country and region. You can choose an ETF basket that covers *developed* or *emerging* markets, or some combination of the two. You can trade emerging markets either as a group or individually. ETFs cover each of biggest emerging markets. There's nothing left out. They can also be charted and analyzed like an individual stock or any other market. Exchange-traded funds offer the best of both worlds. They do that by combining features of both open-end mutual funds and stocks. They offer a basket approach to trading similar to a mutual fund, which offers instant diversification. At the same time, they offer the same simplicity involved in buying or selling an individual stock.

▦ Stock Market ETFs

The first ETF issued in the U.S. market was the SPDR S&P 500 (SPY), which was launched in 1993. It has also been the largest traded fund since then. The SPY is a fund that is designed to track the S&P 500 Index. The S&P 500 is considered to be the main benchmark for the U.S. market. That's why the S&P 500 Index is used as the basis for all relative strength comparisons between individual stocks as well as market sectors.

Did You Know. . .?

SPDR stands for Standard & Poor's Depositary Receipts.

More information on the SPY can be found at www.spdrs.com, which is run by State Street Global Advisors. That's also the home to the SPDR Dow Jones Industrial ETF (DIA). The site also lists other popular ETFs like the SPDR Gold Shares (GLD), SPDR Barclays High Yield Bond ETF (JNK), and the SPDR S&P Dividend ETF (SDY). More information on the nine select sector SPDRs can be found at www.sectorspdrs.com. It's always a good idea know which stocks are in those sectors and how they're weighted. That information is available on that site.

Another very popular stock ETF is the Power Shares QQQ Trust (QQQ), which is based on the Nasdaq 100 Index (NDX). That index includes 100 of the largest domestic and international nonfinancial companies listed on the Nasdaq market based on market capitalization. Of the seven sectors included in the NDX, technology is by far the biggest, with a weighting of 66 percent. By comparison, the second-biggest weighting (16 percent) belongs to consumer discretionary. That's why the Power Shares QQQ Trust is viewed as a proxy for the technology sector. More information on the QQQ and other Power Shares offerings (including commodities and currencies) can be found at www.powershares.com.

Although Vanguard has a smaller ETF market share than iShares and State Street Global Advisors, many of its stock ETF offerings are highly regarded by Morningstar. Vanguard's lower expense ratios are one of the attractions. Some of the more popular Vanguard ETFs are Vanguard Total Stock Market (VTI), Vanguard Dividend Appreciation (VIG), and Vanguard FTSE All-World ex-US (VEU). More information on Vanguard ETFs can be found at www.vanguard.com.

▦ Bond ETFs

Most of the major bond ETFs can be found on the iShares web site (www.ishares.com). The offerings listed on that site cover every bond category as well as every part of the yield curve. One of the more popular offerings is the iShares Barclays 7–10 Year Treasury Bond Fund (IEF). That ETF approximates the rate of return on the intermediate-term sector of the U.S. Treasury market as defined by the Barclays Capital U.S. 7–10 Year Treasury Bond Index. Since bond ETFs are based on bond *prices*, they trend in the opposite direction of bond *yields*. The time to buy the IEF, therefore, is when the 10-year yield is dropping. The same is true for the iShares Barclays 20+ Year Treasury Bond Fund (TLT), which tracks returns on the long-term sector of the Treasury market. That ETF is especially popular when long-term rates are falling. Both of those bond ETFs usually trend in the opposite direction of the stock market, which makes them especially popular during periods of stock market weakness. iShares also offers a Treasury Inflation Protected Securities Fund (TIP), which offers bond investors some protection against rising inflation.

There are several bond categories besides Treasuries, along with ETFs to track and trade them. The iShares S&P National Municipal Bond Fund (MUB) tracks municipal bond prices. Also offered are a number of corporate bond funds. One of the most popular is the iBoxx Investment Grade Corporate Bond iShares (LQD). Another is the iBoxx High Yield Corporate Bond iShares (HYG). Corporate bond funds don't always trend the same way that Treasuries do.

Treasuries are considered to be the ultimate safe haven during periods of economic stress and stock market weakness, because they're backed by the full faith and credit of the U.S. government. Corporate bonds are more closely tied to the fortunes of corporations that issue them. That's especially true of high-yield (junk) bonds. That's why high-yield bond ETFs often act more like stocks than bonds. If you're looking for safety, Treasury bond ETFs are the place to be. If you're optimistic about the economy, corporate bond ETFs might be a better choice. High-yield bond ETFs offer the most profit potential in good economic times, but are also the riskiest when things turn bad. Municipal bond ETFs also carry the additional risk of defaults.

■ Commodity ETFs

Less than a decade ago, it was nearly impossible to get involved in commodity markets outside of the futures markets. That's no longer the case. Exchange-traded funds have opened up that asset class to the individual investor and have made trading them as easy as trading stocks. Exchange-traded funds offer a basket approach to commodity trading as well as individual commodities. PowerShares is the biggest provider of commodity baskets. The PowerShares DB Commodity Index Tracking Fund (DBC) is composed of futures contracts on 14 of the most heavily traded commodities. Commodity group offerings include the DB Agricultural Fund (DBA), the DB Base Metals Fund (DBB), the DB Energy Fund (DBE), and the DB Precious Metals Fund (DBP). PowerShares also offers ETFs for individual commodities like gold, silver, and oil (www.powershares.com).

Other providers offer individual commodity ETFs. The most popular is the SPDR Gold Trust (GLD). Another popular one is iShares Silver Trust (SLV). ETFs also exist for copper, palladium, platinum, crude oil, gasoline, heating oil, natural gas, corn, coffee, and sugar. Some of those, however, are lightly traded. Weakness in the U.S. dollar over the last decade has made commodity markets a more attractive alternative to bonds and stocks. That's because commodity prices usually rise when the dollar falls. Fortunately, that alternate asset class is now included in the exchange-traded fund universe and easily available to the public.

Did You Know. . .?

The Market Vectors Gold Miners ETF (GDX) offers exposure to gold and silver shares, which are closely tied to the trend of gold and silver.

■ Currency ETFs

Commodities aren't the only markets that have benefited from the falling dollar over the last decade. So have foreign currencies. Fortunately, exchange-traded funds now offer investors a way to participate in currency trends. One of the most popular is the CurrencyShares Euro Trust (FXE), which is provided by Rydex Investments. The FXE is designed to track trends in the Euro. Rydex Investments launched the NYSE listed CurrencyShares Euro Trust in 2005. It was the first exchange-traded fund to offer investors foreign currency exposure. Since then, Rydex has issued CurrencyShares for the Australian dollar (FXA), British pound (FXB), Canadian dollar (FXC), Chinese renminbi (FXCH), Japanese yen (FXY), Mexican peso (FXM), Russian ruble (FXRU), Swedish krona (FXS), and Swiss franc (FXF). Some of those newer currency offerings are still lightly traded, however. More information on CurrencyShares can be found at www.currencyshares.com.

WisdomTree also offers currency ETFs that include the Brazilian real (BZF), Chinese yuan (CYB), Indian rupee (ICN), South African rand (SZR), and Emerging Currency Fund (CEW). The CEW offers a basket approach to 11 emerging currencies including Mexico, Brazil, Chile, South Africa, Poland, Israel, Turkey, China, South Korea, Taiwan, and India. Always check on the liquidity of newer currency offerings to make sure they're mature enough for trading (www.wisdomtree.com).

■ Trading the Dollar

In addition to the commodity offerings mentioned previously, PowerShares also offers a way to trade trends in the U.S. dollar. The most popular one is the PowerShares DB US Dollar Bullish Fund (UUP). The UUP is based on the Deutsche Bank Long U.S. Dollar Futures Index (USDX), and is designed to replicate the performance of being long the U.S. dollar against the euro, Japanese yen, British pound, Canadian dollar, Swedish krona, and Swiss franc. The euro's 57 percent weighting in the UUP makes it the dominant foreign currency in the ETF. The yen is a distant second at 13 percent, and the British pound third at 12 percent. That gives the UUP a high inverse correlation with the trend of the euro. The UUP is the vehicle that I use most often in my intermarket analysis. I also play close attention to the euro. The UUP is only suitable if the dollar is rising. When it's falling, the DB U.S. Dollar Bearish Fund (UDN) is a better choice. The UDN rises when the dollar drops.

Powershares also offers the DB G10 Currency Harvest Fund (DBV). That ETF is comprised of currency futures contracts on certain G10 currencies that are associated with relatively high interest rates that tend to rise in value relative to currencies with relatively low interest rates.

■ Foreign ETFs

The simplest way to invest in a basket of foreign *developed* stock markets is to buy MSCI EAFE Index iShares (EFA). That index is generally viewed as the benchmark for foreign stock markets. Ninety percent of its holdings are concentrated in 10 foreign developed markets in Europe and Asia, with its two biggest holdings in the United Kingdom (22 percent) and Japan (21 percent). The problem with the EFA is that it doesn't include anything from North or South America. That leaves out Canada and big Latin American countries like Brazil. An alternative to EAFE iShares is the Vanguard FTSE All-World ex-US ETF (VEU), which offers exposure to 46 countries outside the United States. Unlike the EFA, the VEU includes Canada. The VEU also has a 25-percent weighting in emerging markets, which include Latin America. For one-stop shopping in foreign markets, the Vanguard VEU has more to offer than EAFE iShares.

Another popular foreign basket is MSCI Emerging Market iShares (EEM). Ninety percent of its holdings are concentrated in the 10 largest emerging markets, with its biggest weightings in Asia and Latin America. The four biggest holdings are China (16 percent), Brazil (15 percent), South Korea (14 percent), and Taiwan (10 percent). The EEM includes the four BRIC countries that are Brazil, Russia, India, and China. The MSCI BRIC Index Fund (BKF) offers exposure to those four large emerging markets by themselves. MSCI also offers exchange-traded funds in more than 20 individual countries. *Inverse* global ETFs also exist to take advantage of falling foreign markets. With every part of the world covered by ETFs, all you need is a set of charts and you're all set to span the globe for trading opportunities. You can do most of your foreign shopping right on the floor of the New York Stock Exchange.

■ Inverse and Leveraged ETFs

ProShares is the world's largest provider of *leveraged* and *inverse* funds with exposure to U.S. and foreign equities, market sectors, fixed-income markets, commodities, and currencies. The ProShares *inverse* ETFs allow you trade in the opposite direction of most of the ETFs already listed in this chapter. That's especially helpful in falling markets either for hedging purposes or for profit. Two popular inverse ETFs in the U.S. market are ProShares Short S&P 500 (SH), which trends in the opposite direction of the S&P 500, and ProShares Ultra Short QQQ (QID), which trades inversely to the Nasdaq 100 and twice as fast.

Inverse ETFs are also called *bear* funds for a reason: They rise in value when a market is in decline. They lose value when a market is rising. For that reason, inverse (or bear) funds are not suitable as long-term holdings. They're better employed as short- to intermediate-term trading tools. *Leveraged* (ultra) funds are designed to trade two or three times faster than their benchmark. For that reason, they're better left to expert traders with short-term time horizons. They're probably too risky for the average investor.

■ Summary

My main purpose in this chapter is twofold. One is to increase your awareness of the large number and scope of ETFs that are currently available and where to get more information on them, what they're designed to do, and what goes into their construction. A second purpose is to explain why they're so important to traders and investors, and how much easier they have made it for us to study so many markets at the same time and to make trading choices from among them. You'll be shown lots of chart examples of how to use ETFs throughout this book. If you like to chart, you'll also like ETFs. Since they trade just like stocks (with price and volume information), they can also be charted just like stocks.

This chapter ends Part III of the book. Chapter 8 showed how the four-year business cycle influences intermarket trends and asset allocation choices. It also explained why it's important to take longer-term economic cycles into consideration, including the Kondratieff Wave and the 18-year real estate cycle. Chapter 9 explained how the business cycle influences sector rotations within the stock market, and how rotating sector leadership offers clues about the state of the business cycle and stock market. That chapter included several visual tools to help keep track of which sectors, and individual stocks, are showing market leadership.

The five chapters in Part IV will deal specifically with intermarket relationships that exist between bonds, stocks, commodities, and currencies. We'll start that study in the next chapter with the most reliable of all those relationships: the inverse link between the dollar and commodities.

THE NEW NORMAL

CHAPTER 11

The Dollar and Commodities Trend in Opposite Directions

This chapter demonstrates the inverse correlation between the U.S. dollar and commodity prices, one of the most consistent and reliable intermarket relationships. The chapter also shows the close positive link between commodities and foreign currencies. The Correlation Coefficient helps measure the strength of a relationship between two markets and offers a way to see when that relationship is weakening. Gold doesn't always act like other commodities because of its additional role as an alternate currency. Gold isn't just the world's strongest commodity. It's also the world's strongest currency. The chapter ends with a description of the dollar's impact on other intermarket trends.

◼ Both Markets Need to Be Analyzed Together

One of the most reliable intermarket relationships is the *inverse* relationship between the U.S. dollar and commodity prices. Throughout the inflationary decade of the 1970s, for example, a falling dollar contributed to soaring commodity prices. A dollar bottom during 1980 contributed to a major peak in commodity prices that led to two decades of falling prices and disinflation. Bond and stock prices rose during those two decades while commodities fell out of favor. In the 20 years between 1970 and 1990, every important turn in commodity prices was either preceded by, or coincided with, a turn in the U.S. dollar in the opposite direction. During the bear market years of 1990 and 1994, a falling dollar contributed to rising commodity prices, which weakened bonds and stocks. An upturn in the dollar after those two bearish years pulled commodity prices lower and helped boost bond and stock prices.

Since our main concern in this book is with intermarket events that have transpired since the 1997–1998 Asian currency crisis and the emergence of deflationary trends since then, we'll begin our comparisons there. As we work our way from then to the present, you'll see that the inverse relationship between the U.S. dollar and commodity prices has remained very constant. From an investing standpoint, that means that both markets are closely linked to one another and should be analyzed together. It's a mistake to analyze one without the other.

The Rising Dollar Contributed to the 1997–1998 Commodity Collapse

Chapter 3 covered the Asian currency crisis that started during the summer of 1997 and lasted well into 1998. A collapse in Asian currency markets raised fears of global deflation, which pushed commodity prices to the lowest level in 20 years. Stocks around the world fell as money poured into U.S. Treasury bonds. I believe that the events of 1997–1998 helped set the stage for the deflationary trends that dominated the first decade of the 21st century. One of the intermarket principles we'll be examining in this chapter is that a rising dollar usually coincides with or leads to falling commodity prices. That's exactly what happened during 1997 and 1998.

JOHN'S TIPS

During times of global financial crisis, money usually flows to the relative safety of the U.S. dollar and Treasury bonds.

Figure 11.1 shows the U.S. dollar and commodity prices trending in opposite directions between 1994 and 1999. The dollar started rising during 1995 (after the *stealth* bear market of 1994) and continued to rally through the balance of the decade (see up arrow). By 1996, the rising dollar started having a negative impact on commodity prices, which started dropping (see down arrow). The fact that the dollar turned up a year before commodities peaked isn't unusual. The dollar often changes direction before commodities and, when it does, becomes a valuable leading indicator that commodities prices are due for a change of direction.

The commodity plunge resulting from the Asian currency crisis started in 1997 and lasted throughout 1998. The collapse in Asian currencies pushed a lot of money into the relative safety of

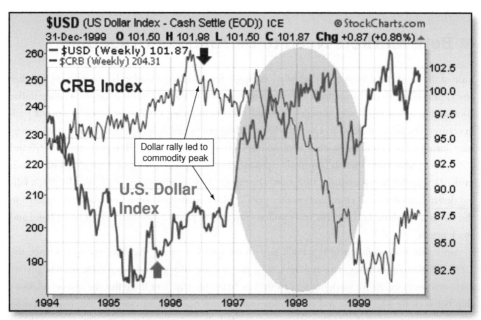

FIGURE 11.1   Rising dollar contributed to commodity collapse during 1997 and 1998

the U.S. dollar (and Treasury bonds). The resulting spike in the dollar during 1997 and 1998 was a major contributing factor to the plunge in commodity prices, which only served to intensify fears of global deflation. Stock prices plunged along with commodities (as bond prices soared), which also heightened deflationary fears. Within five years of the 1997 Asian currency crisis, the Fed embarked on a plan to lessen the resulting deflationary threat. In order to accomplish that, two things had to happen: The dollar had to drop and commodities had to rise. That's just what happened starting in 2002.

JOHN'S TIPS

The Fed adopted the same plan used during the 1930s to boost commodity prices (especially gold) by weakening the dollar.

■ The Falling Dollar from 2002 to 2008 Pushed Commodities Higher

Chapter 5 covered the major peak in the U.S. dollar that occurred during 2002 and the corresponding upturn in commodity markets. The downtrend in the dollar, and the uptrend in commodities, lasted until 2008. The main purpose in this chapter is to demonstrate that the dollar and commodities usually trend in opposite directions. Figure 11.2 demonstrates that very clearly in the years between 1995 and 2008. The two arrows on the chart show the major turns in both markets that started during 2002 when the dollar peaked and commodities bottomed. While the *rising* dollar in the late 1990s contributed to falling commodities, a *falling* dollar after 2002 contributed to a major upturn in commodity markets which lasted for six years until 2008.

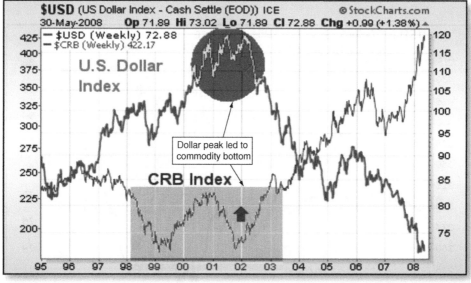

FIGURE 11.2 Falling dollar contributed to commodity rise from 2002 until mid-2008

The Dollar Bottom during 2008 Contributed to Commodity Plunge

An earlier chapter covered the events of 2007 when money fleeing a peaking stock market poured into Treasury bonds. It also showed that falling U.S. interest rates weakened the dollar during the second half of that year, which gave a big boost to gold and other commodities. That wasn't unusual since commodity prices have a history of peaking later than the stock market. In this case, however, the time between the two peaks was unusually long. Although stocks peaked during October 2007, commodities kept rising until the middle of 2008. The falling dollar was the main factor keeping the commodity rally going. A dollar bottom in the middle of 2008, however, finally contributed to a commodity price collapse.

Figure 11.3 shows commodity prices peaking with a vengeance starting in July 2008. From the middle of 2008 to the start of 2009, the CRB Index lost more than 50 percent of its value (which far outpaced its 30-percent drop during 1997 and 1998). The deflationary implications of the 2008 commodity collapse invoked comparisons to the deflationary 1930s and raised fears of another depression. (In the next chapter, we'll explain how the deflationary implications of the 2008 commodity price plunge tightened the correlation between stocks and commodities.) The main point of Figure 11.3, however, is to show that the plunge in commodity prices during the second half of 2008 coincided exactly with an upturn in the U.S. Dollar Index (see arrows). Although the 2008 drop in the CRB Index (−50 percent) was far greater than the rise in the dollar (+20 percent), the dollar bottom was a major contributing factor to the commodity drop. Once again, a change in the direction of the dollar coincided with a change in direction of commodities.

JOHN'S TIPS

While commodity traders need to keep an eye on the dollar, dollar traders also need to keep an eye on commodity markets.

FIGURE 11.3   Dollar bottom during 2008 contributed to commodity plunge

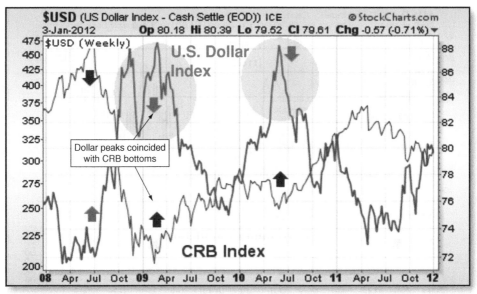

FIGURE 11.4 Dollar peaks in 2009 and 2010 lifted commodities

Dollar Peaks in 2009 and 2010 Lifted Commodities

Figure 11.4 is intended to demonstrate that the dollar and commodities maintained their inverse correlation during the three years after 2008. Most notable are the two dollar peaks that took place during the first quarter of 2009 and the second quarter of 2010. Both of those downturns in the Dollar Index coincided with upturns in the CRB Index (see arrows). Commodity traders during those two years were well served by following trends in the dollar. Sell signals in the dollar during 2009 and 2010 corresponded with buy signals in the commodity pits. From the start of 2009 until the spring of 2011, a 10-percent loss in the dollar coincided with commodity gains in excess of 60 percent. During 2011, however, those trends reversed. A rising dollar that spring resulted in a bad year for commodities (and stocks tied to commodities).

The Dollar Bottom in 2011 Pushed Commodities Lower

A lot of trend changes started to take place during spring 2011. Many of those changes had to do with an upturn in the U.S. dollar. The events of 2011 demonstrated once again why commodities and the dollar have to be analyzed together. Commodity traders who ignored trends in the dollar did so at their own peril. Heading into spring 2011, commodity prices were rising and the dollar was falling. That had been the case for more than two years. During May 2011, however, the Dollar Index hit bottom and started to rise. The dollar rose for the rest of that year. Figure 11.5 shows, however, that the May dollar bottom coincided exactly with a May peak in the CRB Index (see arrows). From that May through the balance of 2011, the dollar rose while commodities fell. Once again, the two markets maintained a strong *inverse correlation*.

JOHN'S TIPS

The spring 2011 commodity peak led to a stock market correction and a rally in Treasury bonds.

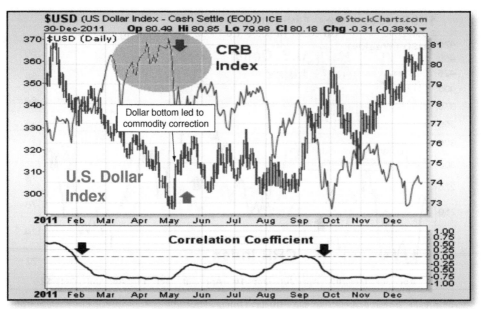

FIGURE 11.5   Dollar bottom in spring 2011 pushed commodities lower

■ Correlation Coefficient

While most of the correlations between markets can be spotted pretty easily on price charts, it's helpful to have those visual impressions confirmed by a statistical measure of the strength of those correlations. The *correlation coefficient* plotted at the bottom of Figure 11.5 shows that the dollar and commodities had a negative correlation of −.75 throughout much of 2011. That confirmed the visual impression shown by the two markets that they were trending in opposite directions.

Did You Know…?

A negative correlation is present when the coefficient is below the zero line.

The correlation coefficient measures the strength of a relationship between two markets. That relationship can be positive or negative. A coefficient of +1.00 means that two markets are perfectly correlated and trend in the same direction 100 percent of the time (which is very rare). Conversely, a correlation of −1.00 means that two markets trend in opposite directions 100 percent of the time (also very rare). Correlations between markets swing between those two extremes. A plus number shows *positive* correlation (same direction), while a minus number shows *negative* correlation (opposite direction). The higher those numbers are in either direction, the higher the correlation (either positive or negative).

JOHN'S TIPS

The most important signals are given when the correlation line moves above or below the zero line.

The correlation coefficient indicator is especially helpful in intermarket analysis, which is based on relationships between markets. It not only allows us to put an objective number on the strength of those relationships, but it allows us to tell when the relationship is strengthening or weakening. The correlation coefficient line at the bottom of Figure 11.5 was in negative territory (below the zero line) throughout most of 2011. That confirmed the negative correlation between the dollar and commodities throughout that year. Notice, however, that the line isn't completely flat. Although it remained below the zero line, it rose and fell throughout the year. The two arrows show that the negative correlation strengthened during February and September 2011. That was a sign to the trader that the dollar was going to have bigger impact on commodity prices. Readings below .50 imply weaker correlation, while readings near .75 suggest strong correlation (either positive or negative). Throughout most of 2011, the *negative correlation* between the dollar and commodities stayed near −.75. While we can usually spot the negative correlations pretty easily by examining the two markets together, we can't always tell when those correlations are getting stronger or weaker. The correlation coefficient indicator does that for us and helps ensure that there's statistical confirmation behind our visual intermarket comparisons.

Did You Know. . .?

Since commodities and stocks were positively correlated during 2011, the negative impact of the rising dollar took a toll on stocks as well.

Gold Isn't Like Other Commodities

When dealing with commodities as an asset class, it's important to recognize that gold isn't just a *commodity*. Gold is also viewed by many as an alternate *currency*. In other words, global traders (and some central bankers) buy gold when they lose confidence in paper currencies. Gold's historic role as a *store of value* makes it especially attractive when other assets look unattractive (or relatively unsafe). That includes paper currencies. That helps explain why gold doesn't always trade in tandem with other commodity markets.

Figure 11.6 compares the price of gold to the CRB Index during 2011. While most commodities peaked during May of that year (when the dollar bottomed), gold kept rising until September. There are several explanations as to why gold held up better than other commodities during the five months between May and September. One explanation had to do with the fact that stocks started to correct that spring along with commodities and fell especially hard during August. Some money leaving a falling

Did You Know. . .?

A strong upsurge in the dollar during September 2011 finally pushed gold into a downside correction.

stock market moved into gold. Another explanation had to do with a plunge in bond yields during 2011. Falling bond yields usually drive money into gold. Another explanation for gold's strength had to do with the fact the most foreign currencies peaked that spring along with most commodity markets.

Did You Know. . .?

Gold usually benefits from a weak stock market.

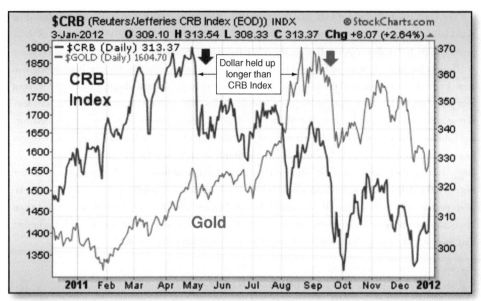

FIGURE 11.6   Gold held up better than CRB during 2011

Did You Know. . .?

Since gold is a *nonyielding* asset, the lower yield offered by falling interest rates increases gold's appeal.

■ Commodities Are Linked to Foreign Currencies

Foreign currencies trend in the *opposite* direction of the U.S. dollar. So do commodity markets. That means that foreign currencies and commodities usually trend in the *same* direction. As a result, they can be charted together and used to confirm each other's trends. At times, turns in either one can warn of turns in the other. Outside of the U.S. dollar, which is the world's reserve currency, the euro is the world's second most influential currency. The euro also has the biggest weighting (57 percent) in the U.S. Dollar Index, which measures the dollar against a basket of foreign currencies. As a result, what the euro does has a huge bearing on the direction of the U.S. currency. Euro direction also has a big influence on the direction of commodity markets.

Figure 11.7 compares the trends in the euro to the CRB Index over the five years between 2007 and 2011. It's clear that they usually trend in the same direction. The most striking event in Figure 11.7 is the fact that the euro and commodities peaked together in mid-2008 and tumbled together (as the dollar rallied). From its July peak, the euro lost 20 percent of its value (which matched the 20 percent gain in the Dollar Index). Commodity-currencies like the Australian and Canadian Dollars fared even worse. The CRB lost half of its value.

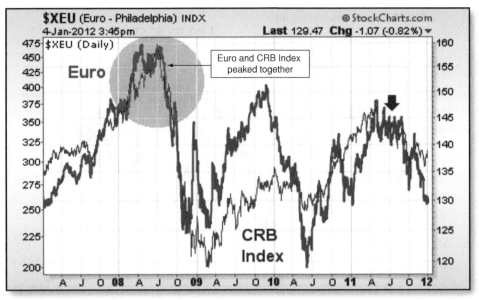

FIGURE 11.7   CRB and euro trend in the same direction

Did You Know...?

Currencies of commodity-producing nations are closely tied to the trend of commodities. They do better when commodities are strong and suffer more when commodities fall.

Figure 11.7 shows the CRB and euro bottoming together in early 2009, which started the commodity rally that lasted into 2011. The down arrow during 2011, however, shows that commodity prices and the euro peaked together in the spring of 2011. The simultaneous drop in most foreign currencies that spring, along with economically sensitive commodities like copper and oil, was viewed as a sign of a weakening global economy. As a result, stocks prices also started to correct downward and lost nearly 20 percent within six months of that spring top. Bond yields also plunged as money rotated out of stocks and into Treasuries. Some of that nervous money moving out of copper, oil, stocks, and foreign currencies found its way into gold.

Did You Know. . .?

The sharp drop in the euro during the first half of 2010 was much bigger than the drop in commodity prices. That was due to a crisis in Europe, which hit that currency especially hard. Foreign currencies tied to commodities held up much better during that period.

FIGURE 11.8   Gold outpaces euro from 2008 through 2011

Gold Outperforms the Euro

Figure 11.8 compares the euro and gold over the same five years as the previous figure. Gold shows a much weaker correlation to the euro between 2007 and 2011. The two most notable examples of their weaker correlation can be seen during 2008 and 2011 (see circles). Although gold corrected downward during the second half of 2008 with other commodities and foreign currencies, its losses were much smaller. At its lowest point during the second half of 2008, gold had lost only half as much as the CRB Index. By the following spring, gold had regained almost all of its losses, while the CRB was still down 50 percent. The euro was down 20 percent. From its 2008 peak to the end of 2011, gold gained more than 70 percent, while the euro lost nearly 20 percent. While gold was rallying, the CRB Index lost 30 percent of its value between its mid-2008 peak and the end of 2011. It seems clear that something beyond its role as a *commodity* accounts for gold's stronger performance. That appears to be gold's additional role as an alternative to paper currencies.

Gold Outpaces Other Commodities

Figure 11.9 is designed to show that gold has done much better than other commodities during periods of dollar weakness and dollar strength. The lower line after 2007 shows the Dollar Index (which measures the dollar against six foreign currencies and is the most useful way to track dollar trends). The upper line is a ratio of gold divided by the CRB Index. The purpose of that ratio is to compare the performance of gold *relative* to the CRB basket of commodities. During the years between 2002 and 2005, the gold/CRB ratio remained relatively flat as the dollar fell. Starting in 2006, however, the gold/CRB ratio started to climb and continued to do so through the end of 2011. During those six years, gold gained more than 200 percent, while the CRB was basically flat.

FIGURE 11.9   Gold outpaced CRB even as dollar rose during 2008 and after

The most striking feature of Figure 11.9 takes place after the middle of 2008 (see circle). Starting in the middle of that year, the gold/CRB ratio spiked dramatically higher. It did so even as the dollar rallied. The ratio also rose during the first half of 2010 and most of 2011, as the dollar bounced. The stronger performance of gold in the face of a stronger dollar certainly seems to suggest that one of the factors behind gold's superior performance is its role as an alternate currency. When the dollar is rising, foreign currencies fall. Rather than moving into the dollar, some of that foreign currency money moves into gold. That gives gold a dual role as a commodity and an alternative currency.

Gold versus Foreign Currencies

Figure 11.9 showed gold outperforming other commodities over the past several years. Gold generally trends in the opposite direction of the U.S. dollar. That means that gold usually trends in the same direction of foreign currencies. But gold doesn't rise at the same *rate* as those currencies. Recent history shows that gold has risen much *faster* than foreign currencies.

Figure 11.10 compares the performance of the world's three strongest major foreign currencies *versus* gold in the five years between 2007 and 2011. The three currencies that are plotted relative to

FIGURE 11.10 Foreign currencies versus gold

gold are the Japanese yen, Australian dollar, and Swiss franc. All three gained ground but not as much as gold. While gold rose 150 percent during those five years, the yen gained 55 percent, and the Aussie dollar and Swiss franc gained 31 percent and 29 percent, respectively. The purpose of Figure 11.10 is simply to demonstrate that all of those foreign currencies fell *relative* to gold during those five years. In other words, gold was not only the world's strongest commodity market. It was also benefitting from its role as the world's strongest currency. That gives gold a dual role as a *commodity* and a *currency*, which explains why it doesn't always act in sync with other commodity markets.

■ The Dollar's Impact on Other Intermarket Trends

This chapter discusses one of the most consistent intermarket themes, which is the *inverse* relationship between commodities and the dollar. The charts are designed to show that the two markets are closely linked and need to be analyzed together. It seems foolhardy, for example, for a commodity trader to analyze commodity charts without also consulting charts of the dollar and foreign currencies. Changes in the trend of the dollar (and foreign currencies) usually coincide with changes in commodity prices. At times, the dollar turns first, which gives advanced warning of an impending change in commodity direction. This chapter also demonstrates that gold serves as both a commodity and a currency, and, as a result, doesn't always act like other commodity markets. The impact of the dollar, however, goes much further than influencing what happens in the commodity pits. Dollar direction has much wider implications.

Over the last decade, the link between the dollar, commodities, and stocks has grown much stronger. The next chapter will show that commodities and stocks have become much more closely aligned, especially since the deflationary collapse during 2008. As a result, the dollar and stocks have developed a more direct inverse relationship. Dollar direction also impacts sector rotations within the stock market.

JOHN'S TIPS

The biggest effect dollar direction has on sector rotation is its influence on stocks tied to commodities.

Chapter 9, for example, discussed the defensive sector rotation that started during spring 2011 when money rotated out of economically sensitive commodity groups, like basic materials and energy, and into defensive sectors like staples, healthcare, and utilities. The rise in the dollar contributed to that rotation out of commodity stocks by pulling commodity prices lower. The correction in commodity-related stocks (which implied economic weakness) contributed to the correction in stocks that started at the same time. Dollar direction also influences the relative attractiveness of U.S. stocks versus foreign stocks.

You'll see in Chapter 12 that a rising dollar usually hurts foreign stocks more than it does those in the United States. That helps explain why foreign stocks fell much further than U.S. stocks during 2011. The rising dollar also explains why emerging market stocks fell much further than those in developed stock markets that year. Emerging markets are more closely correlated with the trend in commodity markets. As a result, emerging markets take a bigger hit when a rise in the dollar causes commodity prices to fall. Those intermarket trends will be demonstrated in the next two chapters. My purpose in mentioning it here is simply to make you aware of the fact that the inverse link between commodities and the dollar is only one link in the intermarket chain (although an important one).

The next chapter, which deals with the close link between commodities and the stock market, will also demonstrate the close correlation between commodity prices and stock groups tied to commodities. Those groups include basic materials, energy, and precious metals. You'll also see why it's a good idea to compare the chart performance of those stock groups to their respective commodities. In many instances, commodity-related stocks change direction ahead of the commodity. You'll see how that happened in spring 2011, and how that helped signal important changes in trend that started that spring in most other markets.

CHAPTER 12

Stocks and Commodities Become Highly Correlated

This chapter discusses the close correlation between stocks and commodities over the last decade, and especially since 2008. The deflationary impact of the housing collapse tightened their correlation even further. Copper influences stock market direction. So does the silver/gold ratio. Silver stocks led the commodity lower in spring 2011. Crude led energy shares lower. Commodities turned down before stocks during 2011. The commodity peak also influenced sector rotations. Gold-miners have underperformed bullion since 2008.

◼ Another Side Effect of the Deflationary Environment

An earlier chapter discussed two events that occurred during the 1990s that contributed to the deflationary climate that has characterized the first decade of the 21st century. One event was the collapse in the Japanese stock market during 1990, which led to a deflationary spiral in that nation's economy. The second deflationary event was the Asian currency crisis that started during 1997 that helped change some key intermarket relationships that still exist to this day. One of those changes was the *decoupling* of bond and stock prices. Prior to 1998, rising bond prices were positive for stocks. After 1998, rising bond prices usually led to falling stock prices.

The second intermarket change was a much closer linkage between the trends of stock and commodity markets. Both of those intermarket changes were reminiscent of trends that existed during the deflationary 1930s when rising commodity prices became a good thing for stocks. The government in effect devalued the dollar during the 1930s in an attempt to boost commodity prices and lessen the deflationary climate that hurt stock values. As a result, stock and commodity prices generally rose and fell together during the 1930s.

The third deflationary event that occurred was the collapse in commodity prices during the second half of 2008. That commodity collapse was a direct result of the financial meltdown that started during 2007, which was caused by a collapse in the housing sector resulting from the subprime disaster. It wasn't just that commodity prices fell. It was how far they fell in such a short period of time.

FIGURE 12.1 Commodities lost half their value during the last half of 2008

Commodities Lost Half Their Value in Just Six Months

Figure 12.1 shows the CRB Index of commodity prices in the three decades since 1980. The CRB Index peaked during 1980 and remained in a downtrend for the next two decades. From its 1980 peak to its 2000 bottom, the CRB lost 46 percent. It took 20 years for it to lose nearly half of its value. During the commodity plunge during 1997 and 1998 (resulting from the Asian currency crisis) the CRB Index lost 30 percent of its value. That loss of a third of its value took two years. By stark contrast, commodity prices plunged 57 percent in the six months after they peaked in July 2008. The fact that commodity prices fell so far in such a short period of time during the second half of 2008 raised fears of another deflationary spiral and helped raise comparisons to the Great Depression of the 1930s. One of the side effects of that deflationary fear was that it tightened the correlation between stock and commodity prices even further.

JOHN'S TIPS

Stocks and commodities became highly correlated after the 1929 stock market crash and during the deflationary decade of the 1930s.

Stock and Commodities Became Closely Correlated after 2008

Figure 12.2 compares the CRB Index and the S&P 500 between 2006 and 2011. The two markets started trending together immediately after the 2008 commodity peak (see circle). Both markets then bottomed together during the spring of 2009 (up arrow) and corrected together during 2011 (down arrow). The correlation coefficient line below Figure 12.2 confirms their stronger relationship. Prior to 2008, the correlation between the two markets swung between positive and negative. During the second half of 2008, however, the correlation between the two markets turned positive (see up arrow) and stayed that way for the following three years (with an average positive correlation around .75).

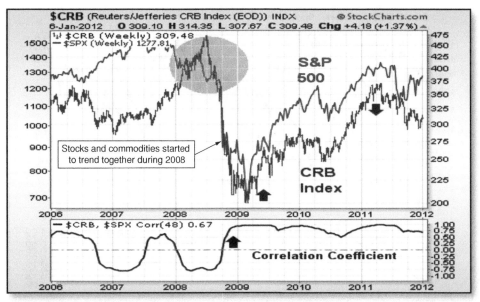

FIGURE 12.2   Stocks and commodities became closely correlated after 2008

The tighter correlation between stocks and commodities after 2008 had important implications for the intermarket analyst. It meant that chart readings in commodity markets could be used to help predict stock market direction (and vice versa). Since the direction of the dollar was an important ingredient in determining commodity direction, it also meant that the dollar was now influencing stock market direction as well. Not all commodities, however, are equal. Some are more important than others in terms of their impact on the economy and stock market. One of the most economically sensitive commodities is copper.

■ Copper Influences Stock Market Direction

Figure 12.3 shows the price of copper and the S&P 500 trending in the same direction since 2000. Both markets fell together during 2001, turned up together during 2003, fell together during 2008, and bottomed together during 2009 (see arrows). The correlation coefficient (below Figure 12.3) shows positive correlation (above zero) for 10 of those 12 years. The only two exceptions were in 2002 and early 2003, when copper (and most commodities) turned up before stocks (owing to a collapsing dollar), and during the first half of 2008, when commodities prices kept rising while stocks plunged. Their correlations have been much tighter since mid-2008.

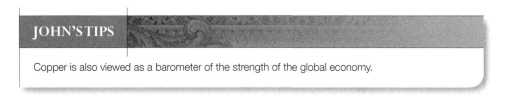

JOHN'S TIPS

Copper is also viewed as a barometer of the strength of the global economy.

Figure 12.4 shows a much tighter correlation between the price of copper and the S&P 500 since the middle of 2008. In fact, the two markets are hard to tell apart during the three years since then. Both markets bottomed together in spring 2009 (first circle) and started to correct together during

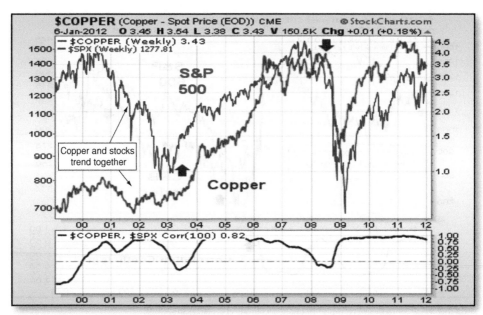

FIGURE 12.3　Direction of copper has influence on stock market direction

spring 2011 (second circle). The correlation coefficient below Figure 12.4 turned positive during the second half of 2008 (see up arrow) and has remained strongly positive in the three years since then. That close linkage carries a lot of important implications for the stock market. Copper is often referred to as the commodity with a Ph.D. in economics (Dr. Copper). That's because copper is viewed as a barometer of the health of the global economy. A rising copper price implies economic health, while a drop in the price of copper suggests a weakening global economy. (In the next chapter, I'll discuss the close linkage between copper and the Chinese stock market, which results from the fact that China is the world's biggest importer and user of copper.)

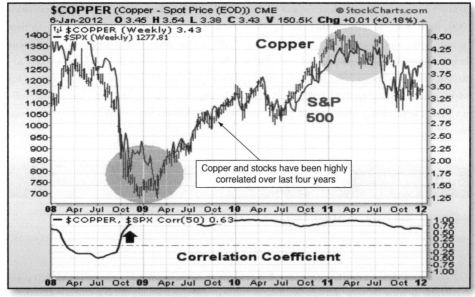

FIGURE 12.4　2009 and 2011 turns in copper coincided with S&P 500 turns

The previous chapter demonstrated that gold doesn't always trend in the same direction as other commodities. That's partially due to gold's dual role as a currency as well as a commodity. Gold's differing performance is also due to the fact that investors often buy bullion as a safe haven when stocks are weak. When they're selling copper, they're often buying gold. That's why analysts plot a ratio of copper prices versus gold to determine stock market direction. The theory behind that ratio is that the stock market and economy are in better shape if the price of copper is rising faster than gold. Accordingly, it's usually a warning sign when the price of gold is outpacing copper. Another ratio that I have found useful for the same purpose compares the performance of silver to gold.

■ The Silver/Gold Ratio Influences the Stock Market

Although silver is considered to be a *precious* metal, it's also an *industrial* metal. It's the industrial role that gives it some value in helping to measure economic trends. Generally speaking, a rising silver price implies economic strength, while a falling silver prices implies the opposite. Using the same rationale that compares the price of copper to gold, the direction of the *silver/gold ratio* can also be employed as a useful stock market indicator. The idea is simple. It's usually better for the stock market when the price of silver is rising faster than gold. Conversely, a falling silver/gold ratio usually implies stock market weakness.

Figure 12.5 compares the silver/gold ratio to the S&P 500 over the 10 years starting in 2002 when commodity prices bottomed. The chart shows that the stock market usually does better when silver

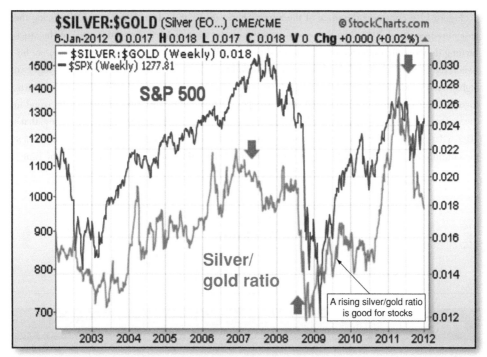

FIGURE 12.5   Silver/gold ratio also influences stock market direction

is rising faster than gold (a rising silver/gold ratio). That was certainly the case between 2003 and 2006. Figure 12.5 also shows, however, that turns in the silver/gold ratio often *precede* turns in the stock market. The ratio peaked at the start of 2007 and fell throughout the balance of that year (first down arrow). Stocks peaked during the second half of that year. Both fell together during the financial meltdown during 2008. The silver/gold ratio bottomed at the end of 2008, which occurred a few months before stocks turned up (up arrow). A peak in the silver/gold ratio in the spring of 2011 also signaled an impending stock market correction (second down arrow). The plunge in the ratio during 2011 was the result of a collapse in the price of silver, which had soared in price to $50 an ounce and resulted in a test of its all-time high reached during 1980. Interestingly, the peak in the price of silver that spring was forewarned by even weaker action in common stocks tied to silver.

◼ Silver Stocks Led Commodity Lower during 2011

Commodity prices were rising during the first quarter of 2011. The one commodity that really caught everyone's attention, however, was silver. During the first four months of that year, silver prices surged over 40 percent, which far outpaced gains in other commodities. During those four months, gold gained a much more modest 10 percent, as did the CRB Index. During the six months leading up to April 2011, silver had climbed from $20 to nearly $50, which put it in position to challenge its 1980 peak at that same level. Unfortunately, that test failed. Silver prices peaked at the end of April and tumbled 40 percent during the following month. The plunge in the price of silver contributed to a sharp drop in most other commodity markets, and eventually led to a correction in the stock market. Interestingly, one of the warning signs that silver was due for a fall came from stocks tied to that commodity.

Figure 12.6 compares the price of the Silver iShares (SLV) and Silver Wheaton (SLW) during the first nine months of 2011. The first down arrow near the start of April shows the price of the stock turning down while the price of the commodity was still rising. That created a *negative divergence* between the two, which signaled a drop in the commodity. A *negative divergence* is present when two highly correlated markets start to diverge from each other during an uptrend. The reason the downturn in Silver Wheaton was a warning is that stocks tied to a commodity (like silver) usually trend in the same direction as the commodity. When either one (the stock or the commodity) stops rising, that's often a danger sign for the other. Interestingly, stocks tied to commodities often change direction *before* the commodity. That's what happened to silver during April 2011, and it was pretty clear at the time.

a **negative divergence** is present when two highly correlated markets start to diverge from each other during an uptrend

Did You Know. . .?

The SLV is an ETF based on the price of silver.

FIGURE 12.6   Silver Wheaton turned before Silver twice during 2011

A Market Message that I posted on the Stockcharts.com web site (StockCharts.com) on April 26 of that year was headlined: "Silver May Be Putting in Climax Top near $50 Target—Weakness in Silver Stocks Also Warns of Profit-taking in Precious Metals." The following paragraph was taken from that message:

SILVER STOCKS WEAKEN: Stocks related to silver have been rising along with the commodity. Chart 4 shows the close correlation between the price of silver and the Global X Silver Miners ETF (SIL) over the last six months. To the upper right, however, the SIL failed to exceed its high at 31 while the commodity kept rising. Yesterday's downside reversal in the SIL on higher volume forms a potential *negative divergence* between silver stocks and the commodity. Chart 5 shows Silver Wheaton slipping below its 50-day line yesterday. It's been falling on rising volume since the start of April. The same negative divergence is seen between the price of gold and gold shares. It seems likely that both commodities are due for a correction. Silver, however, appears to be the most over-extended and the most vulnerable to profit-taking.

(April 26, 2011: StockCharts.com).

The price of silver hit its final peak on April 28 and plunged nearly $20 over the following two weeks. The Global X Silver Miners ETF (SIL) had peaked three weeks earlier on April 8. Silver Wheaton (SLW) also peaked on April 8. In that instance, the downturn in silver shares provided an early

---

Did You Know. . .?

As the name implies, the SIL is an ETF of common stocks tied to the price of silver.

JOHN'S TIPS

Any divergence between a commodity and stocks tied to it usually signals a trend change.

warning that the silver surge was nearing completion. That example demonstrates why it's always a good idea to compare a chart of any commodity with stocks tied to that commodity.

Stocks often lead turns in their related commodities at bottoms as well as tops. Figure 12.6 shows Silver Wheaton and the Silver ETF (SLV) plunging together during May. The stock, however, turned up in mid-June (see up arrow), while the commodity didn't turn up until a month later. In both instances (the April top and the June bottom), the silver stock turned before the commodity. The May 2011 plunge in the price of silver pushed the silver/gold ratio sharply lower, which took a negative toll on other commodity markets and the stock market. During the six months after that spring peak, silver lost 40 percent while gold prices rose 5 percent. At the same time, the CRB Index and S&P experienced similar drops of nearly 20 percent.

■ The Influence of Commodities on Sector Performance

We've already discussed how silver shares are tied to the direction of that commodity. The same is true of gold, copper, and energy shares. If you're trading stock market sectors tied to commodities, therefore, it's necessary to know what's happening to those commodities. (I'll demonstrate shortly that the direction of commodity prices also influences non-commodity sectors.) As a general rule, the direction of commodity prices influences the performance of stocks tied to those commodities. That includes *absolute* and *relative* performance.

Let's start with *relative* performance. Figure 12.7 compares the *price* of crude oil (solid line) to a ratio of the Energy SPDR (XLE) divided by the S&P 500. The two lines trended together during 2010 and 2011. The rising price of crude from mid-2010 to spring 2011 contributed to a rising XLE/SPX ratio. In other words, energy stocks were market leaders during that period of rising oil prices. Both lines peaked during spring 2011 and fell together until that October. During the six months after that April peak, falling oil prices caused energy shares to underperform the S&P 500. That's the way it generally works. The price of crude also influences the *absolute* trend of energy shares.

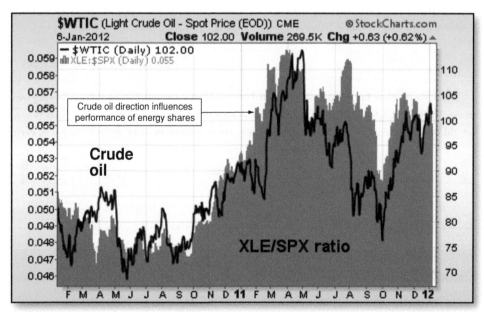

FIGURE 12.7   Direction of oil influences relative performance of energy shares

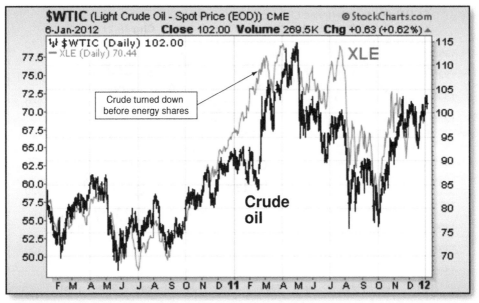

FIGURE 12.8   Crude turned down before energy stocks in spring 2011

Figure 12.8 compares the price of crude oil to the actual trend of the Energy SPDR (XLE) during the same two years as the previous example. Again, a close visual correlation is seen between the trend of crude oil and energy shares. Both rose from mid-2010 until spring 2011, and fell together until that October. Both then rose together during the fourth quarter. In this case, however, the order in which the two lines peaked was different than in the silver example discussed earlier. In Figure 12.8, the price of crude oil peaked at the start of May 2011 and fell sharply throughout that month. The Energy SPDR, however, didn't start to roll over until that August (nearly three months after crude peaked). In that case, the commodity led the stock group lower. The warning was the same, however, in the sense that a turn in one signaled a likely turn in the other. Holders of energy stocks who weren't aware that crude had already peaked were more likely to be surprised when energy stocks fell that summer.

JOHN'S TIPS

It's dangerous to trade energy shares without also charting the direction of crude oil.

Commodities Led Stocks Lower during 2011

The drop in key commodities like copper, oil, and silver during May 2011 had a delayed effect on the stock market, but demonstrated why stock traders need to keep an eye on commodity trends. That's been especially true since 2008, when the two markets became more closely correlated.

Figure 12.9 compares the CRB Index of commodity prices (price bars) to the S&P 500 during most of 2011. Both rose together during that first quarter. Commodities, however, turned down sharply at the start of May (as did the relative performance of stocks tied to commodities). The S&P 500, however, held up better than commodities during the following three months. The close correlation between the two markets, however, should have sent a warning to stock traders that

FIGURE 12.9   The CRB Index led the S&P 500 lower during spring 2011

stocks were becoming more vulnerable to profit-taking. A Market Message that I posted on May 5 carried this headline: "Dollar Bounce Puts More Downside Pressure on Commodities—Breakdown in Copper Hints at Economic Weakness—That's Giving a Boost to Bonds but Leaves Stocks Vulnerable." *(May 5, 2011: StockCharts.com.)* During the six months after the May peak, stocks and commodities lost close to 20 percent.

Did You Know. . .?

Although we're mainly concerned with the interplay between stocks and commodities in this chapter, the dollar and bonds played a key role in market turns that spring. A rising dollar hurt both stocks and commodities, while rising bond prices (falling bond yields) also hinted at economic weakness and a lower stock market.

JOHN'S TIPS

Stocks and commodities bottomed together during the fourth quarter of 2011.

■ The Commodity Peak Also Influenced Sector Rotations

Chapter 9 discussed the defensive sector rotations that started during spring 2011. I'm repeating some of that here to demonstrate that the peak in commodities during 2011 played a role in those sector rotations.

When discussing sector rotation, we're usually referring to *relative* performance between sectors of the stock market. The best way to measure relative performance is through the use of price ratios. Figure 12.10 compares the Energy SPDR (XLE)/S&P 500 ratio (solid line) to a ratio of the Consumer Staples SPDR (XLP) divided by the S&P 500 (solid matter). The two ratios trended in

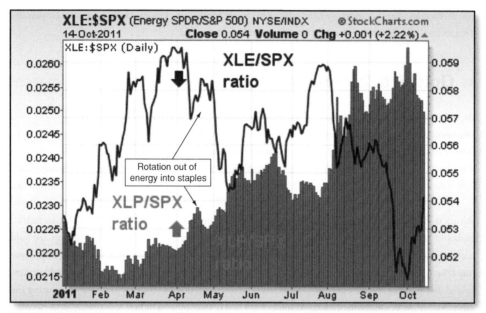

FIGURE 12.10 2011 Rotation Out of Energy Led to Rotation into Consumer Staples

opposite directions during 2011. The Energy SPDR ratio peaked during April just as the Consumer Staples ratio turned up (see arrows). You may recall my explanation in Chapter 9 that rotation out of energy stocks into consumer staples is usually associated with a stock market top. The fact that those defensive rotations were taking place was pretty clear at the time.

JOHN'S TIPS

The drop in energy shares during 2011 was directly related to the drop in the price of crude oil.

A Market Message that I posted during April 2011 regarding sector rotations included the following headline: ". . .Upturn in Relative Performance of Staples and Healthcare Warns of Market Pullback." The opening paragraph in that message included the following excerpt:

. . .Materials and Energy were the two top sectors entering the month of April. Over the last week, energy and materials have reversed to the two weakest sectors. Right on cue, staples and healthcare have reversed to the two strongest. That suggests . . . that market sentiment has turned more defensive which usually suggests a market correction or a period of consolidation.

(April 14, 2011: StockCharts.com).

The point of that April 2011 article was to warn that the downturn in the relative performance of commodity-related stocks was a warning signal not only for commodities and the stock market, but suggested that a change in market leadership was about to take place. The trend changes that started during spring 2011 demonstrate that the downturn in commodity prices (and the upturn in the dollar) impacted virtually every other financial market and suggested a number of possible trading strategies to protect oneself against those trend changes, or to profit from them. One obvious strategy was to rotate out of commodities (and related stocks) and into defensive stock groups (which also pay dividends). Another strategy favored moving some funds out of stocks and into bonds (especially Treasuries). Another strategy might have been to buy some gold.

▪ Gold Stocks versus Gold

As you might expect, the direction of gold has a big impact on the direction of gold mining stocks (and vice versa). However, a change has occurred in their relationship since 2008. Prior to that year, gold stocks usually rose faster than the price of bullion during a bull market in the metal. That hasn't been the case since 2008. Although mining stocks have generally trended in the same direction as bullion, and have done better than the general market since 2008, they've been rising at a much slower pace than the commodity.

Figure 12.11 compares the price of the Market Vectors Gold Miners ETF (GDX) to the price of gold during the bull market in the commodity that started during 2002. The *GDX* is an ETF that includes a basket of precious metal stocks. Although it includes some silver stocks, most of its holdings are gold companies. It can be seen that both lines have risen over the decade since then. And both have done much better than the overall stock market. During the 10 years starting in 2002, gold and gold miners gained 484 percent and 429 percent, respectively, versus a 12 percent gain for the S&P 500 during the same decade. As is usually the case, gold miners did better than bullion in first few years of that decade.

---

the *GDX* is an ETF that includes a basket of precious metal stocks

---

STOCKS AND COMMODITIES BECOME HIGHLY CORRELATED

JOHN'S TIPS

A simple relative strength ratio is the best way to determine whether a gold or a gold-mining ETF is rising faster.

FIGURE 12.11   Miners have underperformed bullion since 2008

The line at the bottom of Figure 12.11 plots a ratio of the GDX divided by gold. The miners/bullion ratio actually started rising during 2001 and continued to rise into 2006. That's not unusual since gold miners often lead the metal higher in the early stages of a new bull market. The relationship changed, however, in a big way during 2008. A plunge in the miners/bullion ratio occurred during that year, when mining stocks fell nearly 30 percent while bullion held relatively flat. The ratio shows that miners have generally matched the performance of bullion since then. They did a little better than the commodity during 2009, but underperformed during 2011. There may be at least a couple of reasons why gold miners have done worse than gold.

Did You Know. . .?

The S&P 500 fell even further than the miners with a loss of 36 percent.

Gold Miners Are Stocks

One of the reasons that gold stocks have lagged behind bullion since 2008 may simply be the fact that miners are stocks. While it's true that they're tied to the price of gold, and benefit from rising gold prices, they're also common stocks. As a result, they're influenced by the direction of the stock market. They suffer when the stock market is weak. That may explain why mining stocks fell so much further than the commodity during 2008. It may also explain why gold stocks underperformed gold during 2011 in what was an unusually volatile year for the stock market, plagued by European debt problems.

It seems plausible that investors and central bankers have turned to gold as a hedge against global debt problems and economic weakness around the world. Gold's role as a currency has also increased its appeal at a time when paper currencies have become less desirable. The emergence of gold ETFs has also made the commodity more easily accessible to investors and institutional traders. In the past, stock investors bought gold-mining shares as a way to participate in a gold uptrend. Over the past few years, they've been able to buy bullion directly through ETFs traded right on the New York Stock Exchange. That may also have reduced the appeal of gold mining shares. It may take a stronger stock market to restore the luster of mining shares relative to the commodity. Or, it might be possible that the relative weakness in mining shares may be an early warning that the next decade might not be as kind to gold assets as the last decade. Either way, it's still a good idea for gold traders to keep an eye on gold-mining shares (and vice versa).

JOHN'S TIPS

Gold ETFs have made the commodity more accessible to stock traders and may have lessened the appeal of gold mining stocks.

Gold Shares Underperform Bullion during 2011

Figure 12.12 compares the Market Vectors Miners ETF (GDX) to the price of gold during 2011. It can be seen that the peaks and troughs in both generally occurred at the same time. It can also been seen, however, that the commodity did much better than the shares during that year. From the start of 2011 to the end of August, bullion rose 35 percent while the shares gained less than half (15 percent).

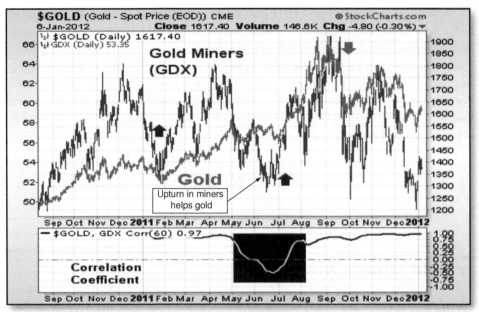

FIGURE 12.12 Comparison of gold and gold miners during 2011

A plunge in mining shares during September (aided by a surge in the U.S. dollar and a drop in the stock market) finally pulled bullion into a downside correction. During 2011, bullion gained 15 percent while mining shares lost 11 percent. At the start of 2012, both were trying to recover from that correction. There may be some possible lessons we can take from a comparison of gold and mining shares in the years since 2008.

One lesson is that they still trend in the same direction. Gold shares still offer a way for more conservative investors to participate in the gold market. Another lesson is that turns in both markets still take place at the same time. An upturn in gold usually has a positive impact on mining shares, and turns in mining shares also have an impact on the commodity. The first up arrow in Figure 12.12 shows miners turning up with gold near the start of 2011. The down arrow shows both turning down together during that September. The most revealing part of Figure 12.12, however, may be what happened between May and July.

JOHN'S TIPS

An uptrend in gold is stronger if gold miners are moving in the same direction.

■ Gold and Miners Relink during July

The Correlation Coefficient below Figure 12.12 shows a positive correlation between bullion and miners during most of 2011. A sharp drop in the correlation line, however, started during May, when shares fell much further than bullion, and resulted in an unusual *negative correlation* between the two (see box). Those negative correlations don't usually last long, and this one didn't. The coefficient turned positive at the start of July, which helped launch a strong rally in the commodity and mining shares. Although gold shares sometimes lag behind the commodity, gold usually does better when gold shares are rising along with it.

Dollar Direction Impacts Foreign Stocks

All of the trend changes that started in spring 2011 began with an upturn in the U.S. dollar (and a downturn in foreign currencies). That had a negative impact on commodity assets and the stock market. The dollar upturn, however, also had a very negative impact on foreign stocks during 2011. As a rule, foreign stocks do worse than U.S stocks when the dollar is rising. That's even truer of ETFs of foreign stocks. That helps explain why foreign stocks did so much worse than those in the United States during that year. I'll demonstrate those global trends in the next chapter when we extend our intermarket analysis into foreign markets.

CHAPTER 13

Stocks and the Dollar

This chapter explores the historical link between the U.S. dollar and the stock market. Over the last decade, the two markets have usually trended in opposite directions. That's due primarily to the fact that commodities and stocks have been positively correlated. The direction of the dollar also has an impact of the relative attractiveness of foreign stocks versus those in the United States. Commodities are closely linked to emerging markets. China influences the trend of copper and the U.S. stock market. A falling euro hurts European shares more than U.S. stocks. Foreign stock indexes bounce off 2010 lows to keep uptrends intact. Canada plays in important role in global intermarket relationships. How to add the Americas to your foreign stock portfolio will be explained.

A Weak Historic Link between the Two

The link between the U.S. dollar and the stock market is one of the most inconsistent intermarket links that I've studied. Historically, stocks have done well during periods of dollar weakness and dollar strength. My 2004 intermarket book suggested that the dollar's impact on stocks needed to be filtered through the commodity markets. A falling dollar, for example, can be bearish for stocks if it produces sharply higher commodity prices (as it did in the 1970s). A falling dollar can coexist with rising stock prices as long as rising commodity prices don't create an inflation problem. At the same time, a rising dollar can coexist with rising stocks as long as commodity prices don't fall into a deflationary trap (as happened during 1998 and 2008).

Did You Know. . .?

It could also be stated that a falling dollar is not a problem until its inflationary impact starts to pull interest rates higher, which is often the result of rising commodity prices.

A Long-Term Comparison of Stocks and the Dollar

Figure 13.1 compares the dollar and the stock market from 1984 to the start of 2012. One thing that becomes immediately clear is that there doesn't appear to be a consistent link between the two markets. An earlier chapter pointed out that a falling dollar during the 1970s was bearish for stocks

FIGURE 13.1 Long-term comparison of stocks and the dollar

since rising commodity prices caused an inflationary spiral that hurt bond and stock prices. A major dollar bottom in 1980 burst the commodity bubble, which led to major bull markets in bonds and stocks starting in 1981 and 1982, respectively. After bottoming in 1980, the dollar rose for five years before peaking in 1985 (first down arrow). The 1985 dollar plunge resulted from the Plaza Accord, a five-nation agreement designed to drive down the price of the U.S. currency. The dollar remained in a downtrend for the next seven years until 1992. Stocks rose throughout that period. The dollar turned up in 1995 and rose for another seven years until 2002 (up arrow). Stocks rose during that period as well.

JOHN'S TIPS

Dollar influence on the stock market needs to be filtered through the commodity markets.

It's too simplistic, however, to suggest that the dollar had no negative effect on stocks during those 20 years. That's where commodity prices enter the intermarket equation. Dollar drops during 1986 and 1989 caused upward spikes in commodity prices, which led to bear markets in stocks during 1987 and 1990 (first two circles). The 1994 bear market in stocks followed another drop in the dollar and an upturn in commodity prices (third circle). A sharp jump in the dollar during 1997 (resulting from the Asian currency crisis) pushed commodity prices to a 20-year low, which hurt stock prices around the world. Our main concern in this chapter, however, is with events that have transpired over the last decade, starting in 2002. The vertical line in Figure 13.1 shows that stocks and commodities became negatively correlated during that year, and have remained so since then. That's where I'll pick up the story.

FIGURE 13.2 Stocks and the dollar have trended inversely over the last decade

Stocks and the Dollar Become Negatively Correlated

Figure 13.2 shows the dollar and the S&P 500 trending in opposite directions since 2002. You may recall from an earlier chapter that a falling dollar during 2002 caused a major upturn in commodity prices. Stocks hit bottom during the fourth quarter of that year and turned up the following spring. The inverse link between stocks and the dollar started during the fourth quarter of 2002 but didn't become a major factor until spring 2003 (see circle). From spring 2003 until the end of 2011, the two markets trended in opposite directions. The stock rally between 2003 and 2007 was accompanied by a falling dollar. A dollar bottom during 2008 coincided with a tumble in stocks (see arrows). The 2009 to 2011 uptrend in stocks took place while the dollar fell. The Correlation Coefficient at the bottom of Figure 13.2 shows the negative correlation between the two markets over the last decade. I believe that the inverse link between stocks is explained largely through the commodity markets.

JOHN'S TIPS

Throughout the last decade, a falling dollar has been supportive to rising stock prices.

The Commodity Impact on the Dollar-Stock Link

I suggested earlier in the chapter that the dollar's impact on stocks needs to be filtered through commodity markets. Once commodities are added to the equation, the inverse link between stocks and the dollar makes more sense. The previous chapter explained that global deflationary concerns over the last decade caused stocks and commodity prices to become more closely correlated, especially after 2008. Since commodities and the dollar have maintained an *inverse* correlation over that decade (and commodities are *positively* correlated to stocks), it stands to

FIGURE 13.3 Dollar upturn during 2011 contributed to stock peak

reason that stocks would trend *inversely* to the dollar as well. (In other words, stocks and commodities have both trended opposite to the dollar.) That implies that the dollar's *negative* correlation to stocks will remain intact until the *positive* correlation between stocks and commodities weakens.

■ The Dollar Bottom during 2011 Hurts Stocks

Figure 13.3 compares the dollar and stocks during 2010 and 2011 and shows both markets traveling in opposite directions. The dollar peak during summer 2010 led to market upturn shortly thereafter. By contrast, a dollar bottom starting in spring 2011 coincided with a peak in the S&P 500 (see arrows). The stock market tumble during August was followed by an upside breakout in the dollar a month later (see circles). The correlation coefficient below Figure 13.3 confirms the negative correlation between the two markets throughout 2011. The correlation line turned positive at the start of 2012 (see circle) as both markets entered that year rallying together. That dollar bounce, however, had more to do with euro weakness than actual dollar strength.

Did You Know. . .?

Commodities peaked slightly ahead of stocks as a result of the dollar upturn.

JOHN'S TIPS

The euro is the heaviest weighted currency in the Dollar Index and has the biggest influence on dollar direction.

The Dollar Impact on Foreign Stocks

This chapter has three goals. The first is to discuss the impact of dollar trends on the U.S. stock market, which we've already done. A second is to demonstrate that global markets are highly correlated. In other words, they rise and fall together. That's why American investors need to know what's going on in foreign markets (and foreign investors need to know what's going on in the United States). The trends in foreign markets have a strong influence on trends in the United States. While global stock markets rise and fall together, however, they don't necessarily do so at the same pace. Some markets rise faster than others, and some fall faster. The dollar has a lot to do with that. The third goal of this chapter is to demonstrate the important influence that the dollar has on the relative performance of foreign stocks versus those in the United States.

The Rising Dollar Hurts Foreign Shares More than U.S.

One of the decisions American investors have to make is how much of their funds to allocate to foreign markets. In order to make that decision correctly, it's important to follow the trend of the U.S. dollar. A falling dollar benefits foreign shares, while a rising dollar benefits the U.S. market. Figure 13.4 shows how that has worked since 2000. The price bars show the trend of the U.S. Dollar Index. The solid line is a *ratio* of the *MSCI World Index—ex USA* divided by the S&P 500. That ratio shows how foreign stocks did *relative* to the U.S. stock market. The *MSCI World Index—ex USA* includes ten of the largest foreign developed and emerging markets.

the **MSCI World Index—ex USA** includes ten of the largest foreign developed and emerging markets

Notice that the two lines in Figure 13.4 have trended in opposite directions. Foreign stocks outperformed U.S. stocks (rising ratio) between 2002 and 2008 as the dollar fell (see arrows). Starting in 2008, however, a stronger dollar has caused foreign shares to do worse than the U.S, which caused

FIGURE 13.4 Rising dollar since 2008 has hurt foreign stocks more than the United States

the ratio to drop (see arrows). That weaker performance by foreign shares was especially noticeable during 2011. While the S&P 500 ended that year basically flat, foreign developed markets (outside of North America) lost nearly 12 percent, while emerging markets fell an even steeper 18 percent. That bigger 2011 loss in emerging markets had something to do with the drop in commodity markets, which resulted from a stronger dollar throughout most of that year.

> **JOHN'S TIPS**
>
> A rising dollar causes commodities to weaken, which, in turn, weakens emerging markets tied to commodities.

Commodities Are Linked to Emerging Markets

Another rule of thumb in international markets is that a close linkage exists between emerging markets and commodity prices. Two of the most notable examples of that are Brazil and China. As a result, not only do the trends of those two markets influence commodity direction (and vice versa), it also means that both of those emerging markets are closely linked to each other. Figure 13.5 shows Brazil and China iShares peaking together during spring 2011 (as the dollar bottomed), with both losing more than 30 percent by October. The solid matter demonstrates the influence that both of those markets had on the CRB Index, which lost 20 percent. Part of the reason for their influence is simply their size. Brazil and China are the world's two largest emerging markets. Their influence on commodity prices (and each other), however, results from differing roles. While Brazil is one of the world's biggest *exporters* of commodities, China is the world's biggest *importer* of those same commodities. A lot of those Brazil exports go to China. That makes China the world's biggest driver of global demand for commodities.

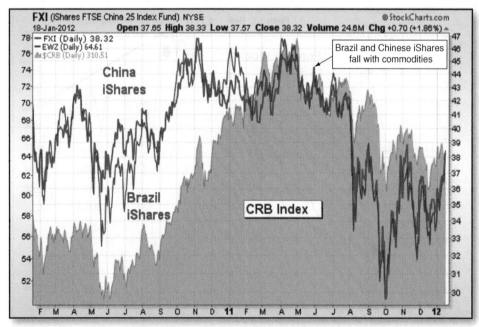

FIGURE 13.5 Brazil and China iShares fell with commodities during 2011

China Influences Copper Trend

The previous chapter mentioned China's influence on the price of copper. That influence can be clearly seen in Figure 13.6, which compares the China iShares (FXI) to the price of copper between 2008 and 2012. It's clear that they rise and fall together. After bottoming together at the start of 2009 (see circle), both markets rallied together until the end of 2010. A peak in the Chinese market started during the fourth quarter of 2010 and was followed a few months later by a copper peak. The fact that the Chinese market turned down first demonstrates one of the benefits of intermarket work: When two markets are highly correlated, and one of them turns down, it's usually an early warning that the other one will turn down as well. That made China iShares a leading indicator for copper.

JOHN'S TIPS

The price of copper is very much influenced by economic reports on the state of the Chinese economy.

It also makes economic sense that Chinese stocks would turn down before copper. The Chinese central bank started to tighten monetary policy in an attempt to combat an inflation problem in that country. That caused Chinese shares to weaken. The resulting slowdown in the Chinese economy reduced demand for global commodities, including copper. That explains why commodity traders need to keep a close eye on the Chinese stock market, since its direction has a big influence on the direction of commodity prices like copper. The previous chapter showed that the price of copper is closely correlated to the U.S. stock market. Since China influences the price of copper, it also influences the U.S. stock market.

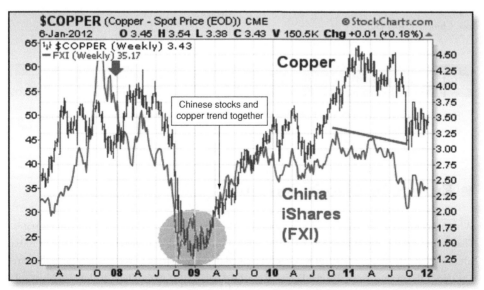

FIGURE 13.6   Direction of Chinese stocks influences price of copper

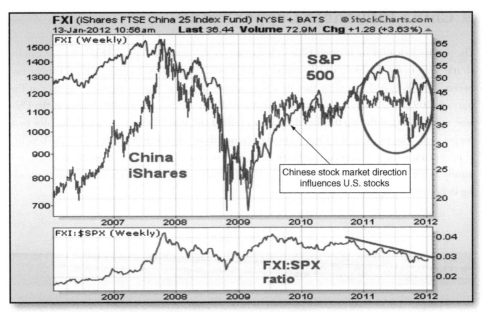

FIGURE 13.7   Chinese stocks underperformed the U.S. during 2011

Chinese Stocks Influence the S&P 500

A more direct connection can be seen between China iShares and the S&P 500 in Figure 13.7. Both peaked together during 2007, rose together during 2009, and fell together during 2011 (see circle). But Chinese shares turned up several months before the S&P 500 at the end of 2008, and peaked several months before the S&P 500 during 2011. That's why it's important to chart foreign stock markets. That's especially true of one as important as China. The ratio below Figure 13.7 divides China iShares (FXI) by the S&P 500. The ratio measures the *relative* performance between the two stock markets. The ratio shows China outperforming the United States during 2006 and early 2007, underperforming during 2008, and outperforming during 2009. The ratio also shows the Chinese market underperforming the S&P 500 from the fourth quarter of 2010 to the end of 2011 (see trendline). Since China has such a big influence on the global economy, it seems safe to assume that the rest of the world does better when Chinese stocks are leading it higher. Global stocks do worse when they lose Chinese leadership.

JOHN'S TIPS

Emerging markets generally rise faster than other global markets during an uptrend, and fall faster during a downtrend.

Europe Is Also Important

What happens in Europe is also important for other global stock markets, including the United States. That was clearly demonstrated during 2011, when European debt problems in a number of EMU countries (and the threat of default by Greece) pushed the euro sharply lower. The plunge in the euro was one of the main reasons that the U.S. dollar rallied during that year. While all global markets suffered downside corrections that year, Europe was one of the hardest hit.

STOCKS AND THE DOLLAR

FIGURE 13.8   Falling EAFE/S&P ratio was caused by falling Euro

Figure 13.8 compares the trend of the euro to a ratio of EAFE iShares (EFA) divided by the S&P 500. EAFE iShares include stocks in European, Australasian, and Far Eastern markets. However, its largest weighting is in Europe (57 percent). Its biggest country weighting is the United Kingdom (22 percent), with an additional 35 percent allocated to other European stocks. It should come as no surprise, then, to see the falling euro having a negative impact on the relative performance of EAFE iShares.

Did You Know. . .?

Europe's 57-percent weighing in the EAFE Index matches the euro's 57-percent weight in the U.S. Dollar Index.

The close correlation between the two lines in Figure 13.8 seems pretty clear. The EAFE underperformed the United States during the first half of 2010 (when the euro fell) and during 2011 when the euro fell again (see circle). From the end of April 2011 to that October, EAFE iShares fell 25 percent, versus 19 percent for the S&P 500. Two of the biggest countries in the EAFE Index, Germany and France, lost more than 30 percent (while Italy fell 38 percent). While all global stock markets fell during those six months during 2011, the falling euro hurt European stocks more than those in the United States.

JOHN'S TIPS

Foreign problems usually drive global funds into U.S. assets like the dollar, Treasury bonds, and stocks.

■ Currency Trends Impact Foreign ETFs More

While a rising dollar causes foreign stocks to underperform the United States, it hurts foreign ETFs even more. Foreign stock ETFs get hit on two fronts. One is because foreign stocks weaken along

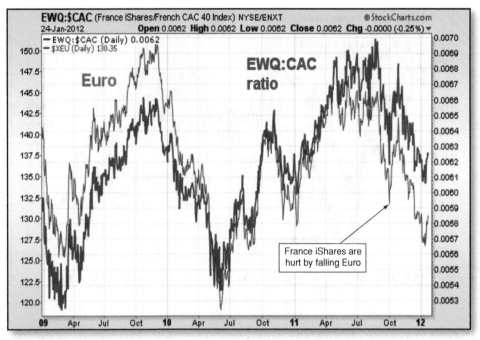

FIGURE 13.9   Falling euro hurts France iShares more than the CAC Index

with their currencies. A second is that a rising dollar causes foreign ETFs to fall faster than their local cash market. That's because foreign stock ETFs are traded on U.S. stock exchanges and are quoted in U.S. dollars. Foreign stock markets are quoted in their local currency. An entity quoted in a stronger currency (like the dollar) will fall faster than an entity quoted in a weaker currency (like the euro). Figure 13.9 shows a close correlation between the trend of the euro and a ratio of France iShares divided by the French CAC Index. The two lines trend together. In other words, the iShares did better than the cash index (rising ratio) when the euro was rising. iShares did worse when the euro fell. Between the spring 2011 top through the following January, the euro fell 12 percent. During those nine months of euro weakness, France iShares lost 26 percent, versus 20 percent for the CAC cash index of French stocks. The bigger drop in the iShares was the direct result of the weaker euro. It works in the other direction as well. A rising euro (or any foreign currency) would cause its stock ETF to rise faster than its cash market.

■ France iShares Hold 2010 Support

The difference in the performance between the iShares and their related cash stock index has important charting implications as well. That's because the effects of currency trends are more directly filtered through the iShares. As a result, foreign stock ETFs often give a truer picture of the trend of a foreign market. That's especially relevant for American investors who are most directly impacted by movements in the U.S. dollar.

JOHN'S TIPS

American investors get a double benefit when a foreign stock market rise is accompanied by a rise in its local currency.

FIGURE 13.10 Comparison of France iShares and CAC Index

Figure 13.10 compares France iShares (EWQ) to the French CAC Index from the start of 2009 to the start of 2012. Both indexes fell during the first half of 2010, along with the euro. The second downturn during 2011 occurred during the second euro crisis. Notice, however, that the France iShares stayed above their spring 2011 lows (see trendline), while the CAC cash index fell below that previous support level. A *support level* is a previous correction low. The two charts gave conflicting messages. The breakdown in the CAC Index was a negative sign for the French market. The ability of the iShares, however, to bounce off that support level was a more encouraging sign for the French market. Those successful tests of support had a positive impact on a regional ETF based on stocks in the European Monetary Union (EMU).

a **support level** is a previous correction low

Did You Know. . .?

German and Spanish iShares also stayed above their spring 2010 lows.

EMU iShares Diverge from Euro

Figure 13.11 compares the euro (solid matter) to EMU iShares (EZU). Figure 13.11 is an example of the type of clues that an intermarket analyst might look for by comparing the trend of the euro (solid matter) to EMU iShares (EZU) entering 2012.

FIGURE 13.11   Positive divergence between EMU iShares and euro

There are two things of note in Figure 13.11. The first is the fact that the EMU iShares are bouncing off the chart support formed during the summer of 2010 (see arrows). That's important because the EMU region was *ground zero* during the global debt problems that surfaced during 2011. The ability of the EMU fund to stay above that support level raised hopes that the euro crisis might be contained.

Figure 13.11 also shows both lines rising and falling together between 2009 and 2012. Both bottomed together in the middle of 2010 (first up arrow). To the far right of Figure 13.11, the chart shows the EMU iShares bouncing off support while the euro has continued to drop into the start of 2012. That created a *positive divergence* between the two lines. The ability of the EMU to stay above its 2010 correction low suggested that the euro selloff was overdone.

JOHN'S TIPS

A *positive divergence* is created when one market starts to rise while another positively correlated market is still dropping.

EAFE and Emerging iShares Stabilize at End of 2011

For investors looking to invest in foreign markets, two of the most popular indexes are EAFE iShares (EFA) and Emerging Markets iShares (EEM). As already explained, the MSCI EAFE Index is based on stocks in 10 of the world's largest *developed* markets in Europe, Australasia, and the Far East. The

FIGURE 13.12 Foreign stock ETFs bounce off spring 2010 support

EAFE is considered to be the main benchmark for foreign *developed* markets. Emerging Markets iShares (EEM) includes stocks in 10 of the world's largest *emerging* markets. Its two biggest holdings are China (17 percent) and Brazil (15 percent). An investor can get a pretty good idea of what's happening abroad by charting those two ETFs.

JOHN'S TIPS

The same charting rules apply to markets all over the world.

Figure 13.12 charts those two foreign stock indexes in the three years since 2009. It's clear that they generally trend in the same direction (which supports the intermarket premise that global stock markets are highly correlated). The two indexes of *developed* and *emerging* foreign stocks have held above their spring 2010 lows (see shaded box). Both will need to build on those gains during 2012 to confirm that a bottom was formed in late 2011. At the very least, both ETFs need to stay over their 2011 lows. Any failure to do so would have very negative implications for stocks all over the world, including those in the United States

Don't Forget about Canada

When looking abroad for trading opportunities, one country that's often overlooked is Canada. That doesn't seem like a good idea, considering that Canada has been one of the world's top performing markets. Over the last decade, Canadian stocks gained 60 percent versus only 14 percent for the S&P 500. Canada is the largest trading partner with the United States, which may explain why Canadian stocks are highly correlated to the U.S. stock market. Canadian stocks are also closely tied to trends in currency and commodity markets. That gives Canada a unique role in the analysis of global intermarket trends.

FIGURE 13.13   Canadian dollar holds up better than the euro

■ The Canadian Dollar versus the Euro

The Canadian dollar is one of only two foreign currencies in the U.S. Dollar Index not tied to Europe. While the Euro carries a 57-percent weight in the Dollar Index, an additional 23 percent is allocated to the British pound, Swedish krona, and Swiss franc. European currencies account for three-quarters of the Dollar Index. The only non-European currencies are the Japanese yen (13 percent) and Canadian dollar (9 percent). That gives the Canadian dollar a role in measuring non-European currency trends, and it doesn't always tell the same story as the euro.

JOHN'S TIPS

The Canadian dollar is more influenced by commodity trends.

Figure 13.13 compares the Canadian dollar to the euro between 2009 and 2012. Although both generally trended in the same direction, there have been wide discrepancies between their relative gains and losses. The two most notable discrepancies took place during 2010 and again during 2011 (see circles). From the fourth quarter of 2009 to the middle of 2010, the euro lost 20 percent, versus a 6-percent loss for the Canadian dollar. From spring 2011 to the end of that year, the euro fell twice as much as the Canadian currency (13 percent versus 6 percent). Upturns in the two currencies, however, usually take place around the same time. The summer 2010 upturn in the euro helped end a minor pullback in Canada. Both then rallied together into 2011 before peaking together that spring.

To the right of Figure 13.13, you'll notice that the Canadian dollar (top line) bottomed during the fourth quarter of 2011 and entered 2012 on a positive note. The euro, however, continued to drop. That created a divergence between the two currencies. If the early 2012 bounce in the Canadian currency continues, that would suggest that the euro is due for a rally as well. Whichever direction the Canadian currency takes from there will have an impact on several other markets during 2012.

STOCKS AND THE DOLLAR

■ Canadian Markets and Commodities

The direction of the Canadian dollar has important implications for the Canadian and U.S. stock markets, as well as commodities. Canadian stocks have a close historical correlation to U.S. stocks. There's also a close historic correlation between the Canadian dollar and Canadian stocks. Both are closely tied to fortunes of commodity markets. Canada is one of the world's biggest exporters of natural resources. Canadian companies that produce energy and basic materials make up half of the Toronto Stock Index. The three markets are, therefore, highly correlated.

JOHN'S TIPS

The direction of the Canadian dollar tells us a lot about the direction of global currencies, stocks, and commodities.

The two solid lines in Figure 13.14 show the Canadian dollar and Canada iShares (EWC) from 2008 through the start of 2012. The close correlation between the two is obvious. The solid matter in Figure 13.14 shows that the CRB Commodity Index usually trends in the same direction as the Canadian Dollar and Canadian stocks. They fell together during 2008, bottomed together near the start of 2009, and rose together into spring 2011. All three markets then corrected together. During the fourth quarter of 2011, all three markets hit bottom together and entered 2012 on more stable footing. The close linkage between the three markets in Figure 13.14 makes Canada an important barometer for global stock, commodity, and currency trends. A bet on Canadian stocks is a bet on global stocks. It's also a bet on the future trend of commodity markets. A rising Canadian dollar would help support both of those trends.

Did You Know. . .?

The Australian dollar is another currency closely tied to commodities. Australia's location in the Pacific Rim also links it to China, which is a big buyer of Aussie commodities. Global traders view the direction of the Aussie dollar as a barometer of trends in that region.

■ How to Add the Americas to Your Foreign Portfolio

Investors wishing to invest abroad can use some combination of EAFE iShares and Emerging Markets iShares. There are, however, a couple of foreign ETFs that offer a form of one-stop shopping for foreign diversification. My favorite is the Vanguard All-World Ex-US ETF (VEU). The VEU includes stocks in 46 foreign countries from developed and emerging markets. One of main benefits of the VEU is that it includes Canada (which is excluded from EAFE iShares). Canada is the second-biggest holding in the VEU (7 percent). A second benefit of the Vanguard fund is that it allocates 25 percent to emerging markets, which includes a 4-percent weighting in Brazil. By combining the world's largest foreign developed and emerging markets, the VEU offers investors a more comprehensive collection of developed markets and a more conservative way to hold emerging markets.

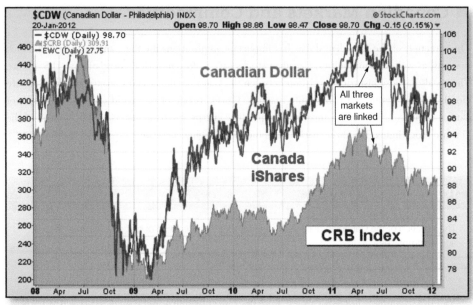

FIGURE 13.14 Close correlation between Canadian markets and commodities

Figure 13.15 compares the performance of the Vanguard All-World Ex-US (VEU) to EAFE and Emerging Markets iShares since 2009. The chart shows the VEU trading in between the other two.

FIGURE 13.15 Comparison of EAFE and EEM iShares to Vanguard ex-US ETF

FIGURE 13.16   Brazil and Canada outperform EAFE iShares

From the start of 2009 to the start of 2012, the EEM was the strongest (77 percent), while EFA was the weakest (27 percent). The Vanguard ex-US fund came in right between the other two (42 percent).

Figure 13.16 shows two reasons why EAFE iShares did worse than the VEU over those three years. Two of the world's best performers since 2009 were Brazil (110 percent) and Canada (71 percent). EAFE iShares include neither one. Another foreign ETF that offers the same choices as the VEU is MSCI ex-US fund (ACWX). That fund did better than the EAFE over the same three years, but lagged behind the VEU. There's no reason to exclude markets in the Americas from your foreign portfolio.

Test Yourself

Answer the following questions.

1. A falling dollar causes commodity prices to _____.

   a. Rise

   b. Fall

   c. Has no effect

2. Gold is viewed as a _____.

   a. Commodity

   b. Currency

   c. Commodity and currency

3. Since 2002, a falling dollar has usually been _____.

   a. Good for stocks

   b. Bad for stocks

   c. Has no effect

4. A rising dollar has the biggest benefit for _____.

   a. Foreign stocks

   b. U.S. stocks

   c. Has had no effect

5. Canadian stocks are closely linked to _____.

    a. U.S. stocks

    b. The Canadian dollar

    c. Commodity prices

    d. All of the above

Answers: **1.** a   **2.** c   **3.** a   **4.** b   **5.** d

CHAPTER 14

The Link between Bonds and Stocks

This chapter covers the important link between the bond and stock markets. It shows how the positive link between bond yields and stocks has existed over the last decade, and how falling bond yields have usually led to lower stock values. Falling bond yields, and lower stock prices, favor dividend-paying stocks, many of which are considered to be defensive in nature. That includes consumer staples and utilities, both of which do better in a climate of rising stock market volatility. Not all bond categories are the same. High-yield corporate bonds act more like stocks than bonds. It's possible to lose money in bonds. The effects of Quantitative Easing and Operation Twist on markets and the yield curve will be studied. TIPS and gold often trend together. Stocks and bond yields diverge at start of 2012. The asset allocation pendulum favors stocks over bonds entering 2012.

179

▪ The Two Markets Compete for Investor Funds

The relationship between bonds and stocks is a very important link in the intermarket chain. Those two markets continually compete for investor funds. When investors are optimistic about economic trends, they favor stocks. When they're pessimistic, they favor bonds. Investment portfolios generally include both asset classes, but not always to the same degree. A standard portfolio usually allocates 60 percent to stocks and 40 percent to bonds. As one grows older, it's advisable to reduce the stock portion and increase the bond allocation. Older investors have less time to recover from a major stock market selloff. While younger investors may be more interested in growth (through stocks), older investors are usually more interested in income (through bonds).

It's important to be able to chart the paths of both asset classes, and to understand how they interact with each other. There are times when it makes sense to overweight bonds, and other times when it's better to overweight stocks. In order to do that, however, it's important to know how to chart the two asset classes and how to compare their relative performances. It's also important to understand the economic forces that drive their relative performance. That includes some understanding of actions taken by the Federal Reserve to influence interest rate direction and asset allocation choices.

Chapter 9 pointed out that the stock market is broken down into sectors and industry groups, which do better at different stages of the business cycle. The same is true of bonds. It's important to know that there are several different bond categories that do different things at different times. Treasury bonds, for example, are usually stronger when the stock market is falling and investors are worried about the economy. High-yield corporate bonds do better when the stock market is rising and the economy looks stronger. This chapter will show how you can compare the trends of those different bond categories by utilizing fixed income *exchange-traded funds (ETFs)*.

> ### JOHN'S TIPS
>
> High-yield corporate bonds and Treasury bonds can even trade in opposite directions.

■ The Positive Correlation between Bond Yield and Stocks

Chapter 3 explained how the relationship between bonds and stocks changed after 1998. Prior to that date, falling bond yields (rising bond prices) were generally positive for stocks. After 1998, that relationship reversed. Since 1998, falling bond yields (rising bond prices) have generally been bad for stocks. I expressed the view in that earlier chapter that deflationary pressures over the last decade were the main reason for that newer relationship between the two markets.

Figure 14.1 shows the positive link between the trend of the 10-Year Treasury note yield and the S&P 500 since 2000. Notice, for example, that sharp downturns in the bond yield either preceded downturns in stocks (as in 2000 and 2007) or coincided with them (see circle and arrows). Chapter 4 showed bond yields peaking in January 2000, eight months before stocks peaked that September. Chapter 6 showed bond yields peaking in June 2007, four months before stocks peaked that October. Bond yields also led stocks lower during 2011, which we'll examine shortly. Plunging bond yields are usually symptomatic of a deflationary environment. Bond yields also fell throughout the Great Depression. Stocks don't usually do that well in a deflationary environment. Attempts by the Federal Reserve Board to combat deflation are also partially responsible for historically low interest rates over the last decade.

FIGURE 14.1 Comparison of stocks and bond yield over last decade

Bond Yield Leads Stocks Lower during 2010 and 2011

Figure 14.2 gives a closer look at the two markets between 2009 and 2011. Again, a positive correlation can be seen between the S&P 500 and the yield on the 10-Year Treasury note. Both rallied together from the start of 2009 to spring 2010. (The first up arrow shows the bond yield turning up first near the end of 2008.) The first down arrow shows the bond yield dropping sharply during spring 2010, which led to a downside correction in stocks. Both then rose together into spring 2011 (second up arrow). The bond yield peaked again during the first quarter of 2011 and fell sharply during the second quarter (see falling trendline). Stocks started falling six months later.

Figure 14.3 gives a closer look at the two markets during 2011 and offers a lesson in how to blend intermarket principles with traditional charting. The yield on the 10-Year T-note peaked that February and fell throughout that summer (see arrows). The S&P 500 starting peaking around the same time, but didn't actually enter a downside correction until that August. The three circles in Figure 14.3 show three peaks forming in the S&P 500 during February, May, and July. Chartists will recognize that chart pattern as a *head-and-shoulders top*. A *head-and-shoulders* top is identified by three prominent peaks, where the middle peak (the head) is slightly higher than the two surrounding peaks (the shoulders). A trendline (called a neckline) is drawn below the two intervening lows. The pattern is complete when prices fall below the neckline, which occurred during August.

a **head-and-shoulders top** is identified by three prominent peaks, where the middle peak (the head) is slightly higher than the two surrounding peaks (the shoulders)

> **JOHN'S TIPS**
>
> This is an example of how intermarket analysis adds another dimension to traditional chart analysis.

FIGURE 14.2   Bond yield led stocks lower during 2010 and 2011

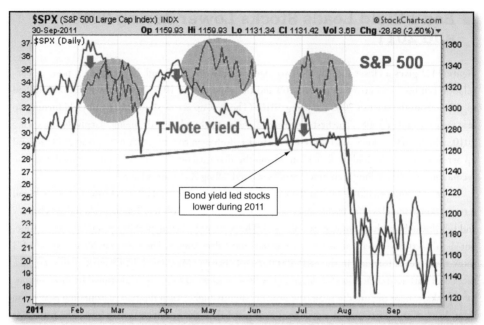

FIGURE 14.3 Fall in bond yield during 2011 warned of stock correction

While the *head-and-shoulders* pattern described previously should have been recognizable to chartists at the time, its bearish warning was further enhanced by the fact that the bond yield was also breaking down. Stocks finally broke down that August, six months after the bond yield peaked. That's a good example of how some knowledge of intermarket principles can be blended with traditional chart analysis. That drop in bond yields during the first half of 2011 also had an impact on sector rotations within the stock market. For one thing, it contributed to a rotation into defensive stock sectors like consumer staples and utilities. It also contributed to a rotation into dividend-paying stocks, which includes both of those defensive groups.

JOHN'S TIPS

Falling bond yields, and a weak stock market, usually drive money into defensive market categories that also pay dividends.

■ The Falling Bond Yield Boosts Dividend-Paying Stocks

Chapter 9 showed the rotation out of economically sensitive stock sectors (like basic materials and energy) that took place during the spring of 2011 and into defensive sectors like consumer staples, health care, and utilities. Part of that rotation was simply a defensive maneuver to protect stock holdings against a potential market downturn. Another factor driving money into those three sectors

Did You Know. . .?

The three defensive sectors (staples, healthcare, and utilities) generally hold up better than other stocks during a downside correction.

was that they are among the market's highest dividend payers. That makes them even more attractive when bond yields are plunging to near-record lows. Income investors search for higher yields. When bond yields are falling, they can often find higher yields in dividend-paying stocks.

Figure 14.4 compares the yield on the 10-Year Treasury note to a ratio of Dow Jones Dividend iShares (DVY) divided by the S&P 500. Both lines trended in opposite directions in Figure 14.4. Each down arrow in the bond yield between 2009 and 2011 was accompanied by an upturn in the DVY/SPX ratio (up arrows). In other words, dividend-paying stocks started to outperform the S&P 500 each time bond yields started dropping during those three years. The most dramatic example of that rotation was visible during 2011, when the February peak in the bond yield (last down arrow) turned the DVY/SPX ratio sharply higher (last up arrow). Dividend-paying stocks were the biggest winners during that unusually volatile year for stocks. That was because dividend-paying stocks also thrive on rising volatility.

Did You Know. . .?

The DVY invests in stocks that pay consistently high dividends.

Consumer Staples and Utilities Thrive on Rising Volatility

Rising volatility usually has a negative effect on most stocks. Some stock sectors, however, benefit from rising volatility. One of them is consumer staples. That happens for two reasons. One is that consumer staples are defensive in nature (since they're not tied to the ups and downs of the business cycle). Another reason for their popularity when volatility rises is because they pay dividends. Dividends cushion the blow from a falling stock market resulting from rising volatility.

FIGURE 14.4   Drop in bond yield boosts dividend-paying stocks

Figure 14.5 is a ratio of the Consumer Staples SPDR (XLP) divided by the S&P 500. The shaded portion represents the CBOE Volatility (VIX) Index. The VIX measures implied volatility for options on the S&P 500. *The VIX* is often referred as the *fear gauge*. The VIX usually trends in the opposite direction of the S&P 500. Therefore, a rising VIX usually coincides with a weaker stock market. Figure 14.5, however, shows a positive correlation between the VIX Index and the *relative* performance of consumer staples. That was especially true during the bear market years from 2000 through 2002, and again during 2008, when a spiking VIX pushed money into defensive stocks (resulting in a rising ratio). It was also true during 2011, when consumer staples were one of that year's strongest sectors. So were utilities.

the **VIX** is often referred as the *fear gauge*

JOHN'S TIPS

Since rising volatility usually results in a weaker stock market, money usually rotates into defensive market sectors.

Figure 14.6 compares a ratio of the Utilities SPDR (XLU) divided by the S&P 500 to the CBOE Volatility (VIX) Index (shaded matter) during 2011. There again, a positive correlation can be seen between the two lines. That was especially evident during that August, when a spiking VIX Index coincided with a sharp drop in U.S. stocks (up arrow). The sharp jump in the utilities/SPX ratio reflected nervous money pouring into dividend-paying utility stocks. Utilities were that year's top sector. The down arrow during October 2011 shows the ratio starting to drop during that fourth quarter as the VIX receded (and the S&P 500 rebounded). That more bullish combination during the fourth quarter caused money to start flowing out of utilities and other defensive sectors. You can buy the VIX through an *exchange-traded note (ETN)* to hedge against a falling stock market. A rising VIX is also a good time to buy defensive dividend stocks.

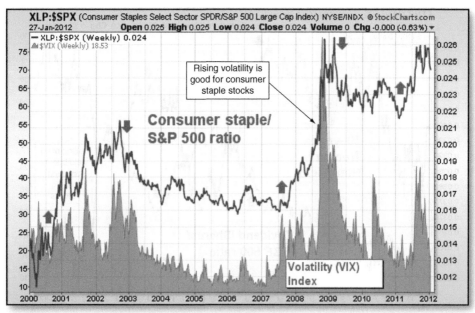

FIGURE 14.5 Rising VIX helps performance of consumer staples

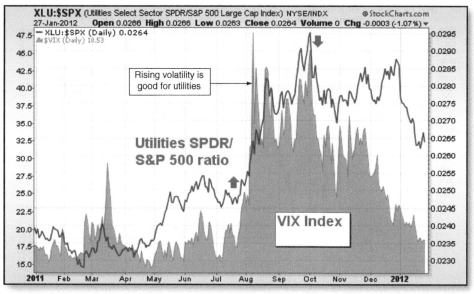

FIGURE 14.6 Rising VIX during 2011 gave boost to utilities

Not All Bonds Are the Same

When discussing bonds, it's important to recognize that not all bonds are alike. In fact, there are at least a half-dozen bond categories that include Treasuries, investment-grade and high-yield corporate bonds, municipal bonds, Treasury Inflation Protected Securities (TIPS), and foreign bonds. And they don't always trend in the same direction. High-yield bonds, for example, act more like stocks than bonds.

Figure 14.7 shows a remarkably close correlation between High Yield Corporate Bond iShares (HYG) and the S&P 500 between 2008 and 2011. It's clear that they generally rose and fell together during those four years. They fell together during 2008, rose together during 2009 and 2010, and fell together during 2011.

> **JOHN'S TIPS**
>
> A rising stock market increases investors' appetite for riskier bond categories like high-yield (junk) bonds.

The correlation coefficient line below Figure 14.7 shows strong positive correlation throughout that period. The reason for their close correlation is based on the fact that high-yield corporate bonds are highly dependent on the fortunes of corporations that issue those riskier bonds. High-yield (or junk) bonds are also considered to be *risk-on* assets. In other words, investors are more inclined to buy junk bonds when they're optimistic enough to assume more risk. The same is true with investment-grade corporate bonds, but to a lesser extent.

While high-yield bonds are more closely correlated to stocks, investment-grade corporate bonds act more like hybrids between stocks and bonds. They are tied to the fortunes of corporations that issue them. They are, however, also sensitive to interest rate trends. That puts investment-grade corporate bonds somewhere between bonds and stocks. They have some characteristics of both. Investment-grade corporates are sensitive to the direction of bond yields, but not as much as Treasuries. They're also sensitive to stock trends, but not as much as high-yield

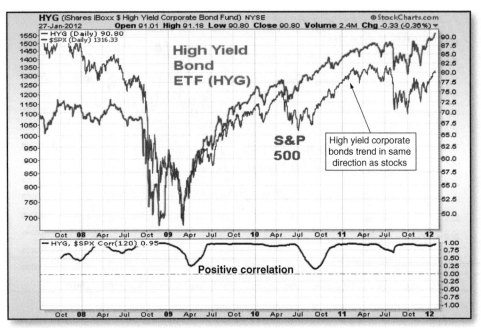

FIGURE 14.7 High-yield bonds track stocks very closely

bonds. When investors are more optimistic about the stock market and the economy, they usually favor corporate bonds over Treasuries. High-yield corporates do best of all when the stock market is rising.

Figure 14.8 compares a ratio of High Yield Bond iShares (HYG) divided by Investment Grade Corporate Bond iShares (LQD) to the S&P 500 (shaded matter) from 2007 through the start of 2012. It seems clear that the two lines trend in the same direction. In other words, riskier high-yield (junk) bonds fall further than investment-grade corporates when the market is weak (like

---

Did You Know. . .?

High-yield bonds are issued by corporations that do not qualify for investment-grade ratings by leading credit agencies. Those issuers must pay a higher interest rate to compensate for the greater risk of default.

---

during 2008 and again during 2011), but rise faster than investment-grade bonds when stocks are rising (2009 and 2010). Bond investors are willing to assume more high-yield corporate bond risk when a rising stock market implies higher corporate earnings. By contrast, they favor the more conservative investment-grade portion when the stock market is weak. Stock market direction also helps determine whether bond investors prefer investment grade corporates over Treasury bonds.

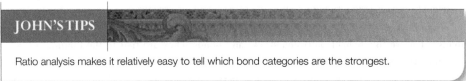

JOHN'S TIPS

Ratio analysis makes it relatively easy to tell which bond categories are the strongest.

Figure 14.9 compares a ratio of Investment Grade Corporate Bond iShares (LQD) divided by 7- to 10-Year Treasury Bond iShares (IEF) to the S&P 500 over the same four years as the previous ex-

FIGURE 14.8 High-yield outperforms investment-grade corporate bonds in rising market

ample. Again, the two lines trend in the same direction. In other words, investment-grade corporates underperform Treasury bonds when the stock market is weak (2008 and 2011), and do better than Treasuries when the stock market is rising (2009 and 2010). That also makes sense. When investors are scared, they gravitate to Treasuries, which are viewed as the safest of bonds. When investors see a rising stock market and feel more confident about corporate profits, they gravitate toward riskier corporate bonds. It's also important to understand that different bond categories can actually lose money under the wrong conditions.

FIGURE 14.9 Investment-grade corporate bonds outperform Treasuries in rising market

FIGURE 14.10   Comparison of high-yield and Treasury bonds in good and bad years.

Did You Know. . .?

The TLT offers the longest maturity bond ETF, which makes it the most volatile Treasury offering. The TLT is the most sensitive to the direction of bond yields and stock market, and trends in the opposite direction of both.

■ Some Bond Prices Can Trend in Opposite Directions

Figure 14.10 compares the actual price trends of High Yield Corporate Bond iShares (HYG) and 20+Year Treasury Bond iShares (TLT) during 2008 and 2009. Their diverging trends can be seen very clearly during those two years, and demonstrate that each bond category can act very differently in good and bad years. While the S&P 500 was falling 46 percent during 2008, high-yield corporate bonds lost 30 percent (first down arrow). Treasury bond prices rose 35 percent (first up arrow) during that period of severe stress (shaded area).

JOHN'S TIPS

Those numbers show that investors can actually lose money in bond funds.

The two bond categories reversed roles after the stock market rallied in early 2009. Treasury prices started to tumble at the start of 2009 (second down arrow) while high-yield bonds turned sharply higher (second up arrow). The long Treasury bond lost 20 percent during 2009, while high-yield bonds gained 30 percent. The shaded area along the bottom of Figure 14.10 shows investment-grade corporate bonds falling during the second half of 2008 (losing 20 percent at one point), which was still less than high-yield bonds. Investment-grade corporate bonds also rallied during 2009 (10 percent), but not as much as their high-yield counterparts.

Figure 14.10 demonstrates that investors can lose money in bonds—even in Treasuries. Of all the bond categories, longer-maturity Treasuries are the most vulnerable to rising bond yields. That hasn't been a problem over the last deflationary decade of falling yields, but could become one in the years ahead when rates eventually start to rise.

Did You Know. . .?

Bond ETFs are based on bond *prices*. Bond *prices* trend inversely to *yields*. When bond *yields* rise, bond *prices* fall.

Here are some guidelines to keep in mind regarding bonds. In a rising stock market, high-yield and investment-grade corporate bonds usually do better than Treasuries (and in that order). In a weak stock market, Treasuries are the safest place to be, and high-yield bonds the riskiest. Investment-grade corporates will usually fall somewhere in between the other two. The existence of exchange-traded funds (ETFS) for all bond categories makes it easier to chart their trends and to measure their relative performance. ETFs also make it much easier to switch between various bond categories to adjust to changing market conditions.

JOHN'S TIPS

The trend of the stock market is an important factor in deciding which bond categories to favor.

■ Quantitative Easing

The Federal Reserve has embarked on three rounds of quantitative easing since the end of 2008. *Quantitative easing* is an unconventional monetary policy used by central banks to stimulate the economy when conventional monetary policy hasn't worked. Normally, the Federal Reserve's main tool for battling deflation is to lower short-term rates. When short-term rates fall to zero, however, the Fed can't lower them any further. In that instance, it can try to stimulate the economy by buying assets of longer maturities in an attempt to lower rates further out on the yield curve. In late November 2008, the Fed launched its first round of quantitative easing by starting to buy $600 billion in mortgage-backed securities. By June 2010, when purchases were halted, the Fed held $2.1 trillion of bank debt, mortgage-backed securities, and Treasury notes. In November 2010, the Fed announced a second round of quantitative easing (called QE2), which involved buying $600 billion of Treasury securities by June 2011. A third round (QE3) was announced on September 13, 2012.

---

quantitative easing is an unconventional monetary policy used by central banks to stimulate the economy when conventional monetary policy hasn't worked

FIGURE 14.11 Impact of quantitative easing on bond yield and stocks

The Impact of Quantitative Easing on Bonds and Stocks

Figure 14.11 shows the impact the first two rounds of quantitative easing had on bonds and stocks. The first vertical bar marks the start of QE1 during the fourth quarter of 2008. Bond yields started rising almost immediately, and were followed by an upturn in stocks a few months later*. The second vertical bar marks the start of QE2 in November 2010. In that instance, bond yields and stocks rose as well. When bond yields rise, bond prices fall. That helps drive money out of bonds and into stocks. Commodity prices rose as well. Immediately after QE1 and QE2 were launched, the U.S. dollar fell sharply and commodities rallied, based on the fear that the injection of too much money into the system would ignite inflation pressures. By the middle of 2011, bond yields started falling sharply again and took stocks with them. That reignited fears of a slowing economy and more deflationary pressures. The Fed then acted a third time, but with a slightly different approach. In September 2011, the Fed responded by announcing the start of Operation Twist.

Operation Twist

During the two rounds of quantitative easing, the Fed acquired $1.65 trillion of federal bonds. Most of those bonds matured in two years or less. In other words, the Fed's growing portfolio of bonds had the effect of lowering short-term rates, but had less impact on long-term bond yields. *Operation Twist* involved the Fed's selling some of its shorter dated holdings and buying more long-term bonds. That would have the effect of driving bond yields lower. The goal was to lower longer-maturity bond yields, which would lead to lower lending rates for businesses and individuals, including lower rates for car loans and mortgages.

* In March 2009, the Fed expanded its mortgage buying program, which gave an added boost to the stock market.

The third vertical line in Figure 14.11 marks the start of Operation Twist in September 2011. As had happened earlier with QE1 and QE2, stocks rallied right after it was announced. Bond yields, however, entered 2012 relatively flat. That also contributed to a flattening of the yield curve.

The Yield Curve

The *yield curve* measures the difference between short- and long-term interest rates. The most common way to measure the yield curve is to plot the difference between 10-year and two-year Treasury rates. When the yield curve is normal, long-term rates are higher than short-term rates. The slope of the yield curve is usually caused mainly by movement in short-term rates, which is controlled by the Federal Reserve. Long-term rates are more influenced by inflationary or deflationary expectations. An *inverted* yield curve occurs when short-term rates exceed long-term rates, and is a danger sign for the stock market and the economy. The yield curve usually *steepens* during a recession as the Fed lowers short-term rates in an attempt to stimulate the economy. During an economic recovery, the yield curve normally starts to *flatten* as short-term rates start to rise faster than long-term rates (or long-term rates fall faster than short-term rates). It's that latter scenario that explains the drop in the yield curve during the second half of 2011.

Thr Impact of Quantitative Easing on the Yield Curve

Figure 14.12 plots the yield spread between the 10-year and two-year Treasury notes, which is the most common way to measure the yield curve. The chart shows that the yield curve steepened after QE1 and QE2 (see arrows). That was the result of a rise in the 10-year yield. The yield curve dropped sharply during the third quarter of 2011, however. That was the result of a sharp drop in Treasury bond yields as money poured into Treasury bonds to offset a weakening stock market.

Did You Know. . .?

Debt problems in the Eurozone also drove global fixed income funds into the relative safety of U.S. Treasuries, as bond prices plunged in weaker European countries and bond yields spiked higher.

FIGURE 14.12   Impact of quantitative easing on yield curve

Figure 14.12 shows that the spread between short and long-term rates stayed relatively flat into the start of 2012 (see circle). That suggested that Operation Twist had some success in achieving the Fed's goal of lowering the long end of the yield curve in an attempt to stimulate the economy. It also appeared to have had the effect of driving investor funds into higher-yielding (and riskier) assets like common stocks, high-yield bonds, and commodity currencies at the start of the new year. That may have helped global stocks get off to a strong start in 2012.

Bond Yield and Stocks Diverge at the Start of 2012

One of the consistent intermarket trends that has existed over the past decade has been the positive link between bond yields and stocks. Over that deflationary decade, falling bond yields usually led to falling stock prices. Figure 14.13, however, shows a divergence between those two markets that existed at the start of 2012 (see trendlines). While the 10-Year Treasury note yield stayed relatively flat during January, the S&P 500 rallied strongly. (Note: The bond yield and stocks recoupled during the second quarter of 2012. The S&P 500 dropped 10 percent while the 10-Year yield fell below 1.5 percent for the first time in history. Stocks bottomed during June and bond yields a month later. By September 2012, both were rising together.)

JOHN'S TIPS

The first quarter of 2012 saw the strongest performance for U.S. stocks since 1998.

Another sign of a growing appetite for risk at the start of 2012 was a 7 percent jump in emerging-market currencies and stocks. That growing optimism was based partially on the Fed's January 2012

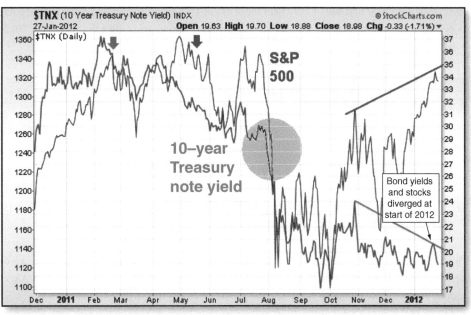

FIGURE 14.13 Bond yield and stocks diverge at start of 2012

announcement that it intended to keep short-term interest rates near zero through the end of 2014. That announcement caused both bond and stock prices to jump (and pushed bond yields even lower). (Note: During that second quarter, emerging market currencies and stocks fell as money left riskier assets [stocks and commodities] for the safety of U.S. Treasuries and the dollar. Those riskier assets rebounded again during the third quarter of 2012.)

TIPS and Gold Rise Together

Immediately after the Fed's January 2012 announcement, Treasury Inflation Protected Securities (TIPS) were among the strongest bond gainers. Another market that rose sharply after the Fed announcement was gold. One of the goals of quantitative easing was to help ensure that inflation did not fall below target. In other words, it was intended to keep deflation at bay. One of the risks was that the Fed's battle against deflation might go too far (or last too long), and eventually lead to higher inflation. That may explain why two of the strongest performing assets since the start of QE1 have been gold and Treasury Inflation Protection Securities (TIPS).

Figure 14.14 shows a close correlation between TIPS iShares (solid line) and the price of gold (solid matter) from the start of 2010 to the start of 2012. Shortly after the Fed announced the extension of its zero-interest-rate policy for the next three years in January 2012, TIPS iShares (TIP) rose to the highest level in a decade. At the same time, gold experienced its strongest January in 32 years. The strong action in those two markets suggested that some investors were hedging their bets against the possibility that the unusually accommodative stance of the Fed (and other central bankers) would eventually lead to higher inflation. (Note: The two markets diverged shortly thereafter. While falling

---

Did You Know. . .?

TIPS offer bondholders added protection by adjusting principal payments for inflation.

bond yields during the first half of 2012 kept the prices of TIPS rising, the surging dollar pushed gold 15 percent lower during that second quarter. Both markets rose together after the September 2012 launch of QE3.)

The Pendulum Swings Back to Stocks at the Start of 2012

Chapter 6 demonstrated how to use ratio analysis to help determine whether bonds or stocks were the stronger asset class. It showed the pendulum swinging back to stocks at the start of 2009. After favoring stocks for the following two years, the pendulum swung back to bonds during 2011.

Figure 14.15 plots a ratio of the 10-Year Treasury note price divided by the S&P 500. The ratio peaked at the start of 2009 (down arrow) and fell until the end of 2010. The falling bond/stock ratio favored stocks during those two years. The ratio turned up sharply in the middle of 2011 and broke a two-year trendline (up arrow) in the process. That year was better for bonds (especially Treasuries) than stocks. That wasn't the case at the start of 2012.

Figure 14.16 gives a closer look at the same Treasury note/S&P 500 ratio entering 2012. It shows the upturn in the ratio during July 2011 when bond prices rose and stocks fell (up arrow). The ratio peaked, however, that October (down arrow) and signaled that the pendulum had swung back to stocks. The chart shows the ratio falling below its October low, which confirmed the asset allocation shift in favor of stocks entering 2012. (Note: The ratio shifted in favor of bonds during that second quarter as stocks corrected downward, before shifting back in favor of stocks during the third quarter. Through the middle of August 2012, stocks outgained 10-year Treasury prices by 12 Percent.)

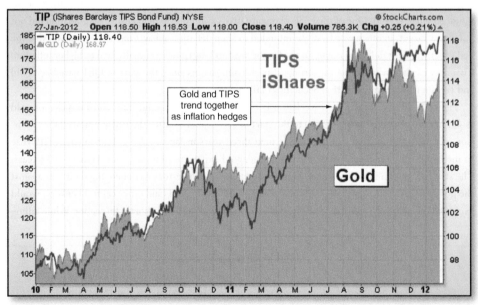

FIGURE 14.14 Gold and TIPS rise together as inflation hedges

FIGURE 14.15   Bond/stock ratio favored bonds during 2011

JOHN'S TIPS

Rising bond yields, and falling bond prices, encourage investors to rotate out of bonds and into stocks.

FIGURE 14.16   Bond/stock ratio favors stocks at start of 2012

■ The Fed Launches QE3

On Thursday, September 13, 2012, the Fed launched its third round of Quantitative easing (QE3), which entailed the monthly buying of $40 billion mortgage-backed securities (which are mortgages backed by Fannie Mae, Freddie Mac, and Ginnie Mae). That was in addition to the $45 billion a month of bonds the Fed was buying under Operation Twist, which was extended until the end of the year. The Fed also extended its pledge of near-zero short-term rates until the middles of 2015. (That came a week after the European Central Bank announced an ambitious program of buying an unlimited amount of government bonds.) Market reactions to QE3 were similar to what happened during QE1 and QE2. The dollar fell to a four-month low as foreign currencies rose. Gold led surging commodities to a six-month high. The Dow Industrials rose to the highest level since December 2007, while the Nasdaq reached a new 12-year high. High-yield corporate bonds rose to new highs along with stocks. TIPS also rose as a hedge against higher inflation. By contrast, the 30-year Treasury bond suffered its worse drop in three years as its yield jumped to a four-month high. QE3 helped strengthen intermarket relationships. Stocks and commodities rose together during Septmeber as the dollar fell. Rising stock and commodity prices helped push Treasury bond prices lower and yields higher. QE3 also helped restore the normal relationship between stocks and bonds. Stocks and T-bond yields rose together (as T-bond prices fell).

CHAPTER 15

The Link between Bonds and Commodities

This chapter explores the link between the bond and commodity markets. Bond and commodity prices normally trend in opposite directions. The 30-year bull market in bonds started shortly after the 1980 peak in commodity prices. Copper is the commodity most closely linked to bond prices and yields. You'll find out what comprises the Thomson Reuters/Jefferies CRB Index. The CRB/Treasury bond ratio helps determine which of the two markets is stronger. That ratio also has an influence on stock market direction, sector rotations, and the direction of emerging markets. Conflicting trends in two Asian giants may help explain how commodity inflation has coexisted with bond deflation

197

■ One of the Traditional Relationships

The previous three chapters examined the *inverse* link between commodity prices and the dollar, the *positive* link between stock and commodity prices, and the *inverse* link between bond and stock prices. This chapter will deal with the last of the intermarket links, which is the relationship between bonds and commodities. This is one of the simplest of the traditional intermarket relationships. Over the last decade, however, deflationary tendencies have dampened the normal relationship between the two markets somewhat. Since 2002, commodity *inflation* has coexisted with interest rate *deflation*, which is somewhat unusual. Some ideas have already been offered in previous chapters as to why that happened, one having to do with the Federal Reserve's attempts to boost commodity inflation by weakening the U.S. dollar. It was argued in Chapter 5, for example, that the major commodity upturn that started during 2002 was a direct result of the Fed's battle against deflation (by weakening the dollar in order to *reflate* the economy). This chapter will offer a couple of other explanations as to why rising commodity prices over the last decade didn't have the normal effect of pulling bond yields higher. But let's start with the normal relationship that usually exists between bond and commodity prices.

◼ Bond and Commodity Prices Normally Trend in Opposite Directions

Treasury bond prices are very sensitive to the threat of inflation. Rising commodity prices are viewed as a leading indicator of inflation. As a result, an *inverse* relationship usually exists between bond and commodity prices. In other words, bond and commodity prices normally trend in *opposite* directions. Rising commodity prices normally cause Treasury bond prices to fall. Falling commodity prices normally result in higher bond prices.

Did You Know. . .?

We're talking here about bond *prices*. Bond *prices* and bond *yields* always trend in *opposite* directions. As a result, commodity prices and bond *yields* normally trend in the *same* direction.

JOHN'S TIPS

Bond *prices* and bond *yields* are *inversely* correlated.

◼ The 30-Year Bond Rally Started with the 1980 Commodity Peak

During the inflationary decade of the 1970s, rising commodity prices resulted in falling Treasury bond prices (and rising bond yields). That all changed with a major peak in commodity prices during 1980 that ushered in a two-decade period of disinflation. *Disinflation* refers to a situation when consumer prices are rising at a *slower* pace. During the last two decades of the 20th century, falling commodity prices resulted in rising bond prices.

---

disinflation refers to a situation when consumer prices are rising at a slower pace

---

Figure 15.1 shows Treasury bond and commodity prices trending in opposite directions between 1981 and 2001. The first down arrow shows the CRB Index peaking during 1980, which was followed one year later by a major upturn in Treasury bond prices (first up arrow). The following two decades saw rising bond prices and falling commodities. (That combination also produced higher stock prices.) A comparison of the up and down arrows during those 20 years also shows that turns in one market usually coincided with turns in the other, and in the opposite direction. A downturn in the CRB Index during 1984, for example, coincided with an upturn in bond prices (see arrows). An upturn in commodity prices during 1993 pulled bond prices lower. During 1997 and 1998, commodity prices tumbled to the lowest level in 20 years as a result of the Asian currency crisis. Plunging commodity prices during those two years pushed bond prices sharply higher. Their inverse relationship lasted into the new century.

◼ The Inverse Bond-Commodity Link between 2003 and 2006

Bond and commodity prices continued their inverse correlation during the first six years after 2000, with one exception. That exception took place during 2002. Figure 15.2 compares the two markets

Chart labels:
$CRB (Reuters/Jefferies CRB Index (EOD)) INDX   © StockCharts.com
31-Dec-2001   Open 192.49 High 193.94 Low 187.73 Close 190.61 Chg -2.05 (-1.06%) ▾

$CRB (Monthly) 190.61
$USB (Monthly) 100.39

CRB Index

Treasury bond price

Bond and commodity prices trended in opposite directions

FIGURE 15.1   Inverse correlation between bond and commodity prices between 1981 and 2001

between 2002 and 2006. The circle area shows both markets trending higher during 2002, which was unusual. (I'll have more to say on why that happened shortly.) Starting in 2003, however, they reverted to their more normal inverse relationship. The first up arrow shows the CRB Index turning up during spring 2003, which coincided with a peak in bond prices (first down arrow). Between 2003 and 2006, rising commodity prices coincided with falling bond prices. A drop in the CRB Index during 2006 (second down arrow) helped produce a bond bounce (second up arrow). Their relationship changed again during 2007.

Did You Know. . .?

The drop in Treasury bond prices during 2003 also resulted from a major upturn in stock prices. Investors sold bonds to buy stocks and commodities.

JOHN'S TIPS

Changes to the normal bond/commodity relationship are usually caused by action in stocks or the dollar.

■ Why They Changed during 2007

Figure 15.3 compares the two markets between 2007 and 2012. You'll notice that both rose together during the second half of 2007 and the first quarter of 2008 before reverting back to their more normal tendency to trend in opposite directions. The reasons for their unusual action starting in mid-2007 were due to trends in two other markets: stocks and the dollar. As explained in Chapter 6, stocks started to fall sharply during the second half of 2007, which caused a major asset allocation

$UST (10-Year US Treasury Note Price (EOD)) INDX   @ StockCharts.com
29-Dec-2006   Open 107.48 High 107.48 Low 107.48 Close 107.48 Chg -0.12 (-0.11%) ▾

Treasury bond price

CRB Index

Rising commodity prices caused bond prices to fall

FIGURE 15.2   Inverse bond-commodity link between 2003 and 2006

shift out of stocks and into Treasury bonds. Aggressive Fed easing to stem the drop in stock prices (resulting from a meltdown in the housing market) also pushed interest rates lower (and bond prices higher). The dollar fell sharply as a result, which pushed commodity prices higher. As a result, bond and commodity prices rose together for three quarters starting in July 2007. It wasn't until the following July that a dollar bottom caused commodity prices to weaken.

The first down arrow in Figure 15.3 shows the CRB Index peaking in July 2008. During the second half of that traumatic year, a plunge in commodity (and stock prices) helped push Treasury bond prices sharply higher (first up arrow). From that point on, bond and commodities prices reverted to their more normal relationship. During 2009, a bottom in commodity prices (and stocks) resulted in falling Treasury prices (see arrows). A commodity bounce during the second half of 2010 saw a bond pullback. A commodity correction starting in the spring of 2011 (falling trendline) helped produce a strong year for Treasuries (rising line).

■ Copper versus Corn during 2002

Figure 15.2 showed bond and commodity prices rising together during 2002. I'd like to briefly return to that unusual year to explain why that happened. One reason was simply the fact that stock prices fell sharply during that year, which helped push bond prices higher. (Chapter 5 also explained that a plunging dollar during 2002 caused commodity prices to turn up before stocks, which was also unusual.)

FIGURE 15.3   Inverse bond-commodity link returns to normal during 2008

Another reason why bond and commodity prices rose together during the second half of 2002 was tied to which commodities did the rising. Figure 15.4 compares the price of corn and copper during 2002. You can see a discrepancy between the two commodities starting at mid-year. Between June and September, corn (and other grain) prices rose sharply as a result of drought conditions in the U.S. Midwest (up arrow). That sharp rise in grain prices gave a big boost to the CRB Index. Copper prices, however, fell during that third quarter (down arrow). Grain markets (which react to weather) were

FIGURE 15.4   Copper matches up with bonds better than corn during 2002

rising, while copper (which is more closely tied to the state of the economy) was falling. All it took to push the grain prices higher was the absence of rain. Copper needed some sign that the economy was getting better. Copper is a better economic indicator than corn. Copper is also a better predictor of bond trends. It appears that bond traders were less concerned by the weather-inspired rally in grain markets during the second half of 2002 and more concerned with the weak economic message being sent by a falling copper price. So they held on to their bonds in the face of a rising CRB Index.

JOHN'S TIPS

The price of copper is *positively* correlated to the trend in stock prices, and *negatively* correlated to bond prices.

Did You Know. . .?

Copper bottomed during October 2002, which is when stock prices also hit bottom. That's when bond prices started to weaken.

■ A Comparison of Copper and Treasury Bond Prices

Bond prices are closely tied to the direction of the economy. As a result, a weaker economy produces higher bond prices (and lower bond yields). Conversely, a stronger economy results in weaker bond prices (and stronger bond yields). Of the 19 commodities in the CRB Index, copper is the most closely tied to the economy. As a result, copper is very closely tied to the trend of the bond market.

FIGURE 15.5 Comparison of copper and Treasury bond price

Copper is also closely tied to the ups and downs of the global economy and stocks.

Figure 15.5 shows the generally inverse relationship between copper and Treasury bond prices that existed between 2000 and 2008. Copper prices fell (along with stocks) during 2001 as Treasuries rose. An upturn in copper during spring 2003 (first up arrow) coincided with a major peak in Treasury bond prices (first down arrow). A downturn in copper during the second half of 2006 (second down arrow) coincided with an upturn in Treasury prices (second up arrow). Both rose together from mid-2007 into early 2008 for reasons explained earlier (having to do with falling stocks and a declining dollar).

Stocks turned up with copper in spring 2003, which also caused money to rotate out of bonds and into stocks.

The circled area in Figure 15.5 shows the two markets diverging in a very dramatic way in mid-2008. During the second half of that year, copper prices plunged (along with stocks), while Treasury prices soared. Rising Treasury bond prices during 2008 and plunging copper prices were also symptomatic of recessionary conditions, which lasted throughout that entire year. So was the plunge in stock prices. During a recession, copper and stock prices usually fall along with interest rates. Treasury bond prices rise, which is exactly what happened. That bearish condition lasted into spring 2009, when all three markets experienced major turns in the opposite direction.

JOHN'S TIPS

Copper is an excellent indicator of the strength or weakness of the global economy.

The Copper Bottom during 2009 Contributed to the Bond Top

Although we're concerned in this discussion mainly with the link between copper and bonds, it's hard to separate those two markets from the stock market and the state of the global economy. When studying intermarket linkages between any two markets, it's important to remember that there are always other forces at work. We saw that during 2002, and again from the middle of 2007 to 2008, when bonds and commodities diverged from their normal inverse relationship. Their inverse link reverted back to normal in mid-2008 and remained intact into 2012.

Figure 15.6 shows copper and Treasury bond prices trending in opposite directions from mid-2008 into the first quarter of 2012. The Correlation Coefficient along the bottom of Figure 15.6 shows negative correlation between the two markets for most of that time period. The most dramatic turn is the plunge in Treasury prices during the first half of 2009 (first down arrow), which coincided with a copper upturn (first up arrow).

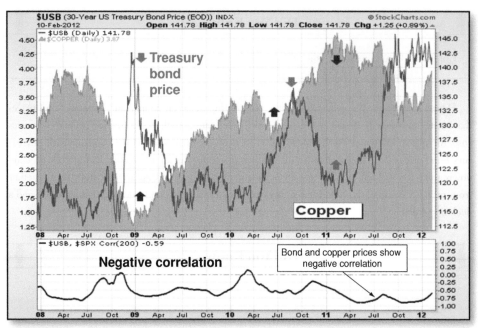

FIGURE 15.6 Inverse correlation between bond and copper prices since 2008

> **JOHN'S TIPS**
>
> This is another example of the value of financial markets in anticipating turns in the economy.

Treasury prices rallied during the first half of 2010 as copper prices corrected (see arrows). Heading into 2011, however, copper prices were again rallying while Treasuries were falling. During spring 2011, however, a downside correction in copper (and most other commodities) contributed to a major upturn in Treasury prices (see arrows). An earlier chapter described how a drop in commodity prices that spring gave warning that global stock markets were vulnerable to a downside correction, which followed shortly thereafter. A crisis in Europe that year also caused the Euro to tumble and the dollar to rise.

The combination of a rising dollar during 2011 and falling commodity prices resulted in a very volatile year for stocks. The rising dollar that year also caused foreign markets to fall further than U.S. stocks. Although U.S. stocks barely escaped a bear market (which requires a drop of 20 percent), most foreign stocks fell well below that bear market threshold. That was especially true of emerging markets like Brazil and China, which are tied to commodities. While commodity markets like copper lost ground during 2011, Treasury bonds had a very profitable year.

Commodities bottomed along with stocks during the fourth quarter of 2011, and entered 2012 on firmer footing. Stocks had one of their strongest annual starts in years. The U.S. dollar weakened

> **Did You Know. . .?**
>
> Stock prices turned up in the spring of 2009, which also caused the bond market to drop. The recession ended in the middle of 2009, which was several months after copper, stocks, and bond yields bottomed.

as the situation in Europe stabilized and the Euro rallied. The weaker dollar in early 2012 also gave a boost to foreign stock markets, which had fallen the most the previous year. Copper rallied as well. The Fed policy of buying longer-dated Treasuries kept bond yields depressed during the first quarter of 2012 in the face of rising stock and commodity prices. (Note: All of those trends reversed during the second quarter when another drop in the Euro (and a rising dollar) caused downside corrections in stocks and commodities (including copper) as Treasury bond prices rose. Those trends reversed again during the third quarter. Treasury bonds weakened as stocks and commodities bounced during the summer of 2012. The September launch of QE3 strengthened the trends of stocks and commodities as the dollar and Treasuries weakened.)

■ The Thomson Reuters/Jefferies CRB Index

Since the CRB Index plays such an important role in intermarket analysis, it's good to know exactly what it is and what's included in it. It is the most widely recognized barometer of trends in the commodity universe. It also has the longest history. The CRB Index was first published by the Commodity Research Bureau in 1958 and originally included 28 commodities. Since then, there have been 10 revisions to the commodity index. That last revision was done in 2005. The Thomson Reuters/Jefferies CRB Index now includes 19 commodities, all of which are traded on exchanges in the United States and London. The CRB Index formula includes commodity contracts that lie within six months of the current date.

The CRB groupings include energy (crude oil, heating oil, unleaded gasoline, natural gas), industrial metals (aluminum, copper, nickel), precious metals (gold, silver), grains (corn, soybeans, wheat), tropicals (cocoa, coffee, sugar), agricultural (cotton, orange juice), and livestock (cattle, hogs). The heaviest weighted commodity group is energy, which always makes up at least 33 percent of the CRB weighting. Crude oil has the single biggest CRB weight of 23 percent. Industrial metals and grains currently have equal weightings of 13 percent each. The two precious metals carry a combined weight of 7 percent (gold at 6 percent and silver at 1 percent). The two most widely followed groups are energy and metals (industrial and precious) because of their impact on inflation and interest rates, as well as global economic trends. (Although the complete name for the index is the Thomson Reuters/Jefferies CRB Index, most market followers use the shorter version (CRB Index).)

> **JOHN'S TIPS**
>
> Exchange-traded funds (ETFs) exist that allow traders to buy and sell a basket of commodities as well as commodity groups.

■ The CRB Index/Treasury Bond Ratio

One of the most useful intermarket indicators that I use is a ratio of the CRB Index divided by the Treasury bond price. I first introduced the CRB/bond ratio in my two earlier intermarket books, and I continue to find it extremely valuable. The most direct use of the ratio is to determine whether bonds or commodities are the stronger asset class at any point in time. But it also has a lot of other applications beyond those two markets, as you'll see in the following charts. Figure 15.7 plots a ratio of the CRB Index divided by the price of a 30-year Treasury bond over the last three decades. The commodity/bond ratio peaked in 1981 (first down arrow) and fell for the following 20 years. Between 1980 and 2000, the falling ratio signaled that Treasury bonds were the better place to be.

The second down arrow shows the ratio plunging during 1997 and 1998 as the result of the Asian currency crisis (which also favored bonds). The ratio also gives the trader a simple way to recognize when the relationship between the two markets is changing. That took place during 2002 when the CRB/bond ratio broke a falling trendline that had been in effect for two decades (see circle). Between 2002 and 2008, a rising ratio favored commodity assets over bonds. The third down arrow shows the collapse in the ratio that occurred during 2008, when commodities plunged and Treasuries soared. Let's pick up the story from there.

JOHN'S TIPS

The CRB/T-bond ratio is the simplest way to tell which asset class is the stronger at any point in time.

■ The Commodity/Bond Ratio Since 2008

Figure 15.8 plots the same CRB Index/30-year T-bond ratio from 2008 into early 2012. The trend-lines drawn on the chart make it easier to spot the turns. The first down arrow shows the ratio plunging in the middle of 2008 during the height of the financial crisis. Clearly, bonds were the preferred asset during the second half of that year. The first up arrow shows the ratio bottoming during the first quarter of 2009 and rising into spring 2011. The rising ratio signaled that commodities were the better market to be in during those two years. The second down arrow shows the pendulum swinging back to bonds during spring 2011. If nothing else, the CRB/bond ratio is a valuable way to measure the *relative* performance of Treasury bonds and commodities, and in deciding which one to favor. But there is something else: how the ratio influences the stock market.

FIGURE 15.7 Commodity/bond ratio over last three decades

FIGURE 15.8   Commodity/Treasury bond ratio since 2008

The CRB/Bond Ratio Influences Stocks

Figure 15.9 adds the S&P 500 (solid area) to the same CRB/bond ratio shown in the previous figure. The chart shows that the direction of the CRB/bond ratio also influences the direction of stocks. Both plunged during 2008 (first down arrow) and turned up together near the start of 2009 (up arrow). They then rose together until spring 2011, when both entered downside corrections (second down arrow). A rising CRB/bond ratio signals that commodity prices are stronger than bonds. Since stocks

FIGURE 15.9   Commodity/bond ratio influences stock market direction

are *positively* correlated to commodities and *inversely* correlated to bonds, a rising ratio has a positive influence on the direction of stocks. A falling ratio is negative for stocks because it implies that bond prices are rising and commodities falling. That makes the CRB/bond ratio a useful indicator for stocks. But that hasn't always been the case.

JOHN'S TIPS

A rising CRB/T-bond ratio also favors economically sensitive stock groups.

■ The History of Commodity/Bond Ratio Influence on Stocks

Figure 15.10 compares the CRB/Treasury bond ratio (solid line) to the S&P 500 (gray area) all the way back to 1990. The purpose of the chart is to show that the influence of the ratio on stocks changed over the last decade. Between 1990 and 1999 (to the left of the vertical line), a falling CRB/bond ratio was good for stocks. After 1999 (to the right of the line), a falling ratio was bad for stocks. The correlation coefficient line below Figure 15.10 shows *a negative* correlation between the ratio and stocks prior to 2000 and a *positive* correlation after 2000.

Chapter 3 explained that the deflationary threat after the Asian currency crisis caused a major decoupling of bond and stock prices (and a closer link between stocks and commodities). Prior to 1998, rising bond prices (and falling commodities) were good for stocks. Since 1998, rising bond prices (and falling commodities) have hurt stocks. The CRB/bond ratio provides us with a simple way to measure the intermarket relationships between the three markets. Since 1999, a rising CRB/bond ratio has been a positive indicator for stocks.

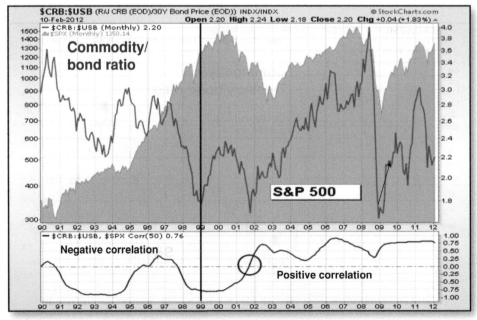

FIGURE 15.10 History of commodity/bond ratio influence on stock market

FIGURE 15.11   Rising CRB/bond ratio favors material Stocks

The CRB/Bond Ratio Also Influences Sector Rotation

Figure 15.11 compares the CRB/T-bond ratio (solid line) to a ratio of the Basic Materials SPDR (XLB) divided by the S&P 500 (solid area). The chart shows that the direction of the CRB/bond ratio also influences the *relative* performance of material stock prices. When commodities are rising faster than bonds (a rising CRB/bond ratio), material stocks usually outperform the stock market. There are two reasons for that. One is simply the fact that material stock prices are tied to the trend of commodity prices. A second reason is that material stocks are also economically sensitive, which means that they do better when investors are more optimistic about the stock market and the economy. (The same is true for other cyclical stock groups like small caps, consumer discretionary, industrial, transportation, and technology stocks.) Figure 15.11 shows that the ups and downs in the relative performance of material stocks were closely tied to the trend in the CRB/bond ratio between 2008 and 2012. The opposite is true of defensive stocks like utilities.

JOHN'S TIPS

A falling CRB/T-bond ratio favors defensive stocks.

Figure 15.12 compares the same CRB/bond ratio (solid line) to a ratio of the Utilities SPDR (XLU) divided by the S&P 500 (solid matter) between 2008 and 2012. You can the two ratios trending in *opposite* directions. Between spring 2009 and 2011, a rising CRB/bond ratio shows underperformance by utility stocks (first two arrows). During 2011, however, a drop in the CRB/bond ratio helped make utility stocks that year's strongest sector (second two arrows). Although the result in Figure 15.12 was the opposite of that in Figure 15.11, the reasoning is the same. When the CRB/bond ratio is rising, investors favor economically sensitive stock groups that benefit from a stronger economy. A falling CRB/bond ratio favors more defensive stocks groups like consumer staples and utilities. That makes the CRB/bond ratio a useful indicator for sector rotation purposes.

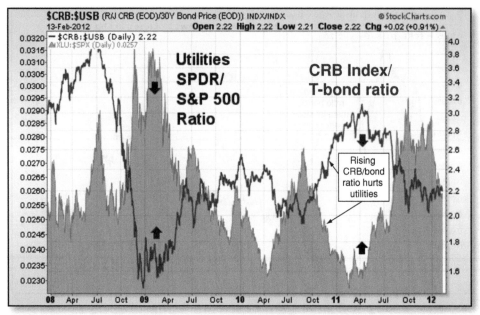

FIGURE 15.12   Rising CRB/bond ratio hurts rate-sensitive utilities

The CRB/Bond Ratio also Influences Emerging Markets

Figure 15.13 compares the same CRB/bond ratio to a ratio of Emerging Markets iShares (EEM) divided by the S&P 500 between 2008 and 2012. Again, a positive correlation can be seen between the two ratios. After falling during 2008, both ratios turned up at the start of 2009 and rose together through the end of 2010. Both ratios corrected downward during 2011 before stabilizing at the start of 2012. A rising CRB/bond ratio sends a positive signal to global traders. When global investors are

FIGURE 15.13   Rising CRB/bond ratio is tied to stronger emerging markets

optimistic, they're more inclined to invest in riskier emerging markets. Since emerging markets are more closely tied to the trend of commodity prices, a rising CRB/bond ratio also sends a signal to traders that the fortunes of emerging markets are improving. (Note: Both ratios weakened during the second quarter of 2012 before firming again over that summer.)

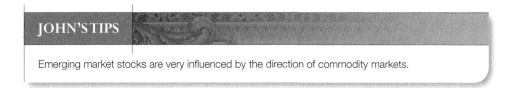

JOHN'S TIPS

Emerging market stocks are very influenced by the direction of commodity markets.

Another aspect of the CRB/bond ratio is its use as a *risk-on/risk-off* indicator. A rising CRB/bond ratio favors *risk-on* assets like commodities, commodity currencies, high-yield bonds, emerging markets, economically sensitive stocks, and stocks in general. A falling CRB/bond ratio favors *risk-off* assets like Treasury bonds, the U.S. dollar, and defensive stock groups. For all of the reasons discussed in this chapter, the CRB/bond ratio is a very useful intermarket indicator.

Commodity Inflation versus Bond Deflation

The preceding charts show that bond and commodity prices maintained an inverse relationship over most of the last decade. As a result, commodity prices and bond *yields* also showed a tendency to trend in the *same* direction most of that time. Bond yields, however, haven't kept pace with rising commodity prices. By the start of 2012, an unusually wide discrepancy existed between the two markets. Figure 15.14 compares the trend in the CRB Index to the 10-year Treasury note yield between 1980 and 2012. The two markets trended in the same direction prior to 2002 (left of vertical bar). Since 2002, however, commodity prices have diverged from the bond yield. That was especially true between 2002 and 2008. Bond yields rose with commodity prices between 2003 and 2007, but not

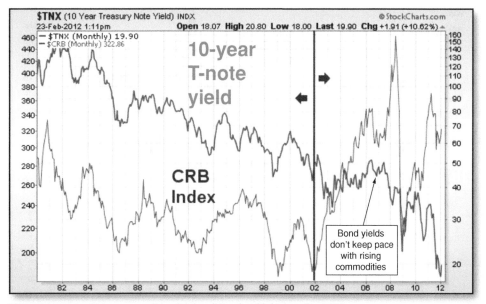

FIGURE 15.14 Rising commodities didn't pull bond yields higher after 2002

nearly as much. Although they diverged more noticeably again during 2010, both declined together during 2011. (Note: The divergence between the two assets was relieved even more during the second quarter of 2012 when a drop to record lows by the 10-year yield accompanied a 20 percent drop in commodity prices. Both then rose together during the third quarter.)

One reason for that discrepancy is that a weak decade for stocks helped push bond prices higher and yields lower. Another reason for bond yields staying low has been the unusually accommodative monetary policy by the Fed to combat deflation. That helped cause the boom in commodity prices, starting in 2002, resulting from the weaker dollar. The deflationary trend in housing after 2007 also had a depressing effect on bond yields and encouraged the Fed to push them even lower. The Fed has kept short-term rates near zero since December 2008. The first two rounds of quantitative easing, combined with the start of Operation Twist in the second half of 2011, contributed to the sharp drop in bond yields by the buying of massive amounts of Treasury securities. The jump in the money supply engineered by the Fed stoked inflation fears, which boosted commodity prices (and weakened the dollar). There may, however, be another explanation why bond yields stayed so low in the face of rising commodity prices. That has to do with competing trends coming from Asia.

Did You Know. . .?

Operation Twist bought longer-dated bonds to push bond yields lower.

FIGURE 15.15   Connection between rising Chinese stocks and commodities

Commodity and Bond Links to China and Japan

Figure 15.15 shows a strong correlation between the Hong Kong stock market and the CRB Index over the last decade. China has been the world's biggest importer of commodities over that decade. It could be argued that commodity inflation is largely tied to an emerging China (which had to tighten monetary policy in order to combat that inflation by the end of the decade). The opposite is true of Japan. Japan's GDP price deflator (a measure of price trends) turned negative in 1998 and remained that way into 2012. That has resulted in 15 years of Japanese deflation.

Figure 15.16 shows a strong correlation between the falling Japanese stock market and the 10-year T-note yield since 2000. It could be argued that Japanese deflation is one of the reasons for the deflation in Treasury bond yields. China and Japan are the world's second- and third-largest economies. One of them is battling inflation, while the other is battling deflation. It doesn't stretch the imagination to suggest that those competing trends in the two Asian giants help explain the coexistence of commodity *inflation* and Treasury yield *deflation* in the United States.

Summary

This chapter ends the fourth and final part of the book. Chapter 11 demonstrated the strong tendency for the U.S. dollar and commodity prices to trend in opposite directions. Chapter 12 showed how stock and commodity prices have become more closely correlated, especially since 2008. Chapter 13 explained the inverse relationship between stocks and the U.S. dollar over the last decade. Chapter 14 examined the inverse link between bond and stock prices. This chapter explored the relationship between bonds and commodities. The linkages covered in those five chapters include all of the major intermarket relationships that currently exist between the four asset classes that are bonds, stocks, commodities, and currencies. Deflationary trends over the last decade have changed some of the

FIGURE 15.16 Connection between falling Japanese stocks and bond yields

traditional relationships that existed during the second half of the 20th century. The current relationships explained in Part IV comprise the *new normal* in intermarket relationships as they exist today.

Those newer relationships will be listed again in the Conclusion, along with some final thoughts on the role intermarket analysis plays in technical market analysis. The Conclusion will also offer some final thoughts on whether the Fed's policy of keeping rates so low for so long is helping or hurting the stock market. History may hold some clues to that answer. The book will end with a glance at some current charts to see what clues they might hold for the coming decade.

Test Yourself

Answer the following questions.

1. Treasury bond and stock prices usually trend _____.
   a. In the same direction
   b. In the opposite direction
   c. There's no correlation between the two

2. High-yield (junk) bonds usually trend _____.
   a. In the same direction as Treasury bonds
   b. In the same directions as stocks

3. Corporate bonds usually outperform Treasuries when stock prices are _____.
   a. Rising
   b. Falling

4. Rising commodity prices usually cause Treasury bond prices to _____.
   a. Rise
   b. Fall

5. A rising CRB/T-bond ratio is usually _____.
   a. Good for stocks
   b. Good for economically sensitive stocks
   c. Bad for defensive stocks
   d. All of the above

ANSWERS:

1. b   2. b   3. a   4. b   5. d

Conclusion

It's All about Relationships

Intermarket analysis is all about relationships. All of the charts included in this book are designed to show how closely related all financial markets are and, more importantly, how that information can be used to improve the forecasting process.

I hope I've succeeded in convincing you that intermarket analysis is also an increasingly important part of technical analysis. Correlations between the various financial markets over the past few years have gotten so strong that it's nearly impossible to understand what's happening in any one market without knowing what's also happening in all of the other markets. The four main markets I'm referring to are bonds, stocks, commodities, and currencies. But it goes further than that. Intermarket analysis plays an important role in asset allocation and sector rotation strategies, both of which are tied to the business cycle. Exchange-traded funds (ETFs) have greatly facilitated the application of intermarket strategies and have made it much easier to keep track of everything.

The influence of foreign stocks also plays a crucial role in the U.S. stock market. Global stock markets are highly correlated. It's dangerous to analyze the U.S. stock market without looking at trends in foreign markets. A financial crisis in the Eurozone has a ripple effect on the trend of the U.S. dollar, commodity prices, Treasury bonds, and the S&P 500. Trends in large emerging markets like Brazil and China also have a big influence on commodity and stock prices. Tune in to any TV business show during the day and you'll get a recap of market events all over the world. What happens *there* impacts what happens *here*.

Fortunately, it's not that hard to keep track of all those markets. All you need is an Internet web site that gives you the ability to chart global markets, and some basic chart reading skills. You don't have to be a charting expert. Most important trend changes are pretty easy to spot. But you have to make sure that you actually *see* those trend changes. In order to do that, you have to look at charts. In addition to some basic chart reading skills, you'll also need some understanding of the basic principles of intermarket analysis. The following is a recap of the most important intermarket principles and relationships.

■ Recap of Intermarket Principles

The basic intermarket principles are these:

■ All global markets are linked to each other.

■ Analysis of any one market should include analysis of the others.

The four asset classes include:

■ Stocks, bonds, commodities, and currencies.

Intermarket relationships:

■ The dollar and commodities trend in opposite directions.

■ Bond prices and commodities trend in opposite directions.

■ Since 1998, bond and stock prices have trended inversely.

■ Since 2008, stocks and commodities have been more closely correlated.

How they interact:

■ Bonds usually change direction before stocks.

■ Stocks usually change direction before commodities.

■ Bond yields peak first, stocks second, and commodities last.

■ Those rotations are more reliable at tops than at bottoms.

Foreign influence:

■ All global stocks are closely correlated.

■ A weaker dollar favors foreign stocks.

■ A stronger dollar favors U.S. stocks.

■ Emerging markets are closely tied to commodity trends.

■ The New Normal in Intermarket Relationships

Although the basic intermarket principles covered in this book remain pretty constant over time, they do sometimes change. When they do change, however, there's usually a reason why. Since the Asian currency crisis that started in 1997, the threat of global deflation has changed some key intermarket relationships. The housing collapse during 2007 and 2008 reinforced that deflationary threat. The major intermarket changes that took place over the last decade are listed below:

■ Since 1998, bond and stock prices have trended in opposite directions.

■ Stock and commodity prices have become more highly correlated, especially since 2008.

■ Stocks and the U.S. dollar have been negatively correlated.

There is, of course, no guarantee that those *new normal* intermarket relationships will continue throughout the coming decade. The threat of deflation after 1998 was the main reason for those newer relationships. There's a possibility that the huge amount of excess liquidity being pumped into the global economy by central bankers will eventually result in higher inflation. That may cause some of the intermarket relationships to shift again to adjust to that new environment. The visual tools shown in this book, however, should help you to spot if and when that happens.

■ Fed Policy May Be Interfering with Normal Bond/ Stock Relationship

Since 2008, the Federal Reserve has embarked on a series of measures to keep interest rates at historically low levels. Three rounds of quantitative easing, plus Operation Twist, were designed to push Treasury bond yields lower and keep them depressed. That was done to boost business and consumer borrowing, and to help revive the housing industry. One goal of that policy has been to encourage investors to move money out of money market funds that pay close to nothing, and Treasury bonds with yields of less than 2 percent, into higher-yielding assets like stocks. While that goal has been partially successful, there's one major problem with it: That very same policy may have kept investors in Treasury bonds for too long, and may actually be preventing a rotation into stocks.

Treasury bond yields peaked in 1981 and have fallen throughout the last 30 years. When bond yields fall, bond prices rise. As a result, Treasury bond prices have experienced a 30-year bull market. Deflationary trends since 2000 have helped bonds to outperform stocks over that decade. With the 10-year Treasury note yield falling below 1.5 percent during 2012 for the first time in history (which is below the rate of inflation), the risk of holding Treasury bonds may exceed potential future rewards. Since bond yields can't go much lower, that puts a cap on how much higher bond prices can go. Treasuries have been a reliable safe haven over the last decade, which has included two major stock market collapses. Any significant improvement in the global economy (combined with higher inflation) in the years ahead, however, should cause bond yields to start trending higher. When bond yields rise, bond prices fall. Falling bond prices drive investors into stocks. Figure 16.1 shows Treasury bond prices rising during the 30 years since 1981, while the 30-year Treasury yield fell from over

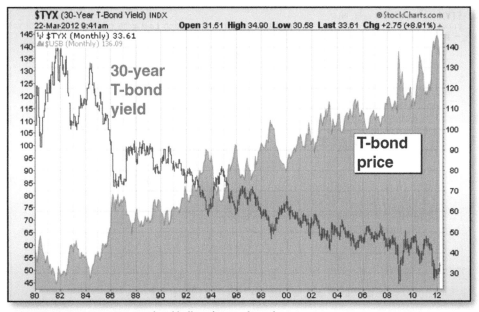

FIGURE 16.1   30-year Treasury bond bull market may be ending

15 percent in 1981 to below 3 percent during 2012. (During July 2012, the bond yield fell below 2.5 percent for the first time since the 1950s.) It seems unrealistic to expect yields to go much lower, which puts a cap on further potential appreciation in bond prices. It's more likely that the 30-year bull market in bond prices (and the 30-year decline in bond yields) is nearing an end.

■ The Fed Also Kept Bond Yields Low during the 1940s

The Fed's current policy of keeping bond yields from rising is also preventing bond prices from falling. That gives bondholders a false sense of security. The last time the Fed tried that form of financial repression was during the 1940s. The Fed started buying Treasuries in 1942 to prevent wartime inflation from pushing yields higher and to pay wartime debt with cheaper money. It wasn't until 1951 that the Fed finally let bond yields take their normal course higher. Although stocks rose during most of the 1940s, it wasn't until bond yields shot up during the 1950s that stocks really took off and continued to do so for the following two decades. It wasn't until the Fed allowed bond yields to rise, and bond prices to fall, during the 1950s that investors sold bonds and bought stocks in a big way.

Figure 16.2 shows the 30-year Treasury bond yield trading flat between 1942 and 1950. That was largely due to Fed policy. It wasn't until 1951 that the Treasury yield broke out to the upside (see circle) and started rising. Stocks turned up that same year. Figure 16.3 shows the Dow Industrials also breaking out of a 20-year basing pattern during 1951 (see circle) and beginning a major uptrend that lasted into the late 1960s. The fact that both markets experienced major upturns together during 1951 wasn't a coincidence. By allowing bond yields to rise during 1951, the Fed also allowed bond prices to fall. That forced investors out of bonds and into stocks.

By keeping bond yields so low in the current environment, the Fed may be interfering with a normal rotation out of bonds and into stocks that usually takes place in the latter stages of deflationary downturn. In so doing, the Fed may actually be keeping a lid on stock prices. Stocks have been locked in a huge trading range since 2000. They may remain stuck in that trading range until the Fed stops intervening in the bond market, and allows market forces to take their natural course. When that happens, I suspect stocks will do better than bonds in the coming decade.

FIGURE 16.2 Fed finally let bond yields rise during 1951

FIGURE 16.3   Dow Industrials broke out of 20-year base during 1951

Asset Allocation Strategies May Start Favoring Stocks

The deflationary decade that started around 2000 has favored bond prices over stocks. That may be changing. Figure 16.4 plots a ratio of the S&P 500 divided by the Treasury bond price since 1980. The rising ratio between 1980 and 2000 favored stocks over bonds. The falling ratio between 2000 and 2008 favored bonds. Since 2009, the rising ratio has favored stocks. Figure 16.4 shows the falling stock/bond ratio confined by two declining parallel trendlines starting in 2000. It bounced off the lower line at the start of 2009. It would have to break through the upper line to signal a major shift back to stocks, but it may be heading in that direction.

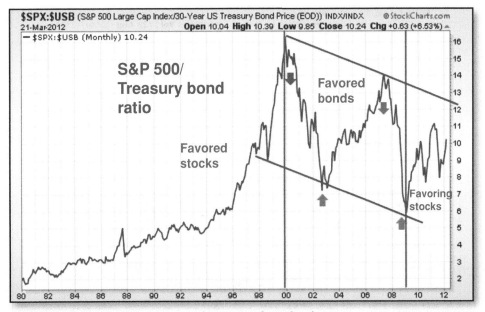

FIGURE 16.4   S&P 500/ T-bond ratio may be turning in favor of stocks

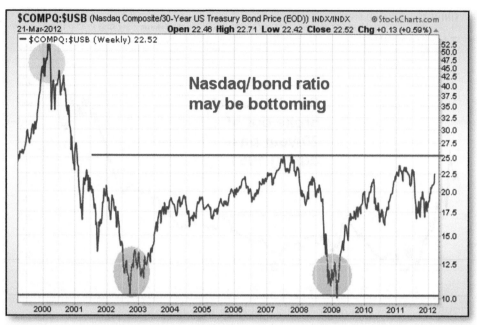

FIGURE 16.5 Nasdaq/T-bond ratio may be bottoming

■ The Nasdaq/Bond Ratio May Be Bottoming

Figure 16.5 paints an even more promising picture in favor of stocks over bonds. It plots a ratio of the Nasdaq Composite Index divided by the Treasury bond price since 2000. The ratio peaked in 2000 when the collapse in the technology-dominated Nasdaq market started the so-called *lost decade* for stocks and turned the bond market sharply higher. The Nasdaq/bond ratio has been trending sideways between its 2002 low and its 2007 peak. During 2009, the ratio bounced from the same level as its 2002 low (see circles) and has risen since then. The ratio is now approaching the top of that decade-long trading range. If and when the ratio exceeds its 2007 peak, that would be a strong signal that the decade of bonds has ended and a new decade for stocks may have begun.

FIGURE 16.6 Nasdaq Composite Index hits 12-year high

The Nasdaq Composite Index Hits a 12-Year High

The collapse in the Nasdaq market during the spring of 2000 started the first bear market of the new century and a bad decade for stocks. (The Nasdaq lost 78 percent of its value.) The Nasdaq may now be leading the stock market out of that losing decade. Figure 16.6 shows the Nasdaq Composite Index moving above its 2007 high during the first quarter of 2012 to reach the highest level in 12 years (see circle). In technical terms, that's a very bullish breakout and suggests that the *secular bear market* in the Nasdaq has ended. A *secular bear market* is a major long-term trend that can last a decade or longer. The solid matter in Figure 16.6 is a ratio of the Nasdaq divided by the S&P 500. That ratio has been rising since 2009 and has also reached a 12-year high. An earlier chapter dealing with sector rotation explained that technology leadership is usually a positive sign for the rest of the market.

a **secular bear market** is a major long-term trend that can last a decade or longer

Banks Show New Leadership

Another encouraging sign for the stock market comes from new signs of strength in banking stocks. Banks have been a huge drag on the stock market since 2007. The plunge in bank shares during 2008 had an especially damaging effect on the rest of the stock market. But that may be changing for the better. Entering 2012, bank stocks looked a lot stronger. Signs of leadership in financial stocks usually occur near the end of an economic contraction and the start of an economic expansion. That's why bank leadership during 2012 is encouraging.

Figure 16.7 shows a chart of the Regional Banking SPDR (KRE) through the first quarter of 2012. The KRE reached its 2010 high, which is an important chart barrier (upper line). A move above that high would be a very strong sign for banking shares and the rest of the stock market. The solid area on Figure 16.7 is a ratio of the KRE divided by the S&P 500. That relative strength line turned up during the fourth quarter of 2011, and made bank shares one of the market's strongest groups during the first quarter of 2012. (Note: Although banking shares slipped back during the second quarter, they still showed market leadership during 2012. From the October 2011 bottom to the following August,

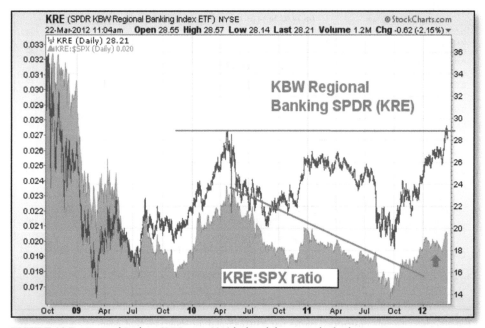

FIGURE 16.7 Regional Banking SPDR tests 2010 high and shows new leadership

regional banks gained 46 percent versus 25 percent for the S&P 500. Financial stocks, in general, gained 30 percent during that same period. During the first eight months of 2012, financials outpaced the S&P 500 by a margin of 17 percent to 12 percent. The regional bank ETF reached a new four-year high immediately after the September 2012 launch of QE3.)

■ Homebuilders Bottom

Figure 16.8 shows Home Construction iShares (ITB) also in the process of testing their 2010 high during the first quarter of 2012. That basket of homebuilding stocks had been trading sideways since 2009. A move above its 2010 high was needed to turn that bottoming formation into a new uptrend (more on that shortly). The shaded matter is a ratio of the ITB divided by the S&P 500. That relative strength line turned up during the fourth quarter of 2011 (along with banking shares) and made homebuilders one of the market's strongest groups during the first quarter of 2012. The fact that both groups showed improvement at the same time is also encouraging, but not surprising. Banks and homebuilders are closely aligned. Banks lend mortgages to people who want to buy those new homes. (Note: The homebuilding index exceeded its 2010 peak during June of 2012. By that August, it had reached its highest level since 2008. It was also the top performing ETF during the first eight months of 2012, gaining 52 percent versus 12 percent for the S&P 500. The ITB doubled in price within 10 months after its October 2011 bottom.)

■ Adding a New Dimension to Technical Analysis

Traditional technical analysis is based on the study of market trends through the use of price charts. Prior to 1990, however, technical analysis was based primarily on *single market* analysis. Each individual market was analyzed all by itself, whether it was bonds, stocks, commodities, or currencies. Traders in those different markets didn't pay much attention to what was going on in other markets. American analysts didn't care much about what was going on in foreign markets, either. Intermarket analysis changed that by encouraging traders to take other markets into consideration. Intermarket

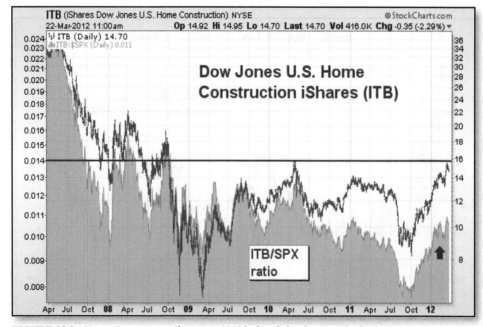

FIGURE 16.8 Home Construction iShares test 2010 high and also show new leadership

analysis doesn't *replace* traditional technical analysis. *It adds another dimension to it.* We still have to analyze each market by itself in order to determine which way it's most likely to trend. In order to do that, we use traditional charting methods. Once that's done, however, it's necessary to take trends in other markets into consideration. That's what intermarket analysis adds to traditional technical analysis. One can't exist without the other. The following list summarizes what I believe intermarket analysis brings to technical analysis.

- It combines global markets into a unified and coherent whole.

- It bridges the gap between fundamental, economic, and technical analyses.

- It increases the value of technical analysis by incorporating economic influences and opens TA to much wider usage.

Reading Up on Charting

Although I haven't written much about traditional charting techniques in this book, it's a very important part of the intermarket process. My book entitled *Technical Analysis of the Financial Markets* (New York Institute of Finance, 1999) offers a comprehensive treatment of the entire field of technical analysis. A second book, entitled *The Visual Investor: How to Spot Market Trends, Second Edition* (John Wiley & Sons, 2009), was written primarily for those readers relatively new to chart analysis and explains how to combine intermarket principles with traditional charting. There are also Internet web sites devoted to charting.

StockCharts.com Chart School

I'm associated with Stockcharts.com, which in 2012 was named "Best Technical Website" for the 11th year in a row by *Technical Analysis of Stocks & Commodities Magazine* (www.traders.com). If you're looking for a web site to begin your charting experience, Stockcharts.com is a good place to start (StockCharts.com). All of the charts shown in this book were created on the StockCharts site. A lot of the charting capability on that site is available free of charge. StockCharts.com also offers a Chart School, which explains everything you'll need to know about charting (www.stockCharts.com/school). There's also an online bookstore that offers a current list of technical books and videos that you can explore.

Neural Networks

Intermarket analysis requires us to look at a lot of markets in order to determine the impact each one is having on another. That has led to the introduction of artificial intelligence software to search for hidden market relationships. That approach utilizes the pattern-recognition capabilities of *neural networks*. Neural networks are excellent at sifting through enormous amounts of seemingly unrelated market data, and finding repetitive patterns between a target market and numerous related markets. Neural networks can be trained to make market forecasts based upon those hidden patterns. *VantagePoint Intermarket Analysis Software* (www.vptraders.com) utilizes the pattern-recognition capabilities of neural networks. That program was developed by Louis Mendelsohn, one of the pioneers in the field of trading software. An educational web site run by his son, Lane Mendelsohn, is devoted to educating investors on market analysis, and trading software in particular (www.traderplanet.com). That site also offers educational tools and articles on intermarket analysis.

Looking Ahead

We'll end the book by looking at four charts that may offer clues about how some intermarket relationships may play out in the future. Figure 16.9 is a chart of the U.S. Dollar Index from 2000 through the first quarter of 2012. After peaking during 2002, the Dollar Index fell sharply for six years before leveling off during 2008, when it rose above the falling trendline that defined the prior downtrend. It has been trending sideways since then between its 2008 low and its 2009 high. The chart raises the strong possibility that the U.S. Dollar is bottoming. To turn the trend of the dollar higher, however, the price would have to rise above the upper trendline drawn over its 2009/2010 highs. The markets that would be most affected by a rising dollar are commodities.

A Dollar Bottom Would Have a Depressing Effect on Commodities

Figure 16.10 compares the falling U.S. Dollar Index since 2002 with rising commodity prices (the CRB Index). The major collapse in the dollar during 2002 was the principal reason that commodities rose so sharply between 2002 and 2008 (see arrows). The dollar bottom in mid-2008 coincided with a collapse in commodity prices during the second half of that year. A dollar bounce during 2011 also caused a downside correction in commodity prices. Dollar direction will play a major role in the future trend of commodity prices, as it's done for the last 40 years.

A 40-Year Trend of the CRB Index

Figure 16.11 shows the trend in the Thomson Reuters/Jefferies CRB Index since 1970. Four major turns in the commodity price trend have taken place over those 40 years. Each of those turns was accompanied by a turn in the U.S. dollar in the opposite direction. The major upturn in the CRB

FIGURE 16.9 Dollar Index may be bottoming

FIGURE 16.10   A dollar bottom would have a depressing effect on commodities

Index during 1972 (first circle) was helped by a falling dollar. The commodity peak in 1980 (first box) coincided with a major upturn in the dollar. The major upturn in commodities during 2002 (second circle) coincided with a collapse in the dollar. The collapse in commodity values during the second half of 2008 (second box) coincided with an upturn in the dollar. Given the historic inverse link between those two markets, it seems reasonable to assume that a more stable dollar going forward would make it much harder for commodities to match the gains of the last decade.

FIGURE 16.11   Major turns in CRB Index have coincided with opposite turns in the dollar

$SPX:$CRB (S&P 500 Large Cap Index/Reuters/Jefferies CRB Index (EOD)) INDX/INDX   © StockCharts.com
23-Mar-2012   Open 4.47 High 4.50 Low 4.41 Close 4.44 Chg +0.03 (+0.59%) ▲
— $SPX:$CRB (Weekly) 4.44

S&P 500/CRB
Index ratio

FIGURE 16.12 S&P 500/ CRB Index ratio is starting to favor stocks

The Stock/Commodity Ratio Favors Stocks over Commodities

Figure 16.12 plots a ratio of the S&P 500 divided by the CRB Index since 1999. The stock/commodity ratio peaked during 1999 and fell until the middle of 2008. Since the middle of 2008, the ratio has risen. Near the end of the first quarter of 2012, the S&P/CRB ratio has reached the highest level in nearly five years, and has risen above a falling trendline extending all the way back to 1999 (see circle). That rising ratio suggests that the decade-long trend favoring commodities is giving way to a new decade when stocks could regain a leadership role.

I suspect that the inverse link between the stock market and the dollar will weaken in the years ahead. That will be especially true if the close link between stocks and commodities weakens. U.S. stocks may even derive some benefit from a firmer dollar. Foreign stock leadership over the last decade was largely the result of a weaker U.S. currency. A more stable dollar in the years ahead would reverse that trend, and make U.S. stocks a more preferred location for global funds.

Trade trends, not opinions

The preceding chart observations are only one person's opinions based on market trends existing at the end of the first quarter of 2012. I don't advise anyone to trade on another person's opinions. Hopefully, you've learned enough in this book to help you to make those decisions for yourself. Market trends change over time. The principles of chart analysis don't. Intermarket trends do sometimes change. But they usually change for a reason. Those changes usually take place over time and can last for a long time. The trick is to spot when those changes are occurring, and to take advantage of them. With some basic chart reading skills, combined with the intermarket principles described in this book, you should have all of the tools you'll need to help you do that.

John J. Murphy is former technical analyst for CNBC and has over 40 years of market experience. He is senior writer for StockCharts.com, an Internet web site that specializes in financial charts and technical analysis education. Murphy has appeared on Bloomberg TV, CNN, FOX, and the *Nightly Business Report,* and has been widely quoted in several other media outlets. In 1992, he was given the first award for outstanding contribution to global technical analysis by the International Federation of Technical Analysts, and is a recipient of the Market Technicians Association Annual Award. In addition to two previous books on intermarket analysis, he also authored two editions of *The Visual Investor*, all of which are published by Wiley. He also authored *Technical Analysis of the Financial Markets.* Murphy has a bachelor of arts in economics and a master of business administration from Fordham University. He is also Director of Research for Briarwood Capital Management Inc. in New York City.

229

T

U

V

Printed and bound by CPI Group (UK) Ltd, Croydon, CR0 4YY

23/04/2025

14660932-0001